A. G. Paddock

**In the Toils**

Martyrs of the Latter Days

A. G. Paddock

**In the Toils**

*Martyrs of the Latter Days*

ISBN/EAN: 9783744665841

Printed in Europe, USA, Canada, Australia, Japan

Cover: Foto ©Lupo / pixelio.de

More available books at **www.hansebooks.com**

# IN THE TOILS;

OR,

## Martyrs of the Latter Days.

BY

MRS. A. G. PADDOCK.

CHICAGO:
DIXON & SHEPARD.
1879.

Copyright 1879, by
**DIXON & SHEPARD.**
(*All Rights Reserved.*)

**GEORGE J. TITUS,**
**Book and Job Printer** 119 Lake St.,
CHICAGO.

Stereotyped by
Chicago Stereotype Works,
85 & 87 Fifth Ave., Chicago.

# PREFACE.

"Of making many books there is no end." Solomon speaks in the present tense, implying that even in his day a great multitude which no man could number, burned with ambition to see their names—on papyrus let us say. If Solomon spake thus of his own era, what would he have said could his prophetic soul have projected itself into the nineteenth century!

Surely, to-day, whoever inflicts an additional volume upon a long-suffering public, ought to be able to set up an unassailable plea in justification thereof.

The present writer feels the full force of this obligation, and desires briefly to explain the *raison d' etre* of the book now offered to the reader.

When you and I were studying geography, a large section of the map of the United States, including the greater portion of the territory lying between the Rocky Mountains and the Pacific Slope, was covered with little dots and conveniently labeled, "Great American Desert."

It is not always easy to outgrow the traditions of our youth, and to multitudes whom neither business nor pleasure has taken across the continent, the Great Desert is yet a reality—but what a surprise awaits them when they *do* make that long-deferred journey.

The Desert is a land, rich in rivers and fountains, "a land that drinketh water of the rains of heaven," a land whose mountains are store-houses of gold and silver, whose ranges are covered with countless flocks and herds, and whose valleys teem with luxuriant vegetation. And here, in the very heart of the traditional waste of sand, upon the shores of the American Dead Sea, lies a valley filled to the brim with living verdure, and manifold blossoms, and rich with the promise of the coming harvest.

## PREFACE.

The Zion built up in these valleys of the mountains, is like Zion of old, beautiful for situation, but alas! there is a crimson stain on every fair picture upon which the eye rests, and over the whole lovely landscape hangs the shadow of hideous crimes. The pioneers of Utah were the apostles of a religion built upon a foundation of lust and blood, and the annals of the people they led, are black with the record of deeds that disgrace humanity, done in the name of God. * * * *

Only a few weeks ago the telegraph flashed over the country the news of a most brutal murder—a little child killed by her father's hand. The deed was rendered doubly hideous by the sacreligious plea that it was done in obedience to a Divine command, and outraged justice at once demanded that the murderer should be held to answer with his life for his unnatural crime; but *here* crimes almost without number, that in magnitude and atrocity surpass the murder of little Edith, have been committed in the name of religion, and no voice is raised to demand the punishment of the perpetrators. On the contrary, they are elected to offices of trust and authority, they make and administer our laws, and hurl defiance at the government, whose subjects they are supposed to be.

The people, leaders and led alike, not only live in open and constant violation of decency and good morals, of the laws of God and man, but to show their contemptuous disregard of Christian marriage, and of the laws which hedge it round, they send as delegate to the Congress of the United States a man who keeps a harem of polygamous wives, and who boasts that he will compel our lawmakers to recognize his right to do so. They have tacitly made this acknowledgment by allowing him to sit among them for six years past, and now he waits in hope for the fruition of these years of effort; the passage of an Act legalizing polygamy, or, failing in this, the admission of Utah as a State, with full power to regulate her own internal affairs, which means, as we who live here know full well, power to remove all obstacles in the way of carrying out the principles of Blood Atonement and Celestial Marriage.

The book herewith presented to the public, claims to show some of the fruits of these principles, as exemplified in the past history of this people, but it deals only with the least repulsive and shocking facts in that history. Scores of incidents properly belonging to the story I have told, I have suppressed as unfit for publication. Multitudes of facts that have come under my own observation during my long residence among this people, I dare not commit to paper. I have listened with feelings of sickening horror to the recitals of those who have suffered most from the workings of this abominable system miscalled religion, but I cannot give their story to the world.

The characters of the story told in this book are real, the incidents are true, but I have told only a small part of the truth.

A complete history of the dwellers in these " valleys of the mountains " will never be written, nor will the crimes hidden under all their outward beauty ever be disclosed until the day when every hidden thing shall be brought to light and the bloody graves of Utah give up their dead.

The leaders of this people and their sympathizers in the East, are wont to say "Why are those whose homes have not been invaded by polygamy the first to cry out against it? What business is it of theirs?"

I leave other writers to reply to this question for themselves My own answer is: "It is my business because I am a woman, and polygamy degrades my sex below the level of humanity; because I am a wife, and polygamy makes that sacred name a byword; because I am a mother, and polygamy makes maternity a curse, and puts the brand of shame on the innocent foreheads of little children. And I am not alone in the determination to make this cause my own. There is a band of noble Christian workers here who are pledged not to intermit their efforts "until,"- as Whittier wrote of the other twin-relic of barbarism, "this evil plant, which our Heavenly Father hath not planted, whose roots have wound themselves about altar and hearthstone, and whose branches, like those of the tree Al Accoub in Moslem fable, bear every accursed fruit, shall be torn up and destroyed forever."

THE AUTHOR.

Salt Lake June 14. 1879

## PUBLISHERS' NOTE.

It is due to the author to state that, owing to the distance of her home from the place of publication it has been impossible for her to read the proof-sheets of the book, and that, therefore, any typographical errors that may be found herein, are to be charged to the compositor or proof-reader and not to her.

THE PUBLISHERS.

# IN THE TOILS:
## OR
## MARTYRS OF THE LATTER DAYS.
# PART I.

# IN THE TOILS

## OR
## MARTYRS OF THE LATTER DAYS.

### PART I.—Chapter I.

THE HAPPY HOME.—THE MYSTERIOUS STRANGER.—PRESENTIMENTS.

It was a cloudy, chilly evening in May, such as often follows a day of the brightest sunshine in our uncertain climate. The wind roughly shook the tender leaves of the young birches and maples, and moaned like an Autumn blast among the pines and hemlocks on the hill. The whole landscape looked colorless and cheerless under the dull gray sky, but in the foreground a human habitation lent to the picture something of the warmth of the life within.

The house substantially built of hewn stone, surrounded by trim fences and neatly painted outbuildings, was evidently the abode of comfort and plenty, while the climbing rose-trees and honeysuckles covering the porch, the carefully-tended flower beds bordering the walks, and the shrubbery dotting the lawn, told of a presiding spirit in love with the beautiful—perhaps the women standing on the steps and looking out along the lane leading to the highway. The presiding spirit of the place she might have been, and yet—she scarcely seemed to belong to it. Let us sketch her as she stands. A superb figure, a noble head, carried somewhat haughtily, coal black hair, braided and worn like a coronet, eyes dark as the hair, and shaded by long silky lashes, mouth and chin "cast in beauty's mold," but indicating pride and firmness, as well as womanly tenderness, and a smooth cheek whose rich bloom told of warmer climes:

"A tint not won
From kisses of a northern sun."

Such in face and form is Esther Wallace at twenty-seven. Years ago, when she was Esther Pryor, her companions called her "Queen Esther," and she looks a queen to-night, rather than the mistress of that pleasant country home. It is her home nevertheless, and the dearest one she has ever known—how dear none can tell but the bird that sings in her heart, as she stands there watching for the coming of the master of the house. The tender light in her dark eyes grows brighter as she watches, and the lines about the proud mouth melt into soft curves.

Love is lord and king to-night and the haughty spirit shrined in that beautiful form, owns his full power. "Love's young dream," ended may be with girlhood, but love's reality, wifely love deepened and strengthened by the passing years, sanctified by suffering, and made more tender a thousand fold by the child-life cradled in her bosom, will never end. Never in her bright youth did Esther Pryor, watching shyly behind the lattice for her lover, look half so beatiful as Esther Wallace, waiting for her husband at the threshold of his home.

"How late it is! What can keep him so long?" she said, half aloud, looking up a little anxiously at the gathering clouds. The wind swept round the house with greater force and a few drops of rain began to fall as she strained her eyes to catch a glimpse of the distant road. At this moment a side-gate was opened and shut noisily, and a bright little girl rushed up the garden path, and across the porch, crying breathlessly:

"Oh, mamma, mamma, what do you think? A great ugly hawk flew down into the yard, and caught one of the white hen's chickens and me and Horace knocked it over with a pole. Horace has got the hawk now and is going to nail it to the side of the barn he says, but the poor little chickie is quite dead; only see, mamma," and unfolding her apron, the child disclosed to view the luckless chicken pinched to death by cruel claws.

"Softly, Winnie dear," responded the mother, " I am very sorry, but was it you or Horace that killed the hawk?"

" Well, mamma, Horace killed it, but I screamed and made him come quick with the pole, so I helped, didn't I?"

" Yes, I think so; but you had better put your chicken away now, and run in and see if supper is ready. Your papa will be home soon."

" I'll go mamma, but I mean to have a funeral to-morrow for this poor killed little creature. How bad her mother will feel;" and carefully wrapping up the dear departed, Winnie turned away.

A smile flitted across the mother's face, but it was quickly followed by a sigh, as her eyes wandered to a distant corner of the garden where a white railing inclosed a little mound on which the violets and forget-me-nots had bloomed for three summers past. She knew only too well how mothers felt when their little ones were taken from them, and her heart ached bitterly yet, whenever her thoughts turned to the soft blue eyes that were closed in such a long sleep and the tender baby-hands that were so cold when she kissed them last.

Lost in a sorrowful reverie, she did not raise her head again to look for her husband's coming, until roused by Winnie's footsteps.

" Hasn't papa come yet mamma? Aunt Eunice is going to have hot cakes and honey for supper and I am so hungry."

" No, dear, papa is not in sight. I hope he will come

soon, for it is going to rain, and he must not get wet. He is not really well yet."

Winnie meantime, not waiting to hear the last words, had run down to the gate and mounted the horse-block.

"He is coming now," she cried. "That is papa just turning into the lane, and there is a gentleman with him, a tall gentleman that I don't know. May I run and meet them?"

"Yes, if you want to. I must go in and tell Aunt Eunice there will be company to supper."

Aunt Eunice, a staid, middle-aged colored woman, who presided in the kitchen of the stone house with a dignity becoming her responsible position, received her mistress graciously as she entered her own peculiar domain.

"Supper mos' ready, Miss Esther, but 'pears like dese yer waffles takes de longest while to bake. Hopes Massa Wallace ain't tired waitin'?"

"No, auntie, he isn't home yet. He has but just turned into the lane and there is a strange gentleman with him. Have we anything very nice for supper?"

"Well now I'd done cooked suthin' better if I'd 's'pected company. S'posin' I jess fry some ham, an' put on de peach jelly?"

"All right, Auntie. Your suppers are always good. Get anything you like and I will go and meet Mr. Wallace and see what company he has brought."

When Mrs. Wallace returned to the porch her husband was already at the gate. His companion, a tall, dark-haired man, in the prime of life, was apparently a stranger to the neighborhood as well as to herself, as Mr. Wallace was pointing out to him the different objects of interest in sight. Advancing up the walk Mr. Wallace presented his guest to his wife.

"My dear, this is Mr. Harwood, an old friend of my father's. I knew him well in my boyhood but he has lived in the West many years, and I had quite lost sight of him."

Courteously acknowledging the introduction, the stranger bent upon her a pair of keen gray eyes whose searching glance gave her a momentary feeling of discomfort. Where had she met that look before, or what was there in the scrutiny bestowed upon her to cause such an undefinable sense of uneasiness, almost of fear.

She chided herself inwardly for her nervousness as she welcomed the stranger with graceful hospitality and led the way to a pleasant sitting room where a bright wood-fire dispelled the chilliness of the evening?

"Truly, Wallace," said Mr. Harwood, "you are wise to adnere thus far to the ways of your ancestors. After a winter's experience of the close stoves that render most of your Eastern dwellings so uncomfortable, this fire is a pleasant surprise. How often have your father and I cracked our walnuts and roasted our apples before just such a blaze on the stone-hearth of the old homestead when we were boys."

While he spoke Mrs. Wallace observed her husband's friend a little more closely. He might have been fifty years of age. His dark brown hair, long and curling at the ends, was slightly sprinkled with gray. A full beard and mustache hid the lower part of his face completely and a well developed forehead, over-hanging brows and a Roman nose made up the remaining outlines of a not very remarkable countenance. But the eyes! These once encountered would not soon be forgotten. They seemed to look you through and through, to discern your most secret thoughts, and they repelled while they mastered you. Mrs. Wallace shrank involuntarily from meeting them again and seated herself where she was not obliged to face her guest. Winnie, who all this time had kept in the background with a shyness rather foreign to her nature, now advanced to her mother's side and Mr. Harwood perceiving her held out his hand.

"Come here, little one, and tell me your name. I think I forgot to ask before."

The child hung down her head and did not stir.

"Winnifred!" said Mr. Wallace, reprovingly.

At the sound of her father's voice Winnie came forward slowly and with evident reluctance and gave her hand to the stranger.

"A very nice little girl," he said, smoothing her curls, "and like mamma. Not afraid of me, I hope?"

A call to supper at this moment saved Winnie a reprimand for not answering. At the table the conversation became general and Mr. Harwood proved himself an entertaining talker. He was intelligent and well read, had traveled much and told amusing stories of his adventures in strange lands. The supper itself was a success, as Aunt Eunice's suppers were apt to be, and everything passed off pleasantly. After the meal Mrs. Wallace excused herself to attend to household duties and did not return to the sitting room again before Winnie's bedtime. While she was preparing the little girl for sleep, she said to her:

"What was it Winnie, that made you act so strangely, when papa's friend spoke to you to-night?"

"Is he papa's friend? I didn't know that, and I am sorry for I can't like him."

"But why not? My little daughter must not be like Willful Winnifred in the story book."

"I don't know, only I feel afraid of him. Sometimes I shiver all over when I am not cold at all and Sarah Morris says I am walking over my grave then and I felt just so when that dark man held my hand."

"Sarah Morris is very foolish to say such things, and you must not listen to her. Kneel down now and ask our dear Heavenly Father to take care of you and then go to sleep like my own good, little girl."

Reverently, with folded hands, Winnie repeated the simple prayer with which she had been taught to commit herself to the keeping of a Heavenly Friend, and then snugly tucked in her white bed and soothed by her mother's tender words and good-night kiss, dropped into the sound, untroubled sleep of happy childhood. Her mother left the room to rejoin her husband and his guest, feeling more uneasy and perplexed than she would have cared to own. What was there about this pleasant, courteous stranger, she asked herself, to make the child shrink from him. Then she recalled her own involuntary sensation of dread and dislike when she first felt his eyes fixed upon her but not wishing to yield to an unreasonable prejudice and being endowed moreover, with too much common sense to be greatly influenced by presentiments, she resolved to put the whole matter out of her mind and exert herself to make Mr. Harwood's visit as pleasant as possible. The evening was spent in listening to their guest's animated description of the Great West; and when they retired for the night Mr. Wallace said he had gained more information with regard to the resources of the country during that one conversation than in his whole life before. He was much interested in his father's friend and hoped to be able to prevail on him to make their house his home while he remained in the neighborhood. His wife said nothing but long after he had sank into a quiet slumber, she turned restlessly on her pillow, striving in vain to banish the unpleasant impressions of the evening from her mind. .

When at last weariness overcame her and she closed her eyes it was only to wake in a few moments with a start, thinking she heard her child's voice calling for help. Falling asleep again she dreamed she saw her husband standing on the crumbling edge of a precipice, apparently unconscious of danger, when suddenly the stranger approached and thrust him over the brink. Frozen with horror she tried vainly to cry out, when all at once the scene changed and she was walking with her little girl along a well known path. Happening to look up she saw a monster hawk circling slowly round and round above them. It drew nearer and assumed gigantic proportions with the head and face of her husband's guest. With a shriek of mortal terror she caught her child in her arms just as the creature swooped down upon them; but too late. The sharp claws were buried deep in the tender flesh and, when with superhuman strength she wrenched her daughter from their hold, it was only to see her droop lifeless in her embrace. She awoke trembling in every limb and with the cold drops of agony standing on her forehead. The frightful dream was so vivid, the impression that some danger menaced her child so strong that she rose from her bed and lighting her night-lamp, went into the little room adjoining her own where Winnie slept. The child whom she had left sleeping so peacefully a few hours before was now tossing from side to side with flushed cheeks and muttering indistinctly, the only word audible being the one that rises first to a child's lips when in trouble; " Mamma."

Her mother watched her for a few minutes, undecided whether to awaken her or not, but she grew quiet and soon her soft, regular breathing showed that her sleep was no longer disturbed.

"Can it be," thought Mrs. Wallace, "that the child's slumbers are haunted as mine have been? If I could bring myself to believe in forewarnings, I would surely think that this man's visit was to cause us trouble. But no; I should be more childish than Winnie to give way to such fancies. My nerves are out of order and Winnie doubtless saw something in my manner toward Mr. Harwood that influenced her. I will go to sleep and think no more about it."

Reasoning thus she returned to her own room but sleep did not come at her bidding and hours passed before she found rest and forgetfulness. The light of the next morning dispelled to a great extent the nervous terrors of the night and scorning herself a little for having been frightened by a dream she greeted her guest cordially when he made his appearance and presided smilingly at the bountiful breakfast table.

Mr. Wallace, as he intimated to his wife the night before, was anxious to keep the guest whose society he found so pleasant, and urged him to stay with them as long as his business detained him in the place, but Mr. Harwood, with many thanks for the hospitable offer, declined, saying he was obliged to attend to affairs that would require his presence in the county town a few miles away most of the time. He, however, promised to make them another visit and Mrs. Wallace united with her husband in assuring him that it would be a great disappointment if he failed to do so; still she was conscious of a feeling of relief when he was gone and found herself secretly hoping he might not return.

We would not have the reader think from this that Esther Wallace was one of those women who tell white lies every day for the sake of not appearing discourteous. She thought it right to second her husband's invitation, and if her manner toward her guest was more cordial than her feelings, it was because she wished to conquer what she assured herself was a very silly prejudice.

In the course of the morning Winnie, who had been out of doors most of the time atttending to the obsequies of the departed chicken, sought her mother in her room to announce that the funeral was over and she would like a piece of card-board to make a monument for the grave.

The card board was hunted up and while Mrs. Wallace was shaping and lettering it according to orders she asked:

"Did you sleep well last night, daughter?"

"Yes, mamma—or no. I forgot to tell you what a bad dream I had."

"What was it, dear?"

"You would never guess, mamma. I dreamed papa gave me away to that strange man and he was going to take me off and papa would not listen, though I cried and begged ever so hard. Then I called 'mamma,' as loud as I could and the man caught me up but you came running and took me away from him. Don't tell papa, please. I should be ashamed for him to know I dreamed such a thing about him—such a good papa."

Mrs. Wallace smiled as she kissed her little girl and gave the required promise, and the monument being now finished to Winnie's satisfaction, she placed it in her hands and the child hurried away to pay the last token of respect to the memory of her downy favorite.

While she is absent on this errand and her mother engaged with the duties of the day, we will go back a few years and introduce more fully to the reader the persons whose future lives will form the subject of this truthful history.

## PART I.—Chapter II.

A SPOILED CHILD AND A SUCCESSFUL MAN—A WEDDING—
THE MORMON ELDER.

Charles Wallace, the owner of the stone house and fertile acres around it, was of Puritan stock. His father was an honest New England farmer who had grown gray tilling the rocky soil of his native state before Charlie's blue eyes opened to the light.

The elder Wallace reared his family according to the traditions of the Pilgrims. Work, hard work, was the law of the household, but it was coupled with the saving gospel of domestic love, homely kindness and mutual helpfulness. The boys were not driven but led to their daily task, and his elder sons did credit to the school in which they were trained. Year after year they followed the plow and wielded the scythe without once troubling their father with the aspirations that commonly take hold of the nineteenth century-youth whenever hard work is required of him,— but Charlie, the youngest of the flock—the mother's golden-haired darling, rebelled against the toilsome and prosaic life that his brothers accepted as their manifest destiny. It was a thousand times pleasanter to lie under the apple trees on a hot summer-day and read of giants and fairies, of knights and troubadors, than to ply a rake in the hayfield under a broiling sun, and the boy, like a good many older people, managed to persuade himself that the easy way was the right way. The father grumbled about his laziness but the mother plead for him and the sun-browned elder brothers took his part. He was their baby almost as much as the mother's. While he yet wore white frocks they rocked his cradle, carried him on their shoulders to the barn and gave him many a ride on the gentle old horse that stood winking sleepily beside the pile of fragrant hay, which was Charlie's throne of state. He was king then and they his loyal subjects, and ever since it had been their pleasure to do his royal bidding. Now it seemed to them altogether right and fitting that he should play while they worked. "He was such a little fellow yet," they argued, and he looked so fair and delicate with his pink cheeks, blue eyes and golden curls, they were sure he was not strong enough for rough farm work. They were very proud of him and so too in his secret heart was the father; proud of his "smartness," his book-learning, his gift for repeating page after page of poetry, and telling wonderful stories as they sat round the winter evening fire.

Thus it came to pass that master Charlie grew up without making an intimate acquaintance with plow or rake. He graduated in his teens from the district school of his boyhood to the village academy, where the youth of two generations, had grappled with the mysteries of $x + y$ and stumbled through a few pages of Latin grammar.

At this institution of learning he soon distanced all competitors and so distinguished himself that the teacher, the minister and the doctor all united in expressing the opinion that the boy would make something if he had a chance and his father ought to give him better advantages than the village afforded. Charlie quite agreed with them but when he made known his views to his father and modestly requested to be sent to college, the old man thought it quite time to clip the wings of his soaring ambition.

"No Charlie;" he said, "I've let you have your own way all along but this is goin' a leetle 'too fur. If I send all my boys to college, what will be left to give them a start or take care of mother, when I am gone? I can't make fish of one and flesh of another. Look at your old father's hands my boy. Think how hard I've worked to bring you all up, and your brothers have worked hard too—no better boys in the country. I ain't complainin' of you Charlie. You've always been a good boy to me and your mother but you're old enough now to think of somethin' besides school. There's more things to be studied in this world than books as you will find out if you live to be as old as I am, and many a boy goes through college without learnin' what he needs to knows most."

Charlie knew very well that there was no appeal from his father's decision and the idea of going to college had to be given up; but farm life was as distasteful to him as ever. So like another younger son he prayed: "Father give me the portion of goods that falleth to me" and like him also when he had gathered all together he took his journey into a far country, but there the parallel ended; for our Charlie, though not fond of hard work, had no disposition to waste his substance in riotous living. He had an uncle in another State, who had made a fortune in trade and to him he went. The merchant, who had no children of his own, received his sister's son cordially and under his advice and management Charlie's small stock of worldly gear was so well invested that he had the satisfaction of seeing it doubled before the year ended. Prosperity continued to attend him and the next year he felt himself rich enough to retire from business and carry out his plans for study but just at this time while making one of his trips across the country with his uncle, he met Esther Pyror and thenceforth a change came over his dreams.

A pair of glorious dark eyes came between him and the pages of his favorite books when he opened them and the dead languages were neglected for the charm of a living voice. It was the old, old story which is as new to-day as when the first pair of lovers wandered hand in hand on the banks of the four rivers that still

> " Yield those murmurs sweet and low
> Wherewith man's life is undertoned."

And Esther? An orphan living under the roof of a distant relative, it was not strange that she yearned sometimes, for closer ties and a nearer companionship than any she had known since her dead were buried out of her sight.

A native of the sunny South, she was homesick often in this cold Northern land, though she had money enough to save her from dependence and her beauty surrounded her with admirers while her affectionate nature and cheerful spirit made fast friends of those who knew her best.

But Queen Esther, bright, warm hearted and gentle to those she loved, was a trifle haughty withal and thus far those who came a-wooing, attracted either by her fortune or her handsome face, had found little favor in her eyes. Secretly she shared the favor of her faithful servitor, Aunt Eunice, that "Dese yere Nordeners warn't much 'count none on 'em rale gentlemen like ole' massa."

When Charlie came in her way, she rated him with the others at first, but as he dared do no more than worship her in secret, she did not feel called upon to be as reserved with him as her acknowledged suitors and meeting him upon the familiar footing of every day acquaintance, she began before long to admit to herself that there were real gentlemen even at the North. Perhaps this change in her views was apparent in her manner toward Charlie; at any rate his visits became more frequent and he found excuses for remaining in the neighborhood week after week. The sequel is soon told.

The soft summer night, the moonlight, the breath of June roses in the air, may have helped to give courage to the timid lover and subdue the heart of the proud Southern beauty, but certain it is that when Charlie was at length summoned to the city and came to say good-bye, the balcony from which they had watched the stars on other nights was the scene of a passionate avowal of love that had never found expression in words before, and he went away carrying with him Esther's promise to be his wife.

If love is not all of life to a woman, it is at least so much to her that life would be worth little with love left out, and Esther Pryor, rich, beautiful and admired had found her life very empty without it. In the dear Southern home where she grew up from infancy to the verge of womanhood an atmosphere of rare tenderness surrounded her. " Too much indulgence has spoiled many children; too much love not one." So wrote one who knew the heart of a child, and Esther, though a dearly loved only daughter, was not spoiled. She was far from being faultless however and bore little resemblance to the good children in books who always die young. Her exuberant vitality, coupled with the mischief into which it constantly overflowed, would have made her a terror to prim teachers and elderly maiden aunts, but happily for the little Esther none of these watched over her childhood, and her real faults, a violent temper and a strong self-will, were wisely dealt with by a mother as firm as she was loving.

" Mothers have God's license to be missed," so Esther thought in the long years that followed, when the tender voice was stilled and the hand that guided her childish footsteps had moldered back to dust. The father's love for his only child was too nearly allied to worship, for him to perceive her faults and Esther remembered him only as the "darling papa," who showered gifts and caresses upon her without limit and for whose coming she always watched so eagerly. Alas! There came a day when her loving watch ended in woe unspeakable.

One bright morning her father mounted his horse and rode away to transact some business with a neighboring planter. He did not expect to return before night and as it drew near sunset Esther, as was her custom, ran gaily down the avenue and stood at the gate to be the first one to meet papa. She could not look far down the road for where their grounds ended a sudden turn hid it from sight; but she could hear the sound of the horse's hoofs a long way off and for this she stood listening when she heard instead the roll of wheels.

As the cariage came in sight she recognized it as one belonging to a friend of her father's who lived a few miles away. The gentleman sat on the box beside the coachman and as they halted at the gate Esther said to him:

"Papa is not at home, but drive right in. He will be here directly."

"My little girl," he answered, "I want to see your Uncle Robert. Will you run to the house and call him?"

As he spoke Esther noticed how white and strange he looked and she turned to do his bidding wondering whether he was sick or anything dreadful had happened at his house. Uncle Robert, her father's brother who was spending a few weeks with them, received her message with surprise.

"Mr. Jerrolds wants me at the gate you say. Why did he not come in?"

But Esther was already gone to tell her mother how sick Mr. Jerrolds looked when he sent her to call her uncle.

Presently the carriage came slowly up the avenue, Mr. Jerrolds and Uncle Robert walking ahead. It stopped before the veranda and Mr. Jerrolds came along into the room where her mother sat. He was paler than ever, Esther thought, and he could hardly speak.

"My dear Mrs. Pryor," he began at length, "Your husband"—

"Has anything happened to him?" she cried, terrified by his white face and trembling utterance," "Tell me all and tell me quickly!"

"My dear madam, be calm, I entreat you. He has been thrown from his horse and hurt."

"Is he badly hurt? Have you brought him home? Let me go to him,"—for Mr. Jerrolds had placed himself before the door.

"Wait a moment, Mrs. Pryor, only a moment. They are bringing him in. He is very badly hurt. He is"—

"I know! I know! He is dead. Do not stop me!" And wild-eyed and tearless the bereaved wife rushed past him into the hall through which four of the men-servants were bearing the body of their master, who had left them that morning so full of life and strength. At the sight of their mistress they paused a moment with their sad burden.

"Give him to me," she said, "Bring him here! He is mine."

In awe-stricken silence they obeyed and laid him down on the sofa in the pleasant room that until now had been the brightest in the house. Esther who all the while had stood as if transfixed, when she saw her father lying there so white and still, threw herself down beside him crying:

"Oh papa! darling papa! wake up! Look at your own little girl! Don't die papa! don't die!"

Alas! the eyes that had always met hers with looks of tenderest love were forever closed and the cold hands, upon which the sobbing child rained passionate kisses would never more clasp "papa's own little girl." The wife uttered no cry, made no moan. With a face as white as the one upon the sofa-pillow she knelt beside her dead, holding the lifeless head as tenderly as though a careless touch could hurt it now and putting back the dark hair from a cruel wound above the temple. An hour passed but no efforts or entreaties availed to move her from the spot until Esther who was awed into forgetfulness of her own grief by the look on her mother's face, clinging to her dress begged between her sobs that mamma would come with her and not leave her all alone.

"Papa's little girl," the stricken woman said softly, looking down on the trembling, childish figure. Then followed a gush of blessed tears and laying her precious burden gently back on the pillow she suffered herself to be led from the room. Through the sad days that followed, the thought of her fatherless child for whose sake she must live saved the widow from sinking utterly under the suddenness of the blow that had bereft them both. But when all was over and sorrowing relatives and sympathizing friends departed leaving them alone in the home from which the light had gone out forever, she felt it impossible to endure life there, where they had been so happy together; where, turn which way she would, her eyes rested on something that re-called the past. Esther too in her childish way expressed the same feeling:

"Mamma," she said, "do let us go away somewhere. As long as we stay here where papa was always with us, it seems as though he must come back, though I know he never will and I cannot bear it; indeed I cannot."

Esther's words decided her mother. Her own early home was in the North and though father and mother, brothers and sisters had long since passed to the other world, she longed to breathe her native air again and look once more upon the familiar scenes of her girlhood; so, leaving her affairs in trusted and safe hands and taking with her only her daughter and the faithful Aunt Eunice who had been Esther's nurse in infancy she sought the quiet village where she was born. Here surrounded by old friends and devoting herself to Esther's education she found, if not a balm for her sorrow, at least strength to bear it uncomplainingly. The lover of her youth, the husband to whom she gave her whole heart was still hers though the curtain of eternity had fallen between them, and she waited patiently for the lifting of the veil—the hour of sweet and indissoluble re-union.

It came soon. Before Esther was sixteen she closed her mother's eyes and was indeed all alone. In the place of her father's tender caresses her mother's loving words, there remained to her only the marble shaft that she could see from her window gleaming through the trees when she looked out toward the churchyard—only that mound in the far South which she had left when the magnolias were dropping their white petals upon it—two graves and nothing more. True, she had been taught and she believed that her father and mother still lived in Heaven but Heaven seemed very far off to the lonely girl. The other world was too shadowy and indistinct for her to picture father and mother living and loving her the same as when she could see them.

> Oh how far,
> How far and safe, God, dost Thou keep thy saints
> When once gone from us! We may call against
> The lighted windows of thy fair June-heaven,
> Where all the souls are happy—and not one,
> Not even my father, looks from work or play
> To ask, "Who is it that cries after us,
> Below there in the dusk?"

But happily it is so ordered in God's good Providence that time soon heals the wounds of grief in young hearts, and though Esther never for an hour forgot her beloved dead and never ceased to miss them, the years took from her sorrow much of its bitterness, and when the new love came to fill her heart and life the world looked as bright to her as to any loving, trusting woman when she utters the vow: "Forsaking all others I will cleave only unto thee."

* * * * * * *

It was June, the month of roses, when she first met Charles Wallace and in October, when as her lover said the earth had put on gold and purple to do honor to a royal bride, they were married. Eight years had passed since then; years so full of sunshine that Esther sometimes feared they were too happy, until the first shadow came and the little grave was made in the garden. Their home was in the country because Esther wished it, but their money enabled them to live very much as they pleased, and Wallace found the life of a gentleman-farmer not so distasteful after all.

He had at length realized the dreams of his boyhood. In his cozy library, surrounded by the books he coveted, he had leisure and opportunity to study as much as he would; but somehow when the patter of Winnie's baby feet began to be heard about the house, his attention was drawn from graver pursuits to watch the development of her wonderful talents. Wife and child were so much to him that he would have found life very pleasant even if literature, science and art had been banished from it altogether; and as the years followed one upon another he realized the truth of his father's words: "There are a great many things in the world to be studied besides books." He did not give up his literary pursuits, but he was by no means absorbed in them; the care of his family, the improvement of his estate and a natural interest in the affairs of the community in which he lived modified his plans of mental culture.

At thirty he was neither a *savant* nor a renowned genius, but an affable, well-informed country-gentleman whose acquaintance was prized by his neighbors and who was elevated by his family to the pedestal upon which living hearts are wont to place a tender husband and fond father—but the great world outside had never heard of him.

At the time our story opens he was slowly recovering from the effects of a lingering sickness—brain fever followed by a general prostration of the vital forces, from which physicians and friends feared he would never rally. Contrary to their prophecies, however, his strength returned and he was now apparently almost as well as ever, but the quick eyes of his wife discovered a subtle change in him. He had grown dreamy and abstracted to an extent that sometimes alarmed her, and when startled from these moods he was irritable though his temper heretofore had been remarkably placid child-like and even. The first fretful words he ever spoke to wife or uttered when roused suddenly from one of his reveries, but both were ready to make loving excuses for an infirmity that was plainly more of the body than the mind.

On the evening of Mr. Harwood's visit he seemed quite like his former self, and the next day he was more cheerful than he had been for months. As they sat round the supper table at night Mrs. Wallace said:

"I don't think your friend told us in what part of the West he was living."

"Did he not? He has lived in different Western States but his present home is in Utah."

"In Utah! Surely he is not a Mormon?"

Mr. Wallace smiled at the startled earnestness with which his wife put this question.

"That is not what he calls himself my dear. He and the people among whom he dwells proclaim themselves 'Latter Day Saints.'"

"Their saintliness must be of a very peculiar sort if the half that is said of them is true."

"My dear wife, we must not allow ourselves to be too greatly influenced by what we hear. Eighteen centuries ago worse things were said of our Saviour and his followers than have ever been urged against the Mormons."

"True, but those who spoke evil of Jesus and his disciples knew all the time that they were uttering wicked and unfounded calumnies, and the Judge before whom the case was finally tried was compelled to say 'I find no fault in Him.'"

"Well, our Mormon friends may one day triumph in like manner over their accusers; but we will not argue that point now. I am not very well informed with regard to their principles or their history, but when Mr. Harwood comes again we will let him plead his own cause. It would be unfair to condemn him and his people without a hearing."

Mrs. Wallace thought to herself that existence would be very tolerable without any further light on the subject of Mormon faith and practice, but she forbore to utter her thoughts aloud, and as she had herself invited Mr. Harwood to come again, she could not well protest against a second visit from the Mormon Elder as she now understood him to be. So with the best grace she could, she resigned herself to the prospect of the infliction of a long discourse on the mission of the Prophet Joseph and the doctrines held by his followers.

## PART I.—Chapter III.

UNDER THE SPELL. "WHITHER THOU GOEST I WILL GO."

Two weeks passed however without bringing any tidings of Harwood and Esther was beginning to hope that he had left the country, when one bright day in June she was surprised by a visit from the aged pastor of the church to which she and her husband belonged.

Father Belden, though trembling on the verge of fourscore, and compelled to leave the active duties of his charge to a younger colleague, still felt a warm interest in all his people and was greatly beloved and revered by them. To Esther as well as her husband he was father, friend and counsellor. Ever since she first knew him she had associated his calm, benignant face with the thought of peace on earth and good-will to men, but to-day there was a shade of anxiety on the placid brow, and the hand that clasped hers in friendly greeting trembled.

"Are you not well Father Belden?" she asked. "You seem hardly as strong as usual."

"Well in body my child, but something has happened lately that causes me much distress."

"Will you not tell us what it is? If Charles or I can help you in any way you know how glad we will be to do so."

"It is on your husband's account that I have felt so much anxiety. I have hesitated for a number of days to speak to you about it, but now I feel that I can no longer avoid it."

It was now Esther's turn to tremble and turn pale. "What can you mean?" she asked.

"If there is anything wrong with him or any danger threatening him surely I ought to know it."

"Doubtless you, his wife, have observed more clearly than his friends outside his home that since his sickness his mind has never quite recovered its former tone."

"I have, but he is much better lately and I am encouraged to believe he will soon be himself again in all respects. You don't think otherwise?"

"I thought as you do that he would be quite well again soon, and such would doubtless have been the case if no disturbing influence had been brought to bear upon him. You had a visitor three weeks ago I think; a Mr. Harwood?"

"Yes, Mr. Harwood spent one evening with us, and Charles seemed much interested in him at the time but he has not called on us since. What has he to do with my husband's state of mind?"

"Much, I fear. Are you aware that Mr. Harwood is a Mormon missionary?"

"I learned after his visit that he was from Utah and a Mormon, but did not hear that he was on a missionary tour."

"Those people never leave home except to make converts or raise money, and Elder Harwood, as he is called, had both objects in view in coming here."

"You don't think he expected to convert *us*?"

Mrs. Wallace smiled in spite of herself at the preposterous idea. Surely her good pastor's mind must be failing a little if his anxiety about her husband arose from such a source.

"I am certain that Elder Harwood expects to make converts in this neighborhood, but I don't think he has any hope of influencing you. With your husband however the case is different. If the Mormon missionary had talked with him six months ago he would not have listened to his sophistries for a moment. Now he is not as you say quite himself. His mind has not fully recovered from the effects of his illness, and he is in just the right state to be influenced by the wily Elder's glowing picture of Christ's temporal kingdom set up in the valleys of the far West and his accounts of the visions, revelations and visits of angels vouchsafed to the chosen people gathered there."

Father Belden spoke so earnestly and with such evident anxiety that Esther for the first time felt a thrill of fear.

"When," she asked, "could Harwood have talked with my husband upon such subjects? Nothing of the kind was mentioned during his visit here, and they have not met since to my knowledge."

"They have met without your knowledge then, for I have several times seen them walking together engaged in earnest conversation, in which Charles was so much absorbed that he did not look up."

"If he has been so deeply interested I wonder he never mentioned the matter at home. You know his open, frank nature and I don't think he has had a secret from me since we were married."

"I do not suppose he has. I know something of his devotion to his wife and his confidence in her and I know how well she deserves both, but, my child, you must remember what you said yourself a few minutes ago and what I have just repeated—your husband is not quite himself now, and one of the first lessons taught by these Latter Day preachers to their converts is to practice concealment and deception toward their best friends."

"You speak almost as though he might be a convert to this imposture already. I know his mind is weakened by illness and in his present state his father's friend may have a temporary influence over him, but it is not possible that such a transparent delusion as Joe Smith's 'revelation' should gain any permanent hold upon him."

"Esther," said the old man sorrowfully, "I would gladly give the poor remnant of my life to save you from such pain as my next words must cause. Charles was baptized into the Mormon faith by this Harwood yesterday."

Esther sank back in her chair dizzy and faint as from a sudden blow. She would have said again "impossible!" but she remembered her husband's absence from home the whole of the previous day, and his strange manner when he returned at night. She recalled too the fact that since Harwood's visit he had seemed to have business at the village very often and had on every occasion staid away much longer than was his custom. All was explained now. The Mormon missionary, on the lookout for some one to entrap, had heard of their circumstances, and of her husband's state of health, and made up his mind that he would be an easy and profitable convert. His visit to their home probably convinced him that Wallace was the only member of the household whom he could hope to influence, and so he had taken measures to secure him at once and keep the whole matter from his friends until it was too late to thwart him.

Deeply distressed, as she was, at this discovery, no thought of reproaching her husband entered the mind of the loyal wife. In his present state she considered him scarcely more accountable for his acts than for words uttered in the ravings of delirium, but she felt a fierce resentment rising in her heart against the man who had stolen into their home under the guise of friendship and dealt this fatal blow to its happiness. She sat in stunned silence, incapable of replying to her pastor's expressions of sympathy and seeing that she would be better alone, he commended her in a few fervent words to the Friend whose love abides when all other loves fail; and left her to seek help from Him.

Long after the good man had taken his departure Esther remained as he left her seeking to realize the nature and extent of the calamity that had fallen upon her.

Only two years before her sympathies were deeply enlisted in behalf of a poor woman whose husband left her and joined the Mormons, being influenced to do so by a specious misapplication of the words "He that loveth wife or children more than me is not worthy of me."

The deserted family having been wholly dependent on the earnings of the husband and father for support, were plunged into the deepest poverty and distress, and Mrs. Wallace, whose charities were always abundant, was appealed to for help by those who knew their circumstances. During the whole of the first winter after they were left alone she fed them from her own table, and the heart-broken wife who was completely prostrated in body and mind by the stroke which left her worse than widowed, clung to Esther as to the only friend she had on earth. How well she remembered now every word of the poor creature's sad story:

"I never blamed my George, Mrs. Wallace. He was a good husband to me and a good father to his children, but it seemed as if he was possessed like, after he heard that man preach, and then he would come here and he and George would sit under that tree there and talk until maybe ten o'clock at night. Things went on in this way for weeks, George leaving his work and everything else to follow the preacher around. I never could bear the man from the day I set eyes on him. He always made me think of a snake, and my poor George was just bewitched by him as they say snakes will charm birds and squirrels. One night after he was baptized he came home in great trouble of mind. He wouldn't go to bed, but just walked the floor till long after midnight. At last he comes to me and says:

'Mary will you be baptized and go with me?'

'Go where?' says I.

'To Zion where the saints are gathering. I must be there to meet the Lord when he comes. It's been been a great trouble to me that you wouldn't listen to the gospel, but you must receive the truth now and go with me or I must go alone. I can't lose my soul, no, not for wife nor children. I love you Mary and I love the little ones, God knows I do, but I must go where he calls.'

Well, I told him I would go with him to the ends of the earth, but I would never be baptized and pretend to believe something that I knew was a lie. Nothing more was said that night, and very early in the morning George got up and went away, telling me he was wanted in town and wouldn't be home to dinner. He didn't come back at night and when I went to the village to look for him (it was ten o'clock and I was almost wild for he never staid away after dark), they told me he went off on the cars in the morning with the Mormon preacher and two or three others. He never left any word for me, not even a line to say good-bye, and I never heard from him afterwards. And there were the children, crying to see me cry, and little Jimmy calling at night for his papa to undress him as he always used to, and I knowing all the time that their father had left us for good. It was more than I could stand up under and when I took sick my poor little baby pined away and died in less than a month. Oh, Mrs. Wallace was there ever any trouble like mine?"

Was there ever? Ah! poor stricken heart, how many betrayed and deserted wives, deserted for this same false and cruel' faith, could give answer if they dared to speak, but those who suffer most from the blighting influence of this religion, that sunders the holiest ties, must suffer in silence, for they are placed where the same remorseless tyrany that crushes their hearts seals their lips likewise. Esther Wallace, sitting with bowed head in the home which the serpent had already entered, asked herself the same question, "Was there ever any sorrow like my sorrow?" Through the open window floated the song of birds, the breath of the flowers and all the sounds of happy life in the world outside.

It was just such a lovely summer day as that on which her father rode away to his death, just such a day, oh woeful thought, as the one on which she first met him who would soon be hers no longer, for she knew enough of the delusion that had mastered her husband to be certain that, once completely under its power, he would be lost to her and his child forever. Yet while her heart was full of bitterness toward the man who had deluded him, for her husband himself she felt the tender pity of a mother for her sick babe.

"Poor Charlie; my poor darling," she said over and over again to herself, "in his right mind he would sooner cut off his hand than do what he has done. He is not to blame. It is I who am to blame for not watching him more closely."

While she still sat thinking over the perplexing and painful position in which she found herself, she heard her husband's well known step on the porch, and a moment after he entered the room, looking pale and tired.

"Alone Esther?" he asked.

"Yes dear, just now. Winnie begged to ride with Horace to the mill and I let her go."

"I am glad she is not here, for I want to talk to you a little while without interruption."

He threw himself wearily into a chair, and the dreamy, far-away look that Esther had noticed so often of late came into his eyes, but he roused himself directly and said:

"Dear wife you and I have made ourselves believe for a

good many years that we were Christians, but in the light of recent experiences I am constrained to think we have been sadly mistaken. The Gospel tells us that Christ's followers deny themselves, bear a daily cross, suffer as he suffered, and are hated by the world. We have been living easy, comfortable lives; most of our days have passed without crosses and the world does not hate us. Do you think we can lay any claim to discipleship?"

"Yes, I think we can, though we have not followed Christ fully I know. There are other tests of discipleship than those you have mentioned, but suppose we take them alone. In one form or another we have found our daily cross, only look back and I think you will admit that. And if we have not literally forsaken all things, I think we have held our possessions subject to a higher will; ready to give them up when called for. Remember, dear love, when the most precious thing we had, our only son, was demanded of us, we gave him up, not without tears it is true, but without rebellious murmurings."

"Yes, I know we gave up our child because it was not in our power to hold him back, but what voluntary sacrifices have we ever made? And then again how can we think we belong to the company of those who have been chosen out of the world, while we still have the world's friendship? I know of but one people who are hated of all men for their Lord's sake, and to them I am commanded to join myself. A voice that I dare not disobey calls me."

Again he relapsed into a dreamy silence, as though he were indeed listening to a voice that others could not hear, while Esther, feeling that her worst fears were confirmed, summoned all her strength to ask the final question:

"Who are these people, and when and how do you propose to join yourself to them?

"They are the people of whom we have spoken once before—those who have forsaken home and friends for the sake of their faith, crossed a savage desert at the peril of their lives, and gathered in the valleys beyond the Rocky Mountains to wait for their Lord, until he comes to reign a thousand years as he foretold. I am already united to them in the faith and hope of the Gospel. I have been united to them by baptism, and now I only await your consent to dispose of all we have here, and to accompany me to join them in the peaceful valleys where, separated from a world that will not receive the truth; they worship God in the way He has commanded."

"But why, dear, have you waited so long to tell me of this? You have always confided in me, why then did you not speak to me at the first of your convictions and purposes?"

"Because I feared you would not see the truth as I saw it. You remember that immediately after Elder Harwood's visit, we talked a little about his people, and you expressed yourself quite strongly in opposition to their views and practices. Knowing your feelings I shrank from speaking to you of my own, while the struggle between my will and the Divine call was going on in my heart. At times it seemed impossible that I should submit to the requirement to forsake all and go whithersoever the Spirit might lead. Judge then how much harder the struggle would have been, if in addition to conquering my own rebellious heart I had been forced to withstand your tears and entreaties."

"And now you say the struggle is ended?"

"Yes. Whatsoever the Lord commands by the voice of his servant, that will I do."

"That means," thought Esther, "that he submits himself entirely to Harwood's dictation," but a look into her husband's face convinced her that he was sincere in believing he obeyed the voice of God. Harwood, whom she could not look upon otherwise than as a designing and unscrupulous villain, was to him a messenger from Heaven, whose every word was to be heard reverently and obeyed implicitly.

She saw too that he had no suspicion whatever of Harwood's real motive in counselling him, as she did not doubt he had done, to obtain her consent to sell their property and accompany him to Utah.

It will be remembered that at the time of their marriage Wallace possessed only a modest competence, while she had what was counted in those days quite a large fortune in her own right. At Wallace's express wish his wife's property was settled on herself in such a manner that he had no control over it. His own money was invested in their home, which of course could not be sold without her consent. Now, Elder Harwood, as she read him, was not at all anxious to take his convert to Zion empty-handed, and he relied on her affection for her husband as a means of securing their property. If she refused to go with him would Charles give up the idea of gathering with the Saints? She thought not, but to place the matter beyond doubt she asked:

"Suppose I cannot see my way clear to dispose of everything we have and go with you, what then?"

"Then Esther, though I love you and our child far better than my own life, I cannot hesitate a moment between the dearest earthly love and a Divine command. I must go alone."

As he spoke his lips were compressed as though struggling with mental pain, but his eyes shone with almost delirious enthusiasm, and he was plainly prepared to go any lengths in making the voluntary sacrifices of which he had spoken. It would avail nothing to reason with him in his present mood. His wife felt this, so she only said gently:

"Give me a little time Charles. All this is so new, so unexpected, that I cannot decide at once as to what I ought to do."

"As much time as you wish dear wife, and I pray and trust that light may be given to show you the only right way. I will leave you alone now that you may be better able to look over the ground and come to a decision."

So saying Wallace withdrew to his study. Esther feeling as though life and hope had suddenly come to an end, after a vain attempt to look over the ground as her husband suggested, lost altogether the self-control she had hitherto maintained, and wept and sobbed like a grieved child.

"Oh mother, mother!" was her first despairing cry, as though the mother whose grave had been green so many years could hear and help her now. Then the words that came to her before, when she was passing through deep waters made themselves audible to her wounded spirit. "The mother may forget her child yet will I not forget thee." "As one whom his mother comforteth so will I comfort you." And calmed and strengthened by the thought of the Infinite Love that is never deaf to the cry of the helpless and distressed, she laid her case before One who has left us the assurance that He will bear all our griefs and carry all our sorrows.

After this her way seemed clear. Hard as it was to decide to leave home and friends, and bury herself and her child in the wilderness, and among a people of whose practices she had heard enough to make her shrink from contact with them, it would be far harder to give up her husband entirely and let him go alone. "He needs me now more than ever before," she thought "I promised to cleave to him till death should part us, and from that promise nothing can absolve me. And who knows?—perhaps he may come to himself in that wretched place, and be as glad to leave it as I shall." If she had been told, as she wove this one bright thread into the picture of their future, that once settled in the valleys of

Utah, she would have little more prospect of leaving them than of returning from her grave, she would have found it hard to believe it. She thought that actual contact with the people whom her husband denominated "the chosen of the Lord" might be the surest means of opening his eyes, and though the experiment was a costly one she decided to make it.

On one point it afforded her some pleasure to know she had it in her power to disarrange Elder Harwood's plans. Her husband might part with his own property if he chose, but not one penny of her money should be handled by that devout saint and successful missionary.

In the midst of her grief and anxiety she almost smiled to think of the Elder's discomfiture, but she felt quite sure he would allow Charles to accede to her terms, since he could not even take with him the price of their home unless she consented to its sale.

Full three hours passed while she was shaping these resolutions, but she did not notice the lapse of time, until recalled to a consciousness of outward events by Winnie, who came bounding into the room to tell the adventures of her wonderful journey of five miles or more.

The sight of her mother's sober face quieted the lively child somewhat, and when her father, as he came from his study, received her eager greeting almost in silence, she felt that something was wrong, but with a discretion acquired since "papa's sickness" she asked no questions.

The subject that absorbed the thoughts of both husband and wife was not mentioned by either, until they retired for the night, and then Esther was the first to speak.

"I think, dear," she said, "that I see my way clearly now; at least as clearly as I ever shall, and my decision is made. 'Where thou goest I will go,' but more than this I cannot say. The God my mother worshipped must still be my God, and you must not ask me to join myself to the people of your choice. I am willing to leave home and friends for your sake, but my conscience must remain unfettered."

"You promise all that I expect or require, Esther. Faith cannot be coerced. If in the future light is given you to see otherwise than you now do, I shall be glad and thankful, but not for worlds would I attempt to bend you to my views, if the truth itself does not constrain you, I am only too happy to know that you will go with me on any terms. I go forth from my country and kindred like Abraham, but like him I am favored in that I am not compelled to leave behind the dear wife, whose love is the crown and blessing of my days."

The tender words, the loving look and tone, were too much for Esther's over-burdened heart, and burying her face in the bosom that had been her refuge in every other sorrow, she wept without restraint. Her husband clasped her in his arms and kissed away her tears as tenderly as though there was no shadow of a barrier between them, and as she clung to him she said to herself "He is mine still. This cruel belief that would separate what God hath joined together cannot take him from me."

The next morning found her in a happier frame of mind than she would have thought possible. As long as she could be sure of her husband's undivided love she could face any trial, and since he was not so wedded to his new belief as to demand that she should share it, as a condition of sharing his heart and home, henceforth, she did not despair of his final restoration to a sound mind, and to the faith of his fathers. She had said nothing to him as yet about the disposal of their property, but she thought it best to do so now in order that Elder Harwood, whom he would doubtless meet and confer with during the day, might have a clear understanding of the terms on which she consented to accompany her husband. So immediately after breakfast she followed Charles into his study and said: "You have not told me yet what you wish to do with our home."

"No, I don't think that was mentioned last night, for then we were talking of matters of more importance. You know, Esther, I have no control over your property, nor do I wish to exercise any. It is right for you to do what you will with your own, but I will sell our home with your consent, and take the proceeds with us to be used as the Lord may direct."

"Well, dear, I can only repeat your words. It is right for you to do what you will with your own. I will consent cheerfully to any disposition of this place that you think best to make, but the money that my father left me is Winnie's inheritance, and we ought not to risk that. It seems to me that we should only take with us what we will be likely to need in making a new home, and leave the remainder here in safe hands until our daughter grows to womanhood."

"Very well. We will then consider our affairs so far settled. And now, how soon will it be possible for you to get ready for the journey? We have a long distance to go, and as it is already the first week in June we have little time to spare if we wish to get settled in our new home before winter. I can find a purchaser for this property in twenty-four hours, so we need wait for nothing but such preparations as must be made for your comfort and Winnie's on the way."

"Two weeks will be sufficient for any preparations that I have to make. Since we have decided to go, the sooner we start the better."

"Well, then, I will ride to town this morning to see what arrangements I can make about the property, and in the meantime you can, if you think best, let the family know of the decision we have come to."

After her husband left, Esther nerved herself for what she felt would be the most difficult task of the day—namely, to acquaint Aunt Eunice with their plans. Her faithful old nurse was the last remaining link between the present and the past. Her mother commended her to Aunt Eunice's care with her dying breath, and the devoted servant would have risked her life to save her young mistress an hour's pain. Esther knew the old woman would consider that in emigrating to Mormondom they were flying in the face of Providence, and courting destruction, but she knew too, that she would go with them, if their way led into the jaws of death. When she entered the kitchen Aunt Eunice was kneading the bread for the day's baking.

"You'se not feelin' berry well to-day I'se feared Mis' Esther," she said in response to her mistress' greeting. "'Pears like you didn't hardly eat nuffin dis mornin."

"Nonsense, Auntie, I am always well, but I have a great deal to think about to-day. Can you sit down a little while? I want to talk with you."

"In a minute, honey, soon's I kiver up dis yer bread."

This important business having been attended to, Aunt Eunice seated herself with a grave and somewhat anxious face to hear what her mistress had to say, when Esther proceeded to tell her what the reader already knows.

"De Lord be good to us chile'," exclaimed the old woman raising her hands, "is you rally gwine to jine dem ar Mormonites?"

"No, no, Aunt Eunice, not to join them, but Mr. Wallace wishes to make his home in Utah, and where he goes I must go."

"Now Mis' Esther honey, you knows I nussed you when

you wor a' picaninny dat might a bin put in dat basket dar, and dere hasn't been a day o' yer bressed life but what yer old Auntie would a' died fur her lamb, so sartin, I wouldn't hurt yer feelin's now, but 'pears like you might a' hendered dis yer."

"No, Auntie, it is something that I cannot prevent. Mr. Wallace really believes that God calls him to go, and he thinks he will lose his soul if he does not obey."

"Its' all de doin's o' dat ar man with rattlesnake eyes. Didn't I feel in my bones when he comed heyar fust, he hadn't come fur no good? An' pore Massa Wallace not like hisself, an' couldn't be 'spected to see through sech as him. I heern tell down to Easton o' some of his goin's on when I wor to meetin' las' Sunday; nebber 'spected though dat he'd bin an' bewitched Massa Wallace; a rail gentleman like him. Dese yer Mormonite preachers ginerally gobbles up de low trash like dem ar Joneses, I heern wor baptized in Easton las' week. Nebber knowed but onct whar dey ketched any cullied people an' dey warnt no 'count. Ye mind, Mis' Esther when yer mar wor livin' to Brampton dere wor Nance, used to wash for us. Nance allus let on to be mighty pious; shout, she would, in de prar-meetin' like to take de ruff off de house. She used ter work fur Missis Nash, berry nice lady and allus did a heap fur Nance, long o' s'posin her to be one o' de Lord's chillen. Well, one day de Missis comes down to Nance's place kinder onexpected like, an' Nance wor havin' a quarrel with some o' de nabors, swarin' an' goin' on like mad. When she seed de Missis a comin' inter der yard she wor tuk back some, but Nance al lus had a drefful sight o' brass, so she axed her in an' brung a cheer. Den de Missis begins fur to tell what she heern her sayin' as she wor comin' to de house, an' how bad she feels.

'Well, now, Missis, says Nance, 'you must please ter

'scuse me dis onct. I didn't go fur to do it, but dem ar niggers wor so aggravatin' I couldn't help it nohow, and I'se gwine to class to-night and I'se gwine to 'fess.' Den de Missus tells Nance here's de place to 'fess to dem what's she's done wrong to, an' Nance she flies up an' says ' What! me git down on my knees to dem niggers? No, I telled em I'd pull ebery spar o' wool out o' dere heads, an' I will ef dey gibs me any more sarse.' Well, ye see, dat kinder opened de lady's eyes an' Nance didn't git no more presents 'count o' bein' on de Lord's side. Den 'long comes de Mormonite preacher a tellin' how in Zion whar he lives de ribbers flow with milk an' honey an' Nance wor jest fool 'nuff to b'lieve him an' packed off long o' some pore white trash in de town to trabbel to Zion. But 'scuse me Mis' Esther, I nebber meant to run on dis yer way. I haint no manners nohow, to talk all de time, stead o' listenin' to what you has to say."

"I have very little more to say Auntie, except to ask, since we must go and go at once, whether you will go with us."

"You didn't need to ask dat, honey. When Massa Pryor called me inter de parlor de night you wor born, an' put you in my arms an' says, 'Take good care of my dear little daughter,' I thinks dis will comfort my pore heart fur my own picaninny what de Lord tuk to hisself. Sence dat night you's bin my own chile, an' if you wor called to go to de bottom of de sea Aunt Eunice would go to."

"I know it, Auntie. I know you will never leave me while I live, and if I should die in that dreadful country, or on my way there, you will take care of Winnie?"

"Don't go fur to talk o' dyin' chile, an' break yer pore ole Auntie's heart. De Lord what went with His chillen t'rough de sea an' t'rough de wilderness He will go with us. Ef Massa Wallace goes, its right fur you to go too an' in de right way de angel ob de Lord will take car' o' dem as puts dere trust in Him."

"Thank you, Auntie for reminding me of that. I am afraid I forgot for a little while His promise to be with us always, even to the end of the world. Only one thing more Aunt Eunice. Don't speak in Mr. Wallace's hearing, as though any of us thought it a hardship to go, and don't let any one talk to Winnie about the Mormons. I should be sorry to have anything said to hurt her father's feelings, and she might repeat something that would wound him."

"Nebber you fear Mis' Esther, I'll take care o' dat. An' now honey you must tell what you want me to do 'bout gettin' yer things ready, 'cause dat ar Sophy ain't no manner o' 'count when dere's anything pertikler for to do, an' she don't need to know 'bout yer goin' away jess yet nohow."

"I will see about that this afternoon Auntie. I am going to to the village now, and I want you to watch Winnie a little. Don't say anything to her about our leaving just yet. I will talk to her myself to-night.

## PART I.—CHAPTER IV.

### CHRISTIAN COUNSEL.—THE DEPARTURE.

Esther's errand to the village was to call on Father Belden and his wife and acquaint them with the step she was about to take. She did not feel as though she could talk with any one else about the matter, and when she came in sight of the parsonage and thought of the remonstrances and entreaties with which her announcement would be received, her courage began to fail, and could she have gone away without seeing even these kind friends, or bidding any one good-bye she would have turned back. She knew however that this could not be, and so suffered herself to be driven to the house with feelings approaching those of a criminal led to execution.

When the carriage stopped at the door, the good pastor and his wife met her with their accustomed cordiality, but in their friendly greeting there was a mixture of sympathy and commiseration, which did not escape her notice. As soon as they were seated in the house, Esther, determined to have the worst over at once, said without preface:

"Father Belden, what you told me last night my husband has himself confirmed. He has cast in his lot with the Mormons, and is so firmly convinced that his salvation depends on his 'gathering with the Saints,' as he terms it, that if I do not consent to accompany him to Utah, he will leave wife, child, and home and go alone. He has not come to this decision without a great struggle and much suffering, and—I cannot let him go alone."

"You do not mean to say that you have decided to risk your own future and that of your child in Utah, and among a people worse than heathen?"

"Yes, Father Belden, I mean that. I cannot possibly prevent my husband going, and I cannot let him go with no one to watch over him or care for him. He is no more fit to take care of himself than a child, and no more responsible for his acts. If he had deliberately chosen to make his home with this people, when in his right mind, the case would be different, but as it is my duty is clear."

"Surely if his mind is in such a state that he is not responsible for what he does, he might be placed under restraint, and hindered from taking a step that he will regret as long as he lives, if he ever comes to himself."

"No, I don't think any such measure could be adopted even if I could bring myself to consent to it. Charles is as capable of transacting ordinary business as he ever was; it is only on religious subjects that his mind is unsettled. I promised to cleave to him in sickness and in health, and in this sickness of the mind, so peculiar in its nature, he has double need of me."

"My dear child, you are right," said the pastor's aged wife, laying her wrinkled hand tenderly on Esther's. "Nothing but deliberate crime on her husband's part can absolve a woman from her vow to cleave to him until death parts them, and I question sometimes if even that can."

"But consider," interposed Father Belden, "the sort of people among whom Esther must make her home. I have taken some pains to inform myself with regard to them, and I am well assured that their practices are on a par with those of the lowest portion of heathendom. Crimes that are a disgrace to humanity are committed by them in the name of religion, and if they choose to make Esther and her child the victims of their barbarous creed, what is to hinder them? They live in the heart of the wilderness, a thousand miles from civilization, in valleys walled in by impassable mountains and surrounded by savage deserts. Once shut up among them, there will be no escape for her."

"She will still be under the care of One who has said, 'When thou passest through the waters I will be with thee, and through the depths they shall not overflow thee. When thou passest through the fire thou shalt not be burned, neither shall the flames kindle upon thee.' In His hands she will be just as safe there as here by our own fireside."

"Well, I ought to be ashamed, I suppose, of the weakness of my own faith. After preaching for fifty years that the Lord is a stronghold in the day of trouble, I should not hesitate to tell Esther to put His faithfulness to the test, only in the present instance I fear that to take the step she intends would be tempting God rather than trusting Him."

"I think," said Esther, "that perhaps a woman's divinely implanted instincts may be the best guide here. My own heart says 'go.' Aunt Eunice whose faithful affection is second only to a mother's love says: 'go with your husband,' and now Mrs. Belden repeats the same thing."

"If your duty is perfectly clear to you, then I have no right to advise otherwise, and if my poor prayers can help you, you know they will go up for you night and day."

"One thing more I have to ask of you, my dear friends, my best friends. I do not feel equal to talking this matter over with any one who may come to bid me good-bye, and I want you, if possible, to stand between me and the questions and remonstrances that I shrink from meeting. Explain my motives to my friends if you think best, but beg them not to speak to me on the subject."

"We will do that willingly, and if there is any other way

in which we can serve you, you have only to let us know it."

A few inquiries with regard to her plans, a few more kind words of counsel and sympathy, and Esther took leave of these friends of many years.

We must now pass over, as briefly as possible, the week that intervened between this time and the day of their departure. Their home was sold for ten thousand dollars; as good a price as it would have commanded under any circumstances. In addition to this sum Esther made arrangements to take with her a small portion of her own money, but the bulk of her fortune, amounting to over one hundred thousand dollars, was invested according to her previous determination. She did not see Harwood while these arrangements were being made, and her husband was not very communicative with regard to him, but she gathered enough to know he was disappointed by the smallness of the amount he had captured with his convert. He accepted the situation, however, with a good grace, and in one respect and only one as Esther thought, proved himself a safe and wise counsellor. He had taken the journey which they contemplated, so often, that he was able to give and did give valuable advice with regard to the preparations they should make. They were to go by rail and steamer to St. Louis, and thence up the Missouri to Florence, a settlement a few miles north of the present site of Omaha. Here they were to join a company of Mormon emigrants, and with them make the long trip across the plains.

Money is a wonderful leveller of difficulties, and in the short space of a fortnight all the arrangements for a journey of nearly three thousand miles were completed.

And this journey, be it remembered, differed somewhat from the trip across the continent which the tourist now makes in a week, without leaving his palace car and without missing any of the comforts of his home.

They must start in June to be sure of reaching their destination before winter, and must endure hardships, and encounter difficulties and dangers of which the traveller of to day can form only a faint idea.

Winnie was perhaps the only member of the family who was thoroughly interested in the details of their journey, or the preparations that were being made for it. Her mother had been careful not to allow her to hear anything about the Mormons, so there was nothing to dampen her delight in the prospect of seeing the beautiful and wonderful country to which her father told her they were going.

Mr. Wallace himself displayed some enthusiasm with regard to the great West, but his mind was too much absorbed in the new faith he had embraced to be very deeply interested in outward things.

As for Esther, having once determined upon the course, she went through the ordeal of preparation for departure with a degree of outward cheerfulness that surprised her friends, but there was a dead weight upon her heart that it seemed to her she must carry forever.

Through the kindness of her pastor and his wife, she was spared the pitying comments, as well as the expostulations of neighbors and acquaintances, and she was able to bid them all good-bye with no more display of emotion than though she had only been going away for a year.

But there was one farewell she felt she must take when no human eye could look upon her. On the very last day that they spent in their beautiful home, and just as the sun was setting, she went alone to the little grave that held the precious dust of the golden-haired baby that was taken from her arms to sleep under the violets.

The mound, such a short one, was bright with summer

flowers, and the branches of the willows drooped low over the marble tablet that bore the inscription. "Arthur, only son of Charles and Esther Wallace, aged nine months."

Her gaze lingered long on these words and on those beneath: "He shall bear the lambs in His arms and carry them in His bosom." Then dropping on her knees and laying her face on the fragrant, flower-decked sod, she moaned, "Oh my lamb; my lamb! my little baby that it was so hard to part with, why did I shrink from giving you up into His arms. You at least are saved from the evil to come. Good-bye, my baby, good-bye."

Only a mother can know the feelings with which Esther took this last farewell of the spot where her baby slept. None else could understand why it was harder to leave this little mound of earth, than the home where her happiest years had been spent. But the mother who has wet her pillow with tears on many a winter night, because the baby that used to nestle safe and warm in her bosom must now lie under the snow, can realize the pain that wrung her heart at the thought of going so far away from the little grave she had watched and tended year after year.

The sun had set and the shadows were gathering, but still Esther lingered until her husband came down the garden path seeking her.

At the sight of the kneeling figure, so shaken with sobs, the first misgivings that he had felt with regard to his course oppressed him, and raising her tenderly in his arms, he asked:

"Is the sacrifice too great, dearest? Have I asked too much of you?"

"No, love; but it is hard to go so far and leave my baby all alone."

"We will not be going farther away from him. He is not here, we know, but safe in our Father's house, and the precious dust that we have watched over for years will be left in his care."

"Yes, I know, and this pain will not last long I hope, but for a little while it seemed more than I could bear to leave this spot."

As they walked back to the house, on this last night that they expected to spend under its roof, calling up many tender memories of the past, Esther could not help wondering that the new and baleful belief which had taken hold upon her husband's mind should retain its power over him, while in every other respect he now seemed himself again. She had avoided conversation on the subject hitherto, and to-night she shrank from anything that would jar upon his feelings in the softened mood in which he appeared, and so the only opportunity of winning him back was lost; for, could Esther have looked into her husband's heart as he stood by his child's grave, she would have seen a relenting of purpose and rising doubts as to whether the call he was obeying at so great a cost was indeed Divine.

The next morning found them in the midst of the hurry of their final preparations for departure. Elder Harwood came to the house, for the first time since his visit in May, with offers of assistance He accompanied them to the cars and said as he took leave of them:

"I may meet you at Florence, but I am not certain. At any rate, I will have the pleasure of meeting you in Salt Lake City this winter."

His manner to Esther throughout was one of deferential courtesy, and for her husband's sake she did not wish to treat him with positive rudeness, but she was heartily glad when the cars bore them away from the spot, and she was free from the night-mare of his presence. Once, just before starting, she saw his glittering eyes fixed on Winnie in a way that reminded her of her dream, and involuntarily she drew the child towards her and threw an arm around her to shield her.

Their journey to St. Louis was not marked by any incident worthy of notice, and was not specially enjoyed by any of the party except Winnie, to whom the voyage down the Ohio was as full of wonders as a trip to Fairy-land.

At St. Louis they stopped long enough to purchase teams and wagons for the transportation of their goods across the plains, and a carriage for their own use. The steamer upon which they took passage up the Missouri was small and crowded. The navigation of this river is attended with considerable difficulty at any time, as those who have tried it know to their cost, and at low water can only be attempted by boats "constructed," as one veracious chronicler assures, us "to run anywhere the ground is a little damp." Our travellers, making the trip in July, did not meet with the delays they would have experienced later in the season; still their progress was sufficiently slow, and the discomforts of their crowded quarters made them very glad of the end of the voyage.

Arrived at Florence they found that only the van of the emigrant company had reached the place before them. These were encamped just beyond the town, waiting for the main body. They were principally converts gathered from the Middle and Western States, and the appearance of most of them fully justified Aunt Eunice's epithet of "Pore white trash." They were in charge of an Elder under whose preaching many of them had been converted; a man with red hair, a red face, and a very loud voice. He was not a prepossessing individual, certainly, still Esther thought she would sooner trust him than Brother Harwood, and his blunt manners and rough speech were quite refreshing to her as contrasted with that gentleman's smooth ways and carefully worded sentences.

When explaining the mysteries of his faith, there was a peculiar twinkle in his small blue eyes which conveyed to an acute observer the idea that he was not very deeply impressed himself with the doctrines he taught, but in his relations to his people he seemed kindly and honest. He fared as roughly as the poorest, and was always ready to lend a helping hand to those who were in trouble.

When the Wallaces arrived on the ground, he waited on them at once with offers of assistance, but was no more attentive to them in this or in any other respect, than to the humblest of his own flock. Esther took note of this, and thought for the sake of his kindness to the poor and the lowly, she could excuse many things in Brother Daniels that undeniably needed the mantle of charity. She was destined to learn, before she had been many days in the Mormon camp, how much more she would have to excuse in Brother Daniels, and in others than she had dreamed.

Among the emigrants was a pale and rather pretty girl of about sixteen, who attracted Esther's attention from the fact that she seemed entirely alone. She gave her name as Lucy Ferris, and was soon won by the kindness Esther showed her, to tell her story. She had been well brought up, and had received a tolerable education, but when she was twelve years old her mother died, and her father married a woman of violent temper, who ruled him and every-one else on the place with a rod of iron. Poor Lucy's life was rendered so miserable by her step-mother's tyranny, against which her weak-minded father never protested, that she more than once formed the plan of running away, and when the Mormon preacher came to their neighborhood and told of the happy homes that were prepared already in "Zion" for all who would embrace the new gospel, she received his words as a message from Heaven, and fled from her father's house in the night, taking nothing with her but the clothes she wore, to join him and his little band of converts. Since then Brother Daniels had provided for her, and brought her thus far on her way.

"But what will you do, my poor child, after you get to Utah?" asked Mrs. Wallace.

"Oh! there are homes there for all, and even if there were none for me, Brother Daniels would provide for me, I am to be sealed to him as soon as we reach Salt Lake."

"Sealed to him! What do you mean?"

"Why, you know, the gospel teaches that a woman must be saved through her husband. I have no husband nor any friend to care for me, so I am to be married to Brother Daniels for eternity, and in the Celestial Kingdom I will be his wife and he will save me."

"Brother Daniels is not married then? I thought I had heard him speak of his family."

"Oh yes! he has a wife and children in Salt Lake, but you do not understand. It is for eternity that I am to be married to him. It is a spiritual marriage."

"What position will he hold toward you then in this life?"

"He has not explained that to me yet. Indeed, it is only since we came here, that he has said anything to me about being sealed to him."

"Lucy, I am afraid of this doctrine, which Brother Daniels preaches and you believe. If you go through a ceremony with him, that makes you, as you say, his wife in eternity, his relations to you here will be such as must be very unsafe for a friendless and helpless girl like you."

"Oh dear Mrs. Wallace," said the girl earnestly, "you don't know Brother Daniels as I do. He is good in every way, and would cut his right hand off before he would harm me."

"Well, Lucy, I only hope he may justify your good opinion of him. I think myself he is well-meaning and kind-hearted, but if I were in your place, I would have him explain fully what he means by a spiritual marriage, before promising to enter into one. You are a good girl, I believe, and don't want to do anything that you would not like your mother to know if she can look down on you from heaven."

"No, no," said poor Lucy bursting into tears, "and if she were only here now to tell me what to do, I should be sure of going right. But I am all alone. I have no friend on earth but Brother Daniels, and if I should be disappointed in him I would not know where to go or what would become of me; but I cannot believe he would wrong a poor girl who has left everything because she thought he came to her with a message from God."

"We will hope he is not bad enough for that. I do not think he is, but, my poor child, you need not say you have no other friend. I will be your friend if you will let me, and if you fail to find a good home elsewhere, you will be welcome to one with me. In the meantime, I will speak to Brother Daniels myself about this new doctrine. I think he is honest enough to tell me just what he means."

Mrs. Wallace was anxious to carry out this promise to Lucy, for more reasons than one. In her own home she had heard vague stories about the Mormon practice of taking more wives than one, but she had paid very little attention to such reports. Now that she was going with her husband to make her home with the people against whom such things were alleged, the question of the truth or the falsity of these charges became of the greatest importance She had ventured to speak to her husband about the matter once or twice before they had started, but he indignantly repelled the idea, and assured her that the whole thing was the coinage of some enemy of the Saints in the West, who wished to find a pretext for the outrage they had committed in driving those inoffensive people from their homes and forcing them into the wilderness. Lucy's story convinced her, however, that there must be some foundation for the charges, and she determined to learn the truth from Brother Daniels if possible.

She did not find an opportunity of speaking with him that day, but on the next afternoon he called at the place where they were encamped to see Mr. Wallace. He and Winnie were both away, but would return, as she informed the Elder, in a couple of hours, and judging this to be as favorable an occasion as she would find for conversation, she asked him to wait for her husband.

It was not a pleasant task that she had undertaken, and she found it rather difficult to state the question that she was so desirous of having answered.

She did not like to use Lucy's name, but finally concluded it would be best to tell him without reserve what had passed between them so she said:

"Brother Daniels, I had a long talk with Lucy Ferris yesterday, on a subject that I would like to be enlightened about. She tells me that as soon as we reach Salt Lake, she is to become your spiritual wife, but she does not know exactly what that relation implies, nor do I, and as I am going to make my home among your people, with my husband and daughter, who must grow to womanhood there, I am as much interested in having this matter explained as Lucy is. Now, I do not know anyone except yourself to whom I can apply for information, and I rely on your kindness and candor for a full answer to my question. Will you tell me just what is meant by spiritual marriage, as practiced by the Latter Day Saints?"

Esther thought that Brother Daniels' ruddy face flushed

a shade deeper as she put this question, and his keen blue eyes were cast down as he answered:

"It is a doctrine of our church that man is the head and savior of women, as Christ is the Savior of man. A woman is saved through her husband, and she must be married to him not only for time but for eternity, to obtain the benefits of the gospel. Marriage for eternity is far more important than marriage for time. This young girl, of whom you speak, I propose to have sealed to me for eternity, to insure her final salvation."

"But you have a wife, have you not? Would it not be better for Lucy to be sealed to an unmarried man?"

The Elder hesitated, and cleared his throat once or twice before attempting a reply to this. At length he said:

"It does not become me to boast of my own attainments, but it is our belief that the higher a man ranks in the priesthood, the greater will be the degree of exaltation which he can confer on his wife in the Celestial Kingdom. Now our unmarried men are very young, mere boys, in fact, and have not had time or opportunity to rise very high, consequently many of the girls who have come among us see the wisdom of being sealed to older men. Besides, there are more women than men in our church, so that it would be impossible for every single woman among our converts to be sealed to an unmarried man."

"Brother Daniels," said Esther, looking fixedly at him, "I have just one more question to ask, and I want you to to answer it honestly. If this girl, Lucy, is sealed to you for eternity, as you say, what will be her relation to you in this life?"

"Mrs. Wallace, there are many of our missionaries who would evade that question, or give an answer not in accordance with the facts, and would think that our peculiar circumstances justified them in doing so, but I will answer honestly, as you have asked me to. If Lucy does not object, I will provide a home for her, take as good care of her as I possibly can, and make her my wife in every sense of the word. If, however, she cannot see this to be right, I will not attempt to coerce her, or to take any advantage of her friendless condition. My views may shock you very much, but I think I am man enough to act fairly toward a helpless girl. If Lucy does not wish to be my wife in this world, I will find a home for her in some good family, and she may marry a young man for time, but she will still be my wife in eternity "

" Your views do certainly shock me, but I appreciate your honesty and manliness, and only wish all your brethren possessed the same qualities. If you are willing to talk freely on this subject, perhaps I may inquire further whether it is the general practice for girls who are sealed for eternity to men already married, to live with them as their wives in this world? "

" It is. Most of the wives who hold purely spiritual relations to their husbands are elderly women, who come here as widows, or who have been cast off by their families for embracing our faith. It is thought by u to be best for the young women that their spiritual husbands should also be their husbands for time. I will tell you my own history if you care to hear it, as it is also the history of hundreds of my brethren, and will serve to set this matter before you in a clearer light than any sermon on our doctrines could do.

"My parents were Presbyterians of the most rigid type, and tried to train me up in the right way as they understood it, but I was a wild boy, and often gave them, I am afraid, a great deal of trouble. Religion, as taught in the catechism I was compelled to repeat, and the long sermons of the stern-faced old minister who filled our pulpit for more years than I could remember, had no attractions for me, and I vowed to myself many times that when I was once a man, and my own master, I would never darken the door of a church.

"I was about eighteen when I first heard the Mormons. One of their missionaries made a number of converts in our town, and I went to their meetings a few times, more because my father had ordered me to keep away from them than for any other reason, but the truths I heard there stirred my heart as nothing had ever stirred it before, and I made up my mind to cast in my lot with them.

"I was baptized secretly, but my father soon found out what I had done, and as neither persuasions nor threats availed to induce me to renounce my new faith, he turned me out of doors.

"I went at once to the missionary, who received me as a brother and gave me a home in his house, and from that day forward I shared the wanderings and the persecutions of the Saints. Soon after we settled in Nauvoo, I married a good and sensible girl, a great deal too good for me I thought her then, and I still think the same. We were very happy together, but the Saints had no rest in Nauvoo. The same spirit that animated those who drove us out of our former homes possessed the people there, and every man's hand was against us. Troubles thickened around us and it soon became evident that we must fight and die for our faith where we were or be driven into the wilderness.

"It was during these perilous times that the doctrine of Celestial Marriage was first proclaimed among us, and then not openly. In our secret meetings our attention was called to the perils which attended us all, and the unprotected state of the females whose families had cast them off when they joined us, and counsel was given to have all the unmarried women sealed to men who could take care of them. My wife's young sister was living with us at the time. Her parents were dead, and as she had no other home or friends I was counselled to marry her.

"You, Mrs. Wallace, could not experience a greater shock, if such a command was laid upon your husband, than I did at first. Little Jane, who was only fifteen, had been to me like my own sister, or like one of my children.

"And then, hardest of all, was the thought of my wife who loved me so much better than I deserved. How should I ever tell her? I pass over the miserable day and night I spent before I found courage to speak to her, and her anguish when she knew all was terrible to see. But hard as it was for both of us, we dared not disobey a Divine requirement.

"As for Jane, she was neither shocked nor distressed as I had thought she would be. She was only a child, and was accustomed to receive without question whatever she was taught, so I think without any misgivings on her part, she became my wife for time and eternity. She has always lived with her sister, and has been, on the whole much the happier of the two. Mary, my first wife, though a sincere believer in the doctrine that has cost her so much, has not yet learned to make the sacrifices demanded of her cheerfully, and I can't wonder at it. The only wonder is that our women bear as well as they do the heavy cross laid on them, and I own that the sight of Mary's patient, sorrowful face almost breaks my heart sometimes."

He paused here, and wiped great drops of sweat from his forehead, while his ruddy color faded to a sickly pallor, and he seemed to be struggling with memories that overpowered him.

Esther watched him as he sat silent thinking.

"There is good in him after all. Oh, for some power to cause the scales to fall from his eyes."

After a few minutes he resumed:

"When we were driven from Nauvoo we crossed the plains with our brethren and sisters and made a home in Salt Lake. Here I was greatly prospered, and was continually urged to take another wife, as I was well able to support a large family. Two years ago I took a young English girl into my house. She was homeless, friendless, and penniless. I married her, gave her a good house to live in, and provided her with every comfort before I started on this mission. She has no children. Mary and her sister each have four. I think I love all my children alike, though my two girls that were born in Nauvoo in the happy days of my first marriage seem nearer to me on some accounts."

Here Esther felt strongly inclined to put a question that she feared might give pain; still she thought it would do him no harm to probe his faith and test its soundness more fully, so she asked:

"Do you love all your wives alike?"

"Ah! Mrs. Wallace, that is a hard question. I treat them all alike as my religion requires, but my natural inclinations are not entirely subdued, and if I answer honestly I must say that Mary has the first place in my heart."

At this point their conversation was interrupted by the return of Winnie and her father, who had been out for a drive across the prairie.

Mrs. Wallace thought that Brother Daniels looked relieved, as he saw her husband approaching, and she could not wonder at it, for the inquisition to which he had been subjected would have been trying to the feelings of a less sensitive man than the Elder showed himself to be.

As Mr. Wallace hospitably insisted that their visitor should remain to supper, and afterwards found much to say to him about his own recent experiences, it was quite late before he took his leave, and Esther found an opportunity of speaking with her husband about the afternoon's conversation.

Remembering how positively he contradicted the reports she had heard of the peculiar marriage customs of the Saints, she expected that he would be still more shocked and surprised than herself, when he learned the facts, but though he looked disturbed as she gave him Brother Daniels' statements, in detail, they did not affect him as she supposed they would.

After hearing all she had to tell he said:

"Brother Harwood never mentioned the subject of celestial marriage to me, so I cannot think that the Saints count it among the most important truths of the gospel. Brother Daniels is a good man, but as you can see, he belongs to a class from whom we may expect more zeal than knowledge. Since we came here, I have learned from him and others something with regard to the nature and object of these spiritual marriages, but I am certain that he lays altogether too much stress on the doctrine. You cannot possibly reprobate the practice of polygamy, as he admits it, more strongly than I do. It is one of those abuses that creep into the church through the weakness and blindness of human nature, but we must not reject the truth because of the error that is mixed with it. Under the present conditions of humanity we will never find a body of believers who hold no mistaken views, and indulge in no erroneous practices. The Latter-day Saints, as I am firmly convinced, hold more truth and less error than any other religious community on earth, and as they are likewise the only people who show their faith by their works, and endure all things for the gospel's sake, I still feel called to join myself to them. I deeply regret the existence of plural marriage among them, but I am sure that when we get there we shall find it practiced principally by the class of people of whom Brother Daniels is a representative, and we need not affiliate with them."

"But think for a moment," said Esther, "of bringing up our daughter in the midst of such surroundings. You know how impressible she is, and how easily influenced by what she sees and hears."

"I will trust her mother's counsel and example to keep her from every snare. There is no danger of her being brought in contact with anything of the sort at home, and you can choose her associates outside of the family."

"We are not certain that we can always avoid receiving the members of polygamous families into our house, and if spiritual marrriage proves to be an important doctrine among the Saints, you will doubtless be visited and admonished by the brethren with regard to your own duty in the matter."

"Esther!" He pronounced this one word so reproachfully and looked so deeply hurt that she half repented of what she had said, but though she saw how shocked and wounded he was now at the bare suggestion that his brethren might think it his duty to take another wife, she knew that the same idea if presented to him again and again in the name of the faith he had espoused, would soon grow to appear less repulsive, and for his sake, for her own, and for the sake of their child she was determined to have a clear understanding with him in regard to the matter, though at the cost of a little present pain. So without giving him time to protest against the possibility at which she hinted, she went on:

"I have been told that the Mormon prophet is the husband of many wives. I meant to have questioned Brother Daniels to-day as to the truth of this report, but you can speak to him yourself about it. It does not seem reasonable, however, that plural marriage would be practised by the people without his sanction, whether he sets them an example in the matter or not."

"The prophet is only a man, and liable to make mistakes like other men. If he has erred so far as to give the name and state of wife to more women than one, I am sorry, but I would not on that account undervalue the good he has done, or reject the truth he teaches. David was a man after God's own heart, yet he erred very sadly in this same way, but we do not therefore throw aside his psalms."

"I do not think Brigham Young could bring the excuses for indulging in such a practice to-day that David had some thousands of years ago, but what he does is of much less consequence to me than what you may do. My chief fear is that a long residence among this people may familiarize you with the idea of plural marriage, and make it less repellant to you than it is now."

"Esther, I did not expect this of you, and I don't think I have deserved it. I have been your husband eight years. What have I done, or failed to do, in all that time to weaken your faith in me?"

"Nothing, dear, I have trusted you all in all, and I don't think the day will come when you will consciously wrong me. It is a change of views, not a change in heart, of which I am speaking. Your views have certainly changed greatly within the past few months, and in this very particular. One year ago you would have found a much stronger term than 'erroneous' to desinate such a practice as plural marriage."

"Well, Esther, if you think it possible for me to change so greatly as to forget the sacredness of my marriage vows, I will give you my solemn, written promise, here, to-night, never to enter into a marriage covenant with any woman save yourself."

"No, Charles. If the promise you made when I gave

the happiness of my whole life into your keeping does not bind you, nothing will."

"But I insist on making such a promise. I don't want to be haunted by the thought that you are living in daily fear of my taking another wife."

And with something of the petulance of a spoiled child, Wallace withdrew in search of his writing materials. Esther looked after him with a sad smile.

In a few minutes he came back with his bond in his hand.

It was a legally worded document, covering about a page, and dated and signed in due formality. He asked Esther to read it and place it with her marriage certificate, and to please him she did so. He was too seriously offended, however, to get over it at once, and for the first time in her married life, Esther laid her head on her pillow without her husband's good-night kiss.

There was pain enough for her even in this temporary estrangement, as any wife will believe. The night passed without sleep, and the next morning found her too ill to rise.

The sight of her pale face touched a very tender chord in her husband's heart, and with all the affectionate care that he would have shown in their honeymoon he tried to make her comfortable, and to efface unpleasant remembrances. He did not, however, allude directly to the last evening's conversation, nor did she, and the subject was not mentioned again during their stay at Florence.

Two or three days after the above occurrence, the English emigrants, for whom they were waiting, arrived in camp. They numbered over eight hundred, and embraced representatives of almost every class of the middle and lower orders of English society. A large proportion of the company were laborers and artizans with their families, but mingled with these were many whose appearance denoted culture and refinement. Among the latter, Esther noticed particularly a lady whose delicate beauty and graceful manners made her seem strangely out of place in that motley throng. The morning after their arrival her husband brought her to Wallace's tent, with a request that they would permit her to remain with them until he could provide better accomodations for her than the emigrant camp afforded. Esther hospitably assured him that it would give them pleasure to have her stay, and Mr. Wallace accompanied the stranger to town. Left alone with her guest, Mrs. Wallace, in order to avoid more dangerous topics, led the conversation to England and the journey she had taken. The lady thought that in the country to which they were going there would be no room for regrets at having left England, or any other land no matter how fair. She had only been married six months, and her parents thought it hard to give her up so soon, but her husband's home was in Utah, and besides her own heart was set on gathering with the Saints. Her husband, Elder Claude Sperry, had brought over most of the present company. He was young, the wife added with pardonable pride, but his converts were already numbered by hundreds. Among them were her sister, and a very dear friend of hers, both of whom had accompanied her and Claude on their journey to Zion.

"Only think, Mrs. Wallace," continued the young enthusiast, with kindling eyes, "what a blessed privilege it will be for us who love each other so dearly to witness together the coming of our Lord. I have but one grief, and that is that my aged parents may miss the sight, but I will spare no efforts to bring them to Zion before the way is closed up. Oh! if the world that lieth in wickedness could only see the truth, the plains that lie beyond us would be covered this summer with the multitudes hastening to the valleys of the mountains."

"Poor child," thought Esther, "what a rude shock your beautiful faith is destined to receive when you reach those valleys;" but she forbore to express her own views, and devoted herself to making the day pass pleasantly for her guest.

Towards evening Elder Sperry called for his wife accompanied by her sister and the friend of whom she had spoken. Both the girls presented a fine type of English beauty, and possessed in perfection the fresh color and rounded outlines so often lacking among their American cousins. They were in high spirits and seemed far more eager to relate the amusing adventures they had met with during the day, than to discourse of the glories of Zion.

Esther could not think that these gay, thoughtless girls were influenced by religious enthusiasm to undertake a pilgrimage to Utah, and before they left she surmised that one of them at least was more interested in the missionary who had "converted" her than in anything else. While marking the coquetries which this young lady directed towards Brother Sperry, she stole a glance at the fair, sweet face of the young wife, and saw there an expression of pained surprise; a look as though a light had dawned to which she would gladly shut her eyes. It was an evident relief to her when her husband proposed starting for their camp, and as she took his offered arm she clung to him with a manner that seemed to imply she felt the need of guarding her treasure.

## PART I.—Chapter V.

##### ACROSS THE PLAINS—"THIS NEW RELIGION IS NOT GOOD TO DIE BY"—"CANAAN"—A MORMON BISHOP.

Two days after this the Mormon camp broke up, and the long march across the plains began. The people were divided into companies of hundreds, each company in charge of a captain.

The missionaries seemed to have made the best arrangements in their power for the comfort and safety of their converts. Brother Daniels, in particular, exerted himself night and day to make suitable provisions for their wants, but the means at his command were small, and it was plain that the poor people must suffer greatly before their dreary journey was ended.

In answer to a question asked by Wallace, Daniels said:

"All who are unable to pay their own way to Utah, are brought over by the church. We have what is termed a Perpetual Emigration Fund for this purpose, and it ought to be sufficient to provide better accommodations for all, and to supply a few comforts for delicate women and little children. The Saints both at home and abroad are taxed heavily to keep up this fund, and in Utah it is augmented by the proceeds of the sale of unclaimed property of every description. In addition to this, all persons whose emigration expenses have been defrayed by the church are expected to pay back the same with interest as soon as possible. Still there never seems to be money enough on hand to supply the people with the commonest necessaries, and there is much suffering among them on the way every year, and much sickness and death that might be prevented. It don't become me to find fault with those who are called to administer the affairs of the church, but it does seem that there must be mismanagement somewhere."

Before they were two weeks on the road, Brother Daniels' statements regarding the distress among the emigrants were abundantly verified. The wagons provided were only sufficient in number to carry the stores and baggage, both of which were scanty enough; so most of the people were compelled to walk the whole dreary way. There were rapid streams to ford, rough mountain passes to climb, and the fearful alkali desert to cross, before reaching Zion, but no matter how toilsome the journey, they must depend on their own unaided strength to accomplish it. Only the aged and feeble women, and the very young children were allowed to ride at all, and numbers of these had to take turns in walking a part of each day.

The hardships of the journey, and poor and insufficient food, told upon the health and strength of many, and on the fifteenth day out they halted to make a grave for one of their number; an old man who had left a comfortable home, and forsaken wife and children that he might see Zion before he died.

He was one of the English company who had been brought over by Elder Sperry, but that devoted missionary was not to be found when the dying man asked for him.

He had made the journey thus far on horseback, in the capacity of escort to the young ladies already mentioned, and on this particular day he galloped on ahead in the morning with his fair charges, and had been some hours out of sight of the carriage in which his wife travelled, and miles in advance of the lumbering, jolting wagon in which the poor old man lay struggling with death.

Wallace's carriage overtook this portion of the train when the sufferer was almost at the last gasp. To Esther there was something terribly inhuman in the spectacle that met her eyes, and with all the eloquence she could command she begged that the wagons might be stopped, at least long enough to allow the poor creature to die quietly. The driver answered surlily that he should have hard work now to reach their camping ground before dark, and applied the whip to his tired mules to urge them to greater speed, but at this moment Brother Daniels rode up, and seeing how matters stood he ordered the fellow to halt at once.

He obeyed, though with a bad grace, and Wallace brought his carriage as near as possible, intending to take the sick man into it if he could bear moving. Brother Daniels, however, thought it would be better not to disturb him by making the attempt, as in all probability he could not live more than an hour.

The old man, as they gathered around him, made an effort to speak but failed. His dim eyes wandered from one kindly face to another with a look of pitiful entreaty, but he strove in vain to articulate a single word. Esther poured a few drops of brandy into a little water, and her husband raised his head and held it to his lips. He swallowed the draught and seemed to revive a little.

"Is there anything we can do for you?" Esther asked, bending to catch the answer. It came, faintly spoken, and with long intervals between the words.

"This new religion is not good to die by. Will not somebody tell me about 'whosoever believeth on Him?'"

Slowly and reverently Esther repeated:

"**God so loved the world** that He gave His only begotten

Son, that whosoever believeth on Him should not perish but have everlasting life."

"Whosoever believeth on Him," the dying man said again. "If I had only remembered that I should be at home now. I could have believed on Him there. Oh! my poor wife."

A momentary convulsion passed over him, then he said more feebly, "Pray," and with all her heart Esther did pray for the soul groping in the dark, seeking something better than this faith that "was not good to die by."

A gray pallor settled upon the pinched features as the last earnest petition was uttered. The labored breathing grew fainter, and without a struggle the spirit passed away, let us hope to Him who has promised rest to all the weary and heavy-laden.

The sun was now setting, and the few who had lingered beside the dying man found themselves left far behind their companions. It would not be safe, they knew, for them to be overtaken by night there alone, so by Brother Daniels' direction a shallow grave was hastily dug, and the body lowered into it.

No prayer was offered, no burial service read, and Esther thought with a shudder as they turned away from the spot, that it might be her fate, or the fate of those she loved, to be buried in the same way before the journey ended.

"Let us get away from here," said Wallace, "This is too horrible."

He drove very fast, and in moody silence until they reached the encampment.

Winnie, who had never been in the presence of death before, except on that dimly-remembered day when her baby brother slept and would not wake, clung trembling to her mother. Aunt Eunice, after the single fervent ejaculation: "De Lord hab marcy on sech misable critters," became silent as the rest, but in her heart she vowed that she would bury her dear master and mistress like Christians, with her own hands, should they die by the way.

That night while their supper was cooking by the camp-fire, word was brought to Esther that Mrs. Sperry wished to see her.

She found her lying in her carriage, supported by pillows, and looking sadly changed since the day they spent together at Florence.

She was deadly pale, as could be seen even by the dim light of the lamp that swung above her. There were dark circles under her eyes, and a look of hopeless suffering on the fair young face, that touched Esther to the heart.

"Sit near me," she said, "and draw the curtains close. I want to talk without being overheard."

When her request had been complied with, she went on:

"You are not a Mormon, Mrs. Wallace?"

"No, my husband has embraced that faith, but I never have, and never will."

"Thank God for that. You at least will pity me then. Oh, Mrs. Wallace! I have believed this new gospel with all my heart. I thought that the men who came to preach it were inspired of God, and my Claude, my husband—"

She stopped and covered her face with her hands.

When she looked up again, there was a fierce light in her eyes, and a bright spot burned in either cheek.

"I will tell you," she cried, "he is my husband no longer. This accursed religion, as I have learned too late, puts a-sunder what God hath joined together. After we had left Florence, and he knew, and they all knew that I could not help myself, Claude began to spend his whole time with Clara and my sister, neglecting me for days together, and when I spoke to him about it, he said, 'Oh, how can I ever tell *you*?' He said I must not expect all his time and attention, for he loved Clara and Julia equally with me, and as soon as we reached Salt Lake he expected to marry them both. I was struck dumb at first; then, as soon as I could speak, I poured out a torrent of reproaches for his perfidy and cruelty. He let me talk till I was tired out, then told me very coolly that if I had nothing more pleasant to say to him when he came to see me, he would take good care to keep away from me in future. He said that when we were once settled in Salt Lake, I would learn better than to make such an ado about his taking other wives; that he not only meant to marry Clara and Julia, but he would have as many more women as he liked; that the Latter-day Gospel commanded a woman to give other wives to her husband, and if she refused, he was to take them without her consent, and she would be destroyed for her disobedience, and finally he said I was a poor weak fool, and he could have married Julia instead of me in the first place, if it had not been for the money my aunt left me.

"I don't think he meant to tell me this, but he got so angry at the last that he did not care what he said, and I have no doubt it was the truth. You love your husband, Mrs. Wallace, and can form some faint idea of what I suffered when all my faith and hope, my happiness, my whole life, received this crushing blow. I did not simply love Claude, I worshipped him. He was more to me than God, or my own soul, but I am bitterly punished for my sinful idolatry.

"Then the religion which had come to me as a direct revelation from Heaven; was that a lie too? I hoped at first that Claude had not spoken truly, when he said his wickedness was sanctioned by the new gospel, and that same day I found an opportunity to speak with Brother Daniels about it. My talk with him brought me small comfort. He owned that he had three wives in Salt Lake, and was about to take a fourth. He was very kind and true to set the matter before me in a different light from that in which Claude had presented it. He said it was a heavy cross for men and women alike, it must be borne, in order that we might be purified here and saved in eternity.

"He talked for more than an hour in the same strain, as though any amount of sophistry could make such a black crime appear white to a woman in her senses, and above all a wife. I have not exchanged a word with him since, except to answer some commonplace inquiries, nor have I spoken to Claude.

"Indeed, I have scarcely seen him. He makes good his threat to keep out of my way, and is far too deeply absorbed in his courtship to bestow a thought on me."

"Then you are quite alone?"

"I should be but for Sarah, the servant I brought with me from England. She has lived in our family a number of years, and is warmly attached to me, and she regards this abominable doctrine of celestial marriage just as I do."

"And your sister; has she deserted you too?"

"She comes sometimes to ask if there is anything she can do for me, but she has enough conscience left to make her feel that she has wronged me beyond reparation, and she keeps away as much as possible. Poor Julia! She was such a good girl once, and loved me, I am sure, and I can't blame her altogether. I know well enough the extent of Claude's influence over her, and the force that his specious reasoning has with her. I pity her too, for he will make her suffer some day, though not as I am suffering now."

Here she paused and sank back on her pillow panting for breath.

Esther begged her not to attempt to talk any more, and after doing what she could for her bodily comfort, left her with her servant. She did indeed attempt to speak a few consoling words to the betrayed and deserted wife, to remind her that there was a love which endured when every earthly love failed. But the cruel wrong she had suffered was inflicted in the name of the God in whom she trusted, and the very foundations of her faith were shattered.

If the religion in which she had believed with her whole heart was a lie, could anything be true? And dark and despairing she turned her face away from the friend who would have comforted her, saying, "If there is a God, I ask only one thing of Him and that is death."

Inexpressibly saddened by what she had seen and heard, Esther returned to her husband and child. She did not speak of what had taken place, for besides the feeling that any allusion to the matter would be the betrayal of a sacred confidence, there was the thought, too dreadful to be entertained, that possibly the same fate might be awaiting her.

She tried with all her strength to put this fear from her, taking refuge in the reflection that a pure and upright man like her husband could not be judged by the same standard as this Claude Sperry, who, by his own admission was a wretch utterly without truth or honor. Still in spite of all her efforts, the spectre, conjured up by the revelations of the past few weeks, continued to haunt her, and all that night while her husband slept as calmly as a child beside her, she strove in vain to banish the foreboding that a gulf deeper and wider than the grave would soon separate him from her.

The next day's journey was marked by another revelation of the saintly character of some of the returning missionaries. Brother Daniels, who on the way was often the traveling companion of the Wallaces, and who, barring his polygamous practices, was really esteemed by both of them, was riding beside their carriage, when they passed a covered ambulance, drawn by a very fine span of mules. There were two men on the front seat, who from their resemblance to each other, might have been father and son, and a more unprepossessing pair Esther thought she had seldom seen.

The eldest of the two was considerably past the prime of life. His iron-gray hair hung like mane on his shoulders, his bushy eyebrows almost concealed a pair of small twinkling black eyes, his face was thin and sallow, and every lineament expressed craft and cruelty. His long, lean hands made one think of vultures' claws, and seemed ready to grasp anything within reach.

His companion was almost his exact counterpart, the only noticeable difference being that the hair of the younger man was of inky blackness, while a mustache of the same hue ornamented his otherwise closely shaven face.

The side curtains of the ambulance were rolled up, disclosing a mattrass in the rear of the seat, on which lay a very old and decrepit woman. A young girl, apparently little more than a child, sat beside her. As the carriage passed, the girl turned her face toward them. It was a beautiful face, framed in heavy masses of golden hair, but pale and sad, and the large blue eyes had in them such a look of mournful appeal that Esther felt almost constrained to stop and ask if she could help her; but the carriage rolled on, and the ambulance with its occupants was soon out of sight.

"If I should tell you the history of those people, Mrs. Wallace," said Brother Daniels, "I fear you would have less faith than ever in our religion. I confess that their story, as I have learned it, is one of those things which shake my confidence, not only in human nature but in the power of the Gospel to change wolves into lambs. The men we have just passed are, as you may have surmised, father and son. The father is Elder Carman, a missionary just returned from England. The son is the husband of the young woman you saw.

"Her husband" interrupted Esther in amazement, "Why she cannot be more than fourteen years old."

"I don't suppose she is, but she is a wife nevertheless, and has been for some months. That bed-ridden old woman is her grandmother. She left England with her husband and this young girl, intending to make the journey to Zion by easy stages. The old man, Brother Leonard, was rich; one of the wealthiest converts, in fact, that we have made lately. When he decided to emigrate to Utah, he converted all his property into money, which he took with him. The party traveled under the escort of Carman, though why they should have chosen such a man passes my comprehension; but the Elder is wise as a serpent, if not as harmless as a dove, and doubtless he made them believe that the Lord has commissioned him specially to take care of them. On the way out, it is said, some matters came to light which caused the old man to distrust Carman, and when they reached St. Louis he decided to part company with him, but before he had made arrangements to do so he sickened and died very suddenly. Thus the poor paralytic old woman and the little grand-daughter Eva were left entirely in Carman's power.

"This may seem a strong expression, but you must rememember that they had come on alone with him and were in a strange country—did not know a soul in the great city where they found themselves. Add to this the fact that the old woman's mind was shattered by her sickness, and that Eva knew no more of the ways of the world than your little Winnie, and you will be better able to understand what followed.

"Carman had been joined at St. Louis by his son a day or two before the old man's death, and as soon as the funeral was over the Elder determined not to let such an amount of money as Brother Leonard died possessed of slip through his fingers, told Eva that she must marry James. The poor girl, terrified and distressed, went to her grandmother for help, but Carman had been before her, and persuaded the poor, weak-minded old woman that her salvation depended on the plan he proposed, and between them they forced her into the marriage. I don't know how her husband treats her, but if her face tells the truth her life with him is miserable enough. She makes no complaint, for the very good reason that she never has an opportunity of speaking to any one, except in the presence of one or the other of the Carmans.

"I travelled with them from St. Louis, and to my knowledge neither Eva nor her grandmother were ever left unguarded for five minutes at a time. The money that Leonard left could not have amounted to less than $150,000, and as there is no one to dispute Carman's claim to it, I presume it is all in his hands or those of his son."

"You say that the girl and her grandmother are not allowed to talk with any one; how then did those facts come to your knowledge?" Mr. Wallace asked.

"Oh, I was in St. Louis when the Leonards arrived, waiting for emigrants who were to go West under my care. Brother Leonard met me there, and for some reason was very communicative about his affairs. In one of our talks he intimated that he had cause to be dissatisfied with Carman, and meant to part company with him. It was only two days after this I was shocked by the news of his sudden death. When James Carman presented himself as Eva's future husband, and she found that her grandmother sanctioned his proposals, she appealed to me in her desperation for help, but what could I do? Her grandmother was her legal guardian, and if she chose to marry her to such a man I had no power to prevent it.

"Indeed, I had little time to consider what steps I should

take, for the marriage ceremony was performed that same evening.

"I shall report the case to the President when we reach Salt Lake, and he may perhaps take some notice of it, but no one can tell. If the Carmans pay their tithing out of their ill-gotten gains, it will be all right anyhow, I suppose."

"Why Brother Daniels," said Esther, "you surprise me. I did not expect to hear you speak in such a way of your Prophet."

"I am not finding fault with him particularly, but it seems that in our church as well as in others, wealth often screens its possessor from richly-merited punishment. Money covers more sins than charity the world over—at least that has been my experience."

If our readers think the picture thus far presented too sombre, and lacking that skillful combination of light and shade which makes the work of the genuine artist, we beg leave to remind them that the fault does not lie with the narrator, who is not inventing incidents, but relating actual occurrences. Still there are redeeming features even in the practical workings of the system whose votaries we are following in their weary march across the plains.

Uncomplaining patience under suffering, self-denial for the sake of any faith, no matter how mistaken, and unhesitating obedience to whatever is recognized as the Divine will, must lift humanity into a higher plane, and the history of the Latter Day Saints furnished examples of self-sacrifice and heroic devotion that might be profitably imitated by the adherents of a purer faith.

Besides, among the people whose fortunes we are portraying, there were occasional exhibitions of native nobleness and uprightness that formed a refreshing contrast to the treachery, cruelty, and rapacity of some of the leaders.

Brother Daniels, aside from his mistaken obedience to

the tenets of celestial marriage, was a thoroughly good man, the friend of the poor, the helper of the weak, and the uncompromising enemy of fraud and oppression. After listening to his emphatic denunciation of the Carmans, father and son, Esther took occasion to inquire what had become of Lucy Ferris, of whom she had seen very little during the journey.

"Oh!" said Brother Daniels, "I thought you knew, or I would have told you about her before. While we were still at Florence, she came to me and asked me to explain just what was meant by celestial marriage, and I told her honestly just as I told you. I never saw any one appear so horrified. She turned so white I thought she would faint, before I finished my explanation, and then began to wring her hands and wish she was dead. 'Why, Lucy,' said I, 'if you cannot believe such marriage to be right you need not enter into one. I will find protectors for you on our journey, and a good home in Salt Lake after we get there, and you may marry according to your own views, or remain single just as you please. I will take care that no one annoys or persecutes you on the subject.' You should have seen how she brightened up at that, and the very same day I took her to Brother and Sister Seagrove, a very worthy couple who have no children of their own."

"They were greatly pleased with her and offered at once to take her under their care, and to make her a daughter if she was willing to stay with them. She has travelled with them thus far, and I notice that she now calls Mrs. Seagrove, 'mother.' She has improved greatly in health and spirits, and is certainly much happier with him than I could have made her, even if she could have accepted plurality."

"I am very glad to hear that," said Esther, "for I have felt anxious about her ever since we left Florence. She seemed to me so completely under the influence of the teachings to which she had listened, that although her woman's nature revolted from polygamy, I feared she might yet plunge into life-long misery through a false idea of duty."

Brother Daniels winced a little at this, but he responded bravely:

"Well, Mrs. Wallace, to tell the whole truth, I must own I am glad myself that the affair has taken such a turn. I know Lucy would have been miserable as a plural wife, and I don't want to make any more women wretched for life."

After this very frank avowal, the Elder, perhaps fearing that Mrs. Wallace would improve the opportunity by asking inconvenient questions, took leave of his companions, saying that he wished to speak to some parties ahead.

Wallace looked after him a few moments in silence, then turning to his wife said:

"That man already sees his life to be a mistake, and he is surely to be pitied. He has taken plural wives for conscience sake, and I think he will be convinced before long that he must put them away for conscience sake, but I am afraid he will find the last step harder to take than the first."

"It is to be hoped then," replied Esther, "that his brethren who are equally conscientious will profit by his experience, and avoid taking steps so difficult to retrace."

A faint flush rose to Wallace's cheek, indicating that he made a personal application of this remark, but he said nothing, and Esther continued:

"I am really thankful for our acquaintance with Brother Daniels, for in spite of the serious mistakes he has made, there is enough real goodness about him to restore my faith in human nature; a faith that has been sadly shaken by the experience of the past few days."

"There are nettles everywhere, but smooth, green grasses are more common still," quoted Wallace, half to himself.

The next day and many days following were repetitions of each other. The emigrant train moved slowly forward over the immense expanse of rolling prairie east of the Rocky Mountains, seldom making more than fifteen miles a day. Those who had light carriages and good teams, and could have travelled faster, were forced to keep back with the main body for protection from the Indians, who were in sight along the whole route. When they camped for the night a strong guard was always set, and during the day armed outriders were continually on the lookout for the savages. But there were other enemies not to be kept out by an armed guard.

Bad water and poor food caused much sickness among them, and death had thinned their ranks perceptibly before the journey was half accomplished. Again and again a portion of the train halted for an hour to make a grave for some one of their number. Many of those who sickened and died were children, and the anguish of the mothers when the bodies of their little ones were thrown carelessly into the shallow trenches dug for the dead, was most pitiable. One poor mother held her dead baby in her arms, hidden by her shawl all day long until the train camped at night, making no sign lest it should be taken from her.

But it was not until they passed the Rocky Mountains and entered the alkali desert that the climax of their suffering was reached. Water, which had been scarce enough before, was now almost unfit to drink when found, and they were obliged to make frequent forced marches to reach the bitter, brackish streams that threaded the plains at long intervals. Then the food provided for the emigrants began to fail, so that it was thought necessary to put them on half rations. Every exertion was now made to increase the speed of the train, and the sick and dying were plainly looked upon as burdens to be got rid of as soon as possible. When they had been about eight days on the desert, an old man named Hall, who was driving one of the teams, fell from his seat and the whole of the heavily-loaded wagon passed over him, breaking one of his legs.

It was near night when the accident happened, and nothing was done for him until they reached their camping-ground, when the broken limb was set by one of the party who had a little experience in surgery.

The captain of the company grumbled audibly at the trouble the old man was likely to be, and the driver of the wagon in which he was placed said with an oath that he might better have broken his neck, but happily for himself he was accompanied by his wife and daughter, and was not allowed to lie uncared for as was the case with many other sufferers.

On the evening of the second day after the accident, his wife went to one of the brethren who had a case of medicines, to ask for a composing draught for her husband, who was in considerable pain.

"Don't you be troubled, sister," he said, "I'll fix him up something that will make him sleep sound enough."

When the mixture was prepared, he carried it to the wagon himself and gave it to Hall.

Half an hour afterwards, the Wallaces, who were camped near by, were awakened by the shrieks of the wife and daughter.

Wallace hurried to the spot and found the old man dead, his face distorted; his hands clenched, and his beard covered with foam.

"Look!" cried the daughter, "they have killed my father. The medicine they gave him made him wild, and he died in convulsions."

"Hush girl," said the harsh voice of the captain, who was standing by, "it will be worse for you if you don't learn to hold your tongue." Then turning to some of the men he ordered them to dig a grave at once.

"You are not going to take him from me now," said the poor wife, "you surely will not be so cruel."

"Cruel," he sneered, "you want us to stay here, I suppose until we starve to death. Let me tell you that I command this company, and I'm not going to risk all our lives for an old woman's whim. Men, do as you are told, and be quick about it."

Wallace here ventured to interpose a request for a little delay, but though the captain answered him more civilly, he was not to be persuaded.

"I don't think I'm anyway inhuman," he said, "but you see it ain't possible to stay the train on account of people's feelings. Here we are on the very worst part of the route, provisions running short, and no water for twenty miles ahead. We must be ready to start in the morning with the first streak of light, and it is better to bury the old man now than to wait half the night. It wouldn't do his friends any real good to wait, and would only keep tired men from their rest."

An hour later it was all over, and the suppressed sobs of two broked-hearted women were the only reminders of the tragedy that had been enacted since the sun went down.

To them alone the whole world had grown dark. Their fellow-travellers were absorbed in their own cares, or bowed down under the weight of their own sufferings, and little disposed to give attention to anything which did not immediately concern themselves. Still, there were a few who remembered the desolate widow, and during the remainder of the journey came to her sometimes with expressions of sympathy or offers of help.

There were whispers too that there was something very

mysterious about Brother Hall's sudden death, but none dare speak their suspicions aloud, for after the Captain's stern warning to the dead man's daughter, the people understood well enough that they too were to hold their tongues, or it would be worse for them, and after all, what was one man's death that they should dwell upon it? Their dead were already numbered by scores, and the mountains that surrounded "Zion" were not yet in sight.

True, it may have seemed to them sometimes, as one after the other dropped by the way, that "Some one had blundered."

But if so, it was their part to bear the consequences of the blunder in silence. Brother Daniels' assertion that much of the yearly suffering and death among the emigrants might be prevented, was borne out by the fact that those who, like the Wallaces, had comfortable carriages, and were abundantly provided for, had thus far escaped serious sickness, but among this more favored class there were sufferers whose ailments were beyond the reach of outward remedies.

The young wife of Claude Sperry drooped from day to day, until at last she was unable to lift her head from her pillow. She prayed for death as she told Esther, every day and hour of that wretched journey, but death does not always come at once to those who are weary of life.

Her husband seldom came near her. He was too much absorbed in his love-making to have a great deal of time or thought to bestow on his dying wife. Perhaps, too, if conscience was not entirely dead, the sight of the wreck he had caused smote him somewhat. His wife did not want outward comforts, for her own means were ample, and abundant provision had been made for the emergencies of the journey. She had beside the constant care of her faithful servant, who waited on her with an unselfish devotion seldom surpassed.

Mrs. Wallace too did all in her power for her, but that was little. She would listen to all expressions of sympathy without reply, and the kind friends who felt such tender pity for her, ceased at length to speak of anything pertaining to her hopeless sorrow; a sorrow beyond the reach of any hand but His " who healeth the broken in heart and bindeth up all their wounds."

A few more days passed, and then the tired, travel-worn company were greeted by the welcome sight of the mountains that girt the Promised Land. To those who still retained the enthusiastic faith with which the journey was begun, the first glimpses of the Wasatch peaks was like a vision of the gates and walls of Paradise, while to all the prospect of the near termination of their toilsome journey was hailed with the utmost thankfulness.

New life seemed infused into man and beast, and the few remaining miles were quickly travelled. When the last ascent was made, and the whole company stood upon the Western declivity of Emigration Canyon, the devout believers in the new Gospel broke forth into songs of praise, and even those whose faith had been sadly shaken by the experiences of the journey, gazed with delighted surprise upon the picture before them.

The beautiful Salt Lake Valley lay at their feet, threaded with sparkling mountain streams. Near at hand were tilled fields and laden orchards; far away the Great Salt Lake was spread out like a sheet of silver, under the soft September sky, while at the base of the Western Mountains the blue waters of the Jordan—

    Ran through the gold and green of pasture lands.

The city itself, with its broad, shaded streets and white-walled cottages, lay to the north, while other green and smiling valleys, links in a seemingly endless chain, stretched away to the south as far as the eye could reach.

No wonder that the emigrants, tired and foot-sore, and with vivid remembrances of the desert over which they had journeyed, parched with thirst and faint with hunger, felt as the Israelites did when the wilderness was passed and they entered the borders of Canaan.

A company of brethren from the valley had been sent out to meet them a few days before, and under their escort they reached the city just at sun-set.

Here those who had friends waiting for them separated from their companions, who were directed to encamp for the night in a large square set apart for the purpose in the heart of the city.

There was one noticeable feature of their reception, which savored more of the wicked world outside than of Zion where all were brethren. The poorer emigrants, ragged, travel-stained and woe-begone, were left to shift for themselves as best they could, while those whose appearance and belongings indicated that they brought money with them, were plied with hospitable invitations.

The Wallaces were waited on by a number of prominent Saints, each one of whom would be delighted to have them make his house their home for an indefinite period. They finally concluded to go with Bishop Williams, a pleasant-faced, courteous old gentleman, whose snowy locks and flowing white beard covering his breast gave one the impression that a patriarch of antediluvian times had stepped down into the nineteenth century.

The good Bishop's residence was in the most pleasant part of the town. The house was large and built, like most of those they saw, of adoba, or sun-dried bricks. The grounds were enclosed by neat palings and on one side of the house there was a well-kept kitchen-garden, with a thrifty young orchard in the rear. A buxom, middle-aged woman appeared on the porch to welcome them, and was introduced to the party by the Bishop as " My wife Ellen."

" Miss Ellen " led the way into a pleasant parlor, where an old lady sat knitting. She rose slowly and feebly as they entered, and the Bishop presented his guests to his wife Elizabeth.

Esther glanced involuntarily at her husband. For her own part she found the situation becoming embarrassing, but her confusion did not seem to be shared by their entertainer, who opened a side door and called to some one in the next room.

A young girl with a babe in her arms presented herself in answer to the summons, and was made known to the new arrivals by the patriarch as " my wife Sophia."

Then the whole party sat down and the Bishop, after making a few inquiries about their journey, launched into an enthusiastic description of the glories of the Zion to which they had come.

The subject was interesting to him, if not to his auditors, and Esther was beginning to fear that he would talk all night, when the old lady, who, as they surmised, was the first wife, and perhaps mistress of the household by virtue of seniority, checked him mildly and intimated that their guests must be very tired and would want a little time to rest before supper.

The Bishop apoligized for forgetting this, but added the hope that they had already found rest and refreshment in breathing the pure air of these valleys of the mountains.

Then " wife Sophia " was commissioned to show the Wallaces' to the guest chamber, while Aunt Eunice, who all this time had remained at the door with her arms folded, and a look of grim determination on her face, was directed to go with "wife Ellen," but she only shook her head and moved a step or two backward saying:

"'Scuse me, I'se gwine to de kerridge to stay with my Missis' things 'till I'se wanted," and before any one could intercept her she made a hasty retreat through the open door and took her seat in the carriage which was still standing at the gate, though the horses had been detached.

The Bishop and his family looked after her in surprise, but Esther, glad that she had got out of the way without speaking her mind more fully, said:

"Never mind Aunt Eunice, she is a faithful servant, but a little peculiar. Let her keep guard over the bundles and carpet-bags for a while if she wants to."

There was another member of the party who was quite as apt to make inconvenient remarks as Aunt Eunice, and as soon as they were left alone in their room Winnie exclaimed! "What a dreadful story-teller that old man must be! First he said that fat woman was his wife, then in the house he called the nice old lady his wife, and afterwards, the girl with the baby." "Hush Winnifred," said her father sharply, "little girls must not speak of old people in such a way." Silenced, but not convinced, Winnie proceeded with the task of getting rid of her outer wrappings resolving meanwhile that she would ask mamma what it all meant, as soon as ever she got a chance.

During the process of dressing for supper, Mrs. Wallace found that she needed some articles from the carriage and dispatched her husband in quest of them. He found Aunt Eunice sitting bolt upright among their posession, keeping a vigilant eye on them but ever and anon glancing uneasily toward the house. When Wallace made his appearance she drew a long breath of relief and said:

"You's come den at last but where's Miss Esther?"

"Up in her room, and she has sent me for the large satchel with her dresses and Winnie's."

"You don't mean Massa Wallace, dat you's gwoine to leave Miss Esther an' dat bressed lamb in de lion's den de whole night."

"Now, Aunt Eunice," said her master in his most conciliatory tone, "don't be unreasonable. We must stay somewhere to-night, and this is as good a place as we shall be likely to find. Your mistress needs you, and you will make it very unpleasant for her if you act so strangely."

"Well, Massa Wallace, if you's 'termined on temptin' de Lord in dis yer way, dere's nuffin fur Aunt Eunice to do but to stan' by dem as she's promised nebber to desart. I tole Miss Esther at de fust, if she's called to go to de bottom ob de sea, I'se bound to go dere to," and with the air of one ready for martyrdom, Aunt Eunice gathered up her mistress' belongings and followed her master into the house.

When the Wallaces were called to supper they found a bountiful repast spread out before them, but only the old lady and Sophia sat down with them and their host, while "Wife Ellen" and a young woman whom they supposed to be a servant waited on them.

After supper as they rose to leave the room a troop of boys and girls filed in and took their places at the table.

"You have a fine family Brother Williams," Wallace ventured to remark, "are these all your children?"

"They are the children of my wives, Ellen and Hannah," indicating by a wave of his hand the young woman who had served at supper. "Elizabeth's children are all grown up and Sophia has none, except the little one in her arms."

The evening's conversation turned upon the doctrines

and practices of the saints, and was sustained chiefly by the Bishop and Mr. Wallace.

Esther did not think it wise under the circumstances to volunteer a statement of her own views, and the two wives present took no part whatever in their Lord's exposition of the latter-day gospel, seldom speaking on any subject unless directly addressed.

The younger woman occupied herself with her baby while the old lady knitted steadily and silently, scarcely raising her eyes.

As she sat thus, Esther's gaze was drawn almost irresistibly to the pale, wrinkled face, bent low over the bright knitting needles.

What a history hers must have been!

Wedded in her fair, fresh girlhood to the man of her choice, the first years of her married life might have been as cloudless as those of the beautiful woman who sat watching her. Then Esther pictured to herself the introduction of the New Gospel into their once happy home the severing of early ties, and the Western pilgrimage undertaken in obedience to the behests of their faith. The measureles anguish the wife must have endured in later years, when with the sons and daughters she had borne her husband growing up around her, she was compelled to yield her place in his house and heart to another, was not a matter for idle speculation. Whatever the sufferings of the past had been, the still face told no tales. It was as immovable as the face of the dead.

Only once throughout the evening did she give the slightest sign of emotion, and that was when her husband, in detailing his experiences, said:

"My elder sons, I am sorry to tell you, have fallen away from the faith they were brought up in. After they grew to manhood they became very restless under the restraint the Gospel imposes, and when we came to Utah they went on to California. I have cast them out of my heart entirely, for they who are not for us are against us, even though they may be of our own household.

At this cruel speech the aged mother's hands trembled violently, and her features contracted with a spasm of pain, but it was only for a moment, then the fixed expression returned and the knitting needles moved steadily and rapidly as before.

Esther felt as though she was in some torture chamber of the Inquisition, a spectator of the agonies of a silent victim, who would neither confess nor recant, and it was an inexpressible relief to her when their host, with a polite apology for keeping them up so late, lighted their bedroom candles himself, and wished them a good nights rest.

"Winnie had already been asleep for an hour with her head on her mother's lap, and the whole party were tired enough to appreciate the soft ample beds, that looked so inviting after the many nights they had spent on the narrow mattress in their carriage.

In spite of sharing to some extent Aunt Eunice's feeling that they were in the lion's den, Esther was so overcome by weariness that she slept soundly until morning, never even dreaming of the perils that environed her, and when she asked her husband, on waking, how he had rested, he answered:

"Never better in my life. I shall have to admit the soundness of Brother Williams' idea that there is rest and refreshment in breathing the air of this valley."

"I am afraid we shall find the spiritual and moral atmosphere less refreshing," returned Esther, "for my own part I felt nearly suffocated last evening in the society of that old man with his three or four wives."

"Speak lower dear," said Wallace with an apprehensive

glance toward the bed in which Winnie slept, "I own I am sorry that our first night in Utah should have been passed in such a place, and especially on that child's account; she sees and hears everything, but we need not remain here many hours. I am determined to have a house of my own before night if there is one to be bought for money in Salt Lake.

True to his purpose, Wallace started out immediately after breakfast with Brother Williams as a guide, in search of a residence, though the latter insisted that there was no need of such haste, as it would give him pleasure to have them remain his guests as long as they would.

Esther, left to herself in the polygamous household, asked permission to spend the morning in her room where with the help of Aunt Eunice she occupied herself with the arrangement of their wordrobe. She devised this employment chiefly for the purpose of keeping Winnie out of the way of the family during the day, as she feared that very plain-spoken young lady would give serious offence to their entertainers by the frankness with which she would be sure to express her views.

Aunt Eunice was ready to explode with suppressed disgust and wrath, but she had "put a lock on her mouth," as she informed her mistress and kept silent thus far.

The day passed quietly enough, the women of the household being occupied with their domestic affairs, and the Bishop and Mr. Wallace away. When they returned in the afternoon Wallace brought his wife the welcome inteligence that he had succeeded in making a bargain for a place that they could take possession of immediately. Their host urged them to remain another night at least, but they declined, pleading the necessity of unpacking their goods as soon as possible, to save them from injury.

Mr. Wallace's purchase consisted of two lots, on one of

which has a small but well-built house. Here Esther thought they could make themselves quite comfortable until Spring, when Wallace said he would build on the other lot, and here they brought their household goods at once.

Brother Williams, who had accompanied them and offered his services to assist in unpacking, observed, as they were admiring the neatness of the little house:

"This place will do nicely for your second wife, Brother Wallace, when you get your new house built."

Wallace drew himself up haughtily. "The house will never be needed for such a purpose" he said, "and I must beg of you not to make any more remarks of such a nature in the presence of my family."

"Oho! that is the way the wind sets is it," said the Bishop laughing good-naturedly, "well brother, I meant, no offence I assure you, but I see we must give you a little time to get used to our ways."

Esther flashed a bright glance at her husband; she had a good cause to be proud of him yet; while Aunt Eunice with an ominous scowl on her ebony features, rattled the furniture about in a manner that boded no good to the Bishop if he could but have understood it.

## PART I.—Chapter VI.

"LAYING ON OF HANDS"—THE WARNING—THE EAVESDROPPER—BROTHER DANIELS WAVERING IN THE FAITH.

In the course of a week the Wallaces were comfortably settled in their new home, which they found even more pleasant than they anticipated. The former owner of the place had set out fruit and shade trees in abundance, and the little plat of ground in front of their house was bright with late flowers. In doors, everything was neat and cheerful. The rooms, though small, were convenient, and after being fitted up with various articles which they had brought with them, "looked like home," as Winnie delightedly asserted.

During the rather tedious process of "getting to rights," they had a number of calls, but Aunt Eunice met the visitors at the door with the announcement that the mistress was too busy to see company now, and would be glad to have them come again after they were settled. The brethren who came to see Wallace in the evening, however, were not to be turned away so easily. Some of them were the great ones of the church, the leaders whose word was law, and Esther, watching them as they conversed with her husband, could not but wonder how they obtained their ascendency over the people. They appeared to be, for the most part, men of little talent and less culture, and almost without exception, bore on their faces the stamp of a coarse and violent, or a brutal and sensual nature.

How Charles Wallace, intellectual, refined and sensitive, could fraternize with those men was inexplicable, yet when they descanted on the mysteries of their faith, and told of the visions and revelations with which the Lord had favored "this people," he listened as to a message from Heaven.

One of the brethren known as Elder Richards, made the gift of healing his especial theme, asseverating that the words "they shall lay hands on the sick and they shall recover," were being literally fulfilled day after day, not only here in Zion, but in all parts of the world where the preachers of the new gospel found believing hearers. There were no physicians in these valleys of the mountains he said, because none were needed. When any of their people were sick they obeyed the Apostolic injunction to call for the Elders of the church to pray and lay hands on them.

"And do your sick recover without the use of medicines under this treatment," asked Wallace. "Always," answered his visitor impressively. "Or," he added after a pause, "If they are not healed it is because of their own lack of faith. You know we are told in the scriptures that there were places where even the Saviour of man himself could not do many mighty works because of their unbelief.

The next evening after this conversation, Elder Richards called early, and invited Wallace to go with him and witness the healing of a person in the last stages of consumption. The invitation was at once accepted, and if the Elder had profited at all by his opportunities for the study of human nature, he must have seen, from the rapt expression on the new convert's face, that no miracle could be claimed for the new gospel which would go beyond his belief.

The scene of the proposed cure was a humble cottage more than a mile away, on the outskirts of the town. When they reached the house, they found a number of the brethren assembled. The place was dimly lighted by a single tallow candle, and when they entered the door they could barely discern, through the gloom, a bed in the farther corner with the figure of a woman bending over it, but the rattling breath of the patient was plainly audible, even above the woman's loud sobs.

Elder Richards pushed his way across the room to the bedside, whispering to Wallace to follow. The sick man lay back among his pillows, seemingly unconscious, and with the stamp of death, as Wallace thought, already on his face.

As the Elder took his place by the bed, a silence fell upon the company. The woman hushed her sobs, and all waited reverently for the invocation of the Healing Power.

Wallace looked on with awe, while the ceremony of anointing with oil in the name of the Lord was performed. In the mood in which he was then, it would have been no surprise to him if a voice from heaven had uttered the words, " Thy faith maketh thee whole," so when the Elder, concluding his prayer with his hands resting on the sick man, pronounced him healed, it seemed quite a matter of course that he should raise himself unaided from his pillow, as he did, and in a clear and natural voice give thanks for his restoration.

Any one a little more inclined to skepticism would have noticed that all the circumstances of the supposed cure were such as to favor deception, and that the whole scene was one which might have been gotten up with very little effort, for the purpose of imposing upon a credulous disciple.

Wallace himself had doubtless witnessed better acting on the stage, but he had come to the place fully satisfied that a miracle was to be performed, and he was not in a frame of mind to demand proofs that the sick was healed by Divine power. Still, somehow, when he reached home he did not feel inclined to tell his wife of the "miracle," and replied to her questions on the subject as briefly and evasively as possible.

He could scarcely have told why he did this; perhaps it was only because he dreaded the fire of keen cross-questioning that would have followed his statement of what he had witnessed, but of late he seldom spoke to Esther of anything connected with his new faith, and as that occupied his mind to the exclusion of almost everything else, it came to pass that confidential talks between the husband and wife on any subject were very few. It was the beginning of the end,——

"The little rift within the Lute."

Esther felt this, and the sense of utter desolation which came with the knowledge that she no longer shared her husband's thoughts, or possessed his confidence, would have crushed even her strong spirit, if she had not been sustained by the hope that he would yet come to himself, and cast aside the delusion that must otherwise prove the bane of both their lives.

Again, when she was tempted to exclaim, " My burdens are greater than I can bear," she schooled herself to patience by the thought of those around her whose lot was incomparably more bitter than her own. The face of the aged woman whose silent misery she had witnessed on the night of her arrival still haunted her, and she could not forget the wistful, pleading eyes of the girl, Eva, though seen only for a moment.

But above all, the fate of the betrayed wife of Claude Sperry made her own sorrows seem light. A few days after they were settled in Salt Lake, her faithful servant Sarah brought them the news of her death.

Deserted by all except this one humble friend, the heartbroken wife breathed her last without receiving one token of tenderness from the man who had vowed to love and cherish her, or one sign that she was remembered by the sister, who for a whole lifetime had shared her every thought.

Just two weeks from the day of her death there was a double bridal. The bereaved and SORROWING husband was united in marriage to the equally afflicted sister and her friend Clara. And the man who furnished this example of utter heartlessness and baseness was a High Priest of the religion Esther's husband had just espoused, in favor with the leaders of the people and applauded by them for "rising above human weakness,"—that is to say for proving himself without either heart or conscience.

Before they had been in Salt Lake many weeks, Esther had an opportunity of learning that Father Belden's charges against the Mormons, and his fears that she and her child might be made, as he said, the victims of their barbarous creed were not without foundation. Among the neighbors who called on them in their new home was a Mrs. Nye. This lady was, like herself, from New York, and Esther was not long in discovering that she had little sympathy with the belief or practices of the Saints.

One afternoon, as it happened, Mrs. Nye came in when she was quite alone. After ascertaining this fact, and giving a cautious glance from the window, she drew a chair near her hostess and said in a low voice:

"Mrs. Wallace, I have been waiting some days for an opportunity to give you a word of warning. It is well understood here that you are not a Mormon, and to my certain knowledge your husband has been counseled to compel you to be baptized or else give you up and take another wife in your place. You are a stranger here and don't know what fate would overtake you if your husband should put you away for such a cause, and if I should tell you, you might find it hard to believe me. Yet great as your danger is, I cannot advise you to do as I did."

She paused a moment, and looked out of the window again to make certain that there was no one in hearing and then resumed:

"My husband embraced Mormonism in New York, and soon after his conversion made up his mind to emigrate to Utah. I loved him too well to give him up, and I came with him. We had not been here more than a week before he was waited on by some of the Elders of the Church, and commanded to put me away unless I would consent to be baptized. I had learned enough in our journey to know what my fate would be if my husband forsook me. I had one little child and life was sweet. Alone, I might have braved death, perhaps, but with my baby in my arms I could not. So, though my whole nature revolted from the teachings of Mormonism, I suffered myself to be baptized, and perjured my soul by taking on my lips the vows they exacted of me. I have never known a happy hour since, and after all I have gained little by my sin, for I have always stood out against 'counsel;'—that is to say, I would not consent to my husband taking other wives, and as for him, poor fellow, I must do him the justice to say he has always refused to take them without my consent. For this we have both been marked, he as weak in the faith, and I as rebellious, and we have been made to suffer every thing that the malice of priesthood could invent. I will give you just one example of their dealings with those who disobey counsel:

"A few weeks before my third child was born, my husband gave serious offence by declining to marry the niece of our Bishop. He must be punished in some way and so he was ordered out of the Territory on a three year's mission. He did not have a dollar to leave with me, as those who sent him away knew very well, and the house which he was building to shelter us during the winter was only finished as far as the outer walls and roof, but that was too good a home for a rebellious wife, and two weeks after my husband left, our house and lot were sold by the city authorities for six dollars' tax, which they claimed was due.

"I should have been left to perish on the street with my little ones, but for the humanity of a neighbor, who bought in the house at the sale and refused to allow me to be disturbed.

"This same good and generous man, though far from rich himself, kept us from starvation during the winter, and when summer came I was able to earn bread for my babes, and we managed somehow to live through the three years of my husband's absence.

"I had watched for his coming as eagerly as any wife would, after such a separation, but his return was only the signal for fresh prosecutions. He has been home about a year now, and nearly every week during that time he has been visited by some of the brethren and reproved by them for his neglect of duty in the matter of taking other wives, and this generally in my presence.

"Often these advisers are good enough to mention the names of different girls that he could marry if he would, and my own wickedness in withholding my consent to such marriages is denounced in language that I will not repeat. In addition to this, I have lately received two or three 'warnings' in regard to my obstinacy,—notes slipped under my door at night; here is a specimen."

Mrs. Nye took from her pocket a dirty and crumbled slip of paper on which a rude representation of a coffin was drawn in pencil. Underneath was written "Thus saith the Lord, the woman who refuses to give other wives to her husband, she shall be destroyed. The time is at hand when the sword of the Lord will be unsheathed, not in word but in deed; therefore prepare to have your blood spilled upon the ground that sinners may take warning and Zion be purified."

Mrs. Wallace looked at the note a moment and then handed it back saying:

'You don't surely attach any importance to this scrawl?"

"Ah! Mrs. Wallace," replied her visitor, "no one but a stranger would ask such a question. Night after night, sitting alone in my home with my sleeping children, I have heard the stealthy steps of the church spies under my windows, and the slightest pretext such as would have been afforded by the presence of a suspected person in my house, or by overhearing any conversation that savored of disloyalty to the Prophet, would have converted these spies into murderers."

"But why have you not appealed to the law for protection?"

"Law! There is no law here but the will of Brigham Young. He is not only the absolute head of the church, but the Governor of the Territory, and every office from the highest to to the lowest is filled by his creatures, so you may judge what protection or redress the law as administered by them would afford."

Mrs. Nye spoke with strong feeling, but still in suppressed tones, scarcely raising her voice above a whisper. Esther, hardly knowing whether to credit what she heard or to think her visitor demented, sat a moment in silence, and then asked:

"If, as I infer, you consider my life in danger under present circumstances, what would you advise me to do?"

"Keep as quiet as possible. Avoid expressing your opinion with regard to any of the doctrines of the church, polygamy especially. If you can rely on your husband, there is no need of drawing the wrath of the Priesthood upon your own head by open opposition to their teachings."

"If you can rely on your husband!"

A few months ago Esther would have resented this as an insult; now she thought, with a deadly sickness at her heart, of the gulf that was widening between them.

Could she rely on him? Even if his heart should not be turned from her, his mind was likely to be so warped by the teachings to which he listened, that he would think he did God service in forsaking her. The possibility was too dreadful to dwell upon, yet she could not banish it from her thoughts. At loss for words in which to continue a conversation that had become so painful, she rose mechanically, and walking to the window looked out as her guest had done. The figure of a man, crouching behind a row of currant bushes at the back of the garden and creeping cautiously toward the house, met her astonished gaze. Putting her finger on her lips, she beckoned to Mrs. Nye, who came forward and looking out said in a whisper: "One of the police, They saw me coming here I suppose. We must sit down and talk loudly enough for him to hear on subjects that will not interest him."

Both ladies accordingly took a seat near the window and began a house-wifely chat on pickling, preserving and so forth. When these important matters had been fully discussed, Mrs. Nye rose to go and Mrs. Wallace accompanied her to the door. A careless side glance made them both aware that the spy had moved along to the corner of the house, to make sure of their parting words. It is to be hoped that their importance rewarded him amply. Here they are:

(Mrs. Nye), "If you'll send over for some of my yeast Mrs. Wallace, I think you will say, after you have tried it, that it makes the best bread you ever ate."

(Mrs. W.———) 'Thank you, Mrs. Nye, I will send for it

certainly, for Aunt Eunice has been quite discouraged about our baking lately?"

Esther staid out of doors some minutes after her visitor left, watching for her husband's return. She was a brave woman, physically and morally, but the revelations to which she had listened were startling enough to unsettle the firmest nerves, and she shrank from sitting down alone in the little room where she could almost hear the breathing of the spy crouching under the window.

The honest black face of Aunt Eunice, who turned the corner at this juncture, with her market basket on her arm, was a most welcome sight to Esther. Somehow, the presence of this faithful servant was more reassuring to her than that of her husband, though she would not have acknowledged as much to herself even.

As Aunt Eunice neared the house, the spy was endeavoring to make his way out as he had come, behind the row of current bushes, when her quick eye caught sight of some moving object, and to Esther's consternation she picked up a large stone and hurled it in that direction with force and precision, crying out :

"Dere's some sort ob critter in de garden Missus, a tramplin down de yerbs,"

The "critter" instantly dropped out of sight, and when Aunt Eunice, after setting her basket down on the steps, seized a stick and rushed into the garden, in hot pursuit of the destroyer of her "yerbs" no living object could be found.

"I clare for't Miss Esther," she said, as she returned panting from her bootless chase, "de berry same ole sarpint what de Good Book tells about, must a bin in de garden, fur sartin as I see you, I seed suthin black a creepin' behind de bushes an' when I gits to de place dere's nuffin' in sight nowheres, an' no tracks 'ceptin ob suthin' crawlin' on de ground."

Esther did not controvert this view of the case, thinking it best for the present to keep the discovery she had made to herself.

The next few weeks passed quietly enough. Mrs. Nye did not call again, her husband spent most of his time at home, and there was a cessation of the avalanche of visitors which descended on them the first month after their arrival.

Whatever counsel Wallace may have received with regard to his marital relations, none but himself was the wiser for it. In his family he never referred to the peculiar marriage customs of the Saints, and a stranger might have supposed he felt no interest in them, but when Winnie, with a childs aptitude for putting awkward questions, asked him why the little girls next door, with whom she played, had to give away their papa, his face flushed and he avoided his wife's eyes while he answered that he did not know.

And when Aunt Eunice freed her mind, as she occasionally did, in relation to the polygamous practices of "dese yere heathen" he betrayed his sensitiveness on the subject by quitting the room abruptly.

They had now been two months in Salt Lake, and in all that time they had heard and seen nothing of Brother Daniels, when one evening he surprised them by calling on them.

After the first friendly greeting, Wallace asked him why he had kept out of sight so long.

He hesitated, glanced at Winnie, who was present and answered that he had been away from the city. As soon as Aunt Eunice had taken the child to her room, Daniels burst out impetuously:

"I suppose I ought not to have come here to-night with such a story as I am about to tell, but I felt as though I must have sympathy from some source, and I didn't know where else to go."

Wallace cordially assured him that if he was in any difficulty in which they could be of service to him, they would gladly do anything for him in their power.

"I don't know that any body can help me," he answered, "and the trouble is one that I have brought on others. You remember my telling you of the young English girl, Eliza Harper, whom I took for my third wife? I knew or might have known, when I married her, that she had no affection for me, and only accepted me as her husband because compelled to do so by her destitute and friendless condition. I can't say that I cared much for her either, but I was persuaded that it was my duty to marry her, and I obeyed counsel. About a year after I took her, I was sent away on this mission. During my absence Eliza, who never loved me and never had any reason to, made the acquaintance of a young man, a Gentile, who stopped here a while on his way to California, and the end of it all was that she ran away with him, just before I got home. According to our belief, and I must say our practice too, she has committed a sin that must be punished with death, and my duty, in the light of the teachings I have received, was to follow her and her lover and kill them both, but I could not do it. I have learned that the young man always conducted himself well while in Salt Lake, and that he wished to marry Eliza honorably as soon as they could get out of the Territory,—would have married her here if he could,—and if the poor child found plural wifehood a burden too heavy to bear, I cannot blame her for trying to escape from it. I am only sorry that she did not know me well enough to wait for my return, and tell me the whole truth, as in that case I would have given her a bill of divorce and let her go in peace."

"I do not quite understand you," said Mrs. Wallace. "Do husbands divorce their wives here themselves?"

Practically they do. It only costs ten dollars to dissolve a plural marriage. In this case I would have gone to President Young and told him that Eliza and I had mutually agreed to separate, and upon payment of the customary fee the divorce would have been granted by him, and no questions asked.

"And are women divorced in this manner free to marry when they please?"

"Free to marry any Saint. Inter-marriages with Gentiles are not countenanced. The young man who wished to marry Eliza would have been obliged to identify himself with us, outwardly at least."

"And now I suppose Eliza's sin in leaving you without such a divorce is counted much less than the one she commits in marrying a Gentile."

"That is true, and it is also true that if a woman forsakes a Gentile husband and marries a Saint, she is told that she has done her duty and God will reward her, but I cannot view such things just as I have been taught to."

At this stage of the conversation Brother Daniels glanced uneasily toward the windows just as Mrs. Nye had done, but noticing that the heavy wooden shutters on the outside were closed, he seemed reassured and continued his story.

"When I came home and found Eliza gone, I lost no time in ascertaining the direction she had taken, but not as my brethren supposed for the purpose of following her and shedding her blood. I had a far different object in view, for I not only forgave the poor girl with all my heart for leaving me, but I wished to save her and her lover from the bloody and cruel death they would be sure to meet with at other hands, if I was known to be neglecting my duty. I left Salt Lake six weeks ago on their track, and without doubt my friends in the church think they have received their punishment."

He stopped here and scanned the faces of his listeners. Wallace, marking his hesitancy, said:

"You need not be afraid to tell us the truth. We at least will not blame you for listening to the dictates of humanity."

"I know you will not, but it is enough to make one over-cautious to live in a community like this, when a man's bosom friend may any day become his executioner. Then too I have been in Salt Lake long enough to know that the walls have ears, and that there is no spot in Zion where it is safe to speak above one's breath. I have no cause to blush for what I have done. In the sight of God I feel that I am justified in allowing Eliza to escape,—in aiding her escape in fact, for that is what I have done, though she does not know it. If they have followed the directions they have received, they are safely out of the Territory to-night, but I shall not feel quite easy about them until I hear that they have reached San Francisco."

"Brother Daniels," said Esther impulsively, "I think if ten men like you can be found here this Sodom may yet be saved."

"Better speak a little lower my dear," suggested her husband. "You forgot what Brother Daniels has just been saying,—that the walls have ears."

Then turning to his guest he added, "You have acted rightly; there can be no doubt about that, I think. It is true that Moses commanded those guilty of adultery to be put to death, but it was One greater than Moses who said 'Neither do I condemn thee, go and sin no more.'"

"Adultery!" exclaimed Esther, her cheeks scarlet and her eyes blazing. "It was to escape a life of adultery that the poor child fled from this accursed place. Shame on you,

Charles Wallace, for coupling her name with such a word for trying to get where she could lead a pure life."

Wallace looked at his wife in amazement. He had never seen her in such a mood before and could hardly believe his senses now. Was this the calm, sweet-voiced woman who had walked by his side for years?

He made no attempt to reply to her indignant words, but Brother Daniels, with his customary frankness spoke up at once:

"That is rather bitter Mrs. Wallace, but I for one won't reject the truth because it is unpalatable. I have taken plural wives because I was made to believe it my duty to do so, but my experience in Polygamy has gone a long way toward convincing me that such a system cannot have a divine origin."

"Then why not abandon it at once?"

"Because I cannot. The only plural wife that I have now does not wish to leave me, and I don't see my way clear to divorce her against her will. She has never given me any cause of complaint, and I could not urge my own changed views as a reason for making application to the President for a bill."

"I don't see why you could not."

"Well, perhaps it would be nearer the truth to say I dare not. I don't like to own myself a coward, but I am not ready to brave the consequences of coming out openly in opposition to Polygamy."

"And what might those consequences be?" asked Wallace, speaking for the first time.

"Don't ask me" was the answer. "You will find out soon enough for yourself most likely."

"Ye who would live holy depart from Rome. All things are allowed here except to be upright", quoted Esther.

"I wish that were not true of our Zion, but I almost begin to fear that it is. You remember the Carmans, father and son, whom we saw on the plains. As soon as we reached Salt Lake, I went to President Young as I told you I should, and gave him a full history of their transactions. He heard me attentively and promised to look into the matter, but since my return to the city this week I have learned that Elder Carman has made his own statement to the President and been acquitted of all blame. I have also learned from trustworthy sources that six thousand dollars of poor Brother Leonard's money has been paid into the tithing fund, and I am afraid it is this second fact which explains the first."

"I recollect your prophesying something of that sort when you told us the story," said Mrs. Wallace, "but the robbery they were guilty of was a light crime compared with blighting the whole life of the poor child they sacrificed for the sake of her money. Where is she now? Her face has haunted me ever since I saw her, but I have never heard a word of her since the day we passed them on the plains."

"Her fate is indeed the saddest part of the story. She is not here. James Carman only stopped one night in Salt Lake and in the morning started with the girl and her grandmother for a ranch that he owns more than a hundred miles south. I have been there, and a more desolate place could not well be be imagined;—a log cabin and a shed for cattle, with nothing in sight but endless stretches of sagebush, and not a human habitation of any description within ten miles. Think what a home that must be for a girl brought up delicately, as Eva was,—and there James has left her and left her alone unless there is some creature with her that he has hired to watch her, for her grandmother died on her way to the place, died as mysteriously as her husband did in St. Louis."

"I don't see your object in telling us these things," said Wallace, with a sudden sharpness of voice, and a face indicating great mental disturbance: "Do you want to convince us that instead of gathering with the Saints we have fallen into a den of thieves?"

"God forbid!" answered the other earnestly. "There are Saints here, men and women who came to Zion with the purest motives, and who are leading lives of devotion and self-sacrifice that I verily believe are without a parallel anywhere in the world. That there are also wolves in sheep's clothing among us ought not to be a matter of surprise. It is not that which unsettles my faith, and makes me fear as I do that I have been following cunningly-devised fables. I have believed the teachings of Mormonism as firmly as I believe in God, but I can no longer be blind to the fact that many of our doctrines bear evil fruits."

"Well then," said Wallace, "it seems to me the part of wisdom to follow the advice given long ago: 'Prove all things and hold fast that which is good.' If there are errors in Mormonism I will reject them, but hold fast the truth that I know has been revealed in these latter days."

"You are right in that, but I must warn you that such a sentiment cannot be proclaimed from the housetops here in Zion. It is claimed that all our doctrines, are equally worthy of belief because all have been made known to us by direct revelation from Heaven, and to doubt one of them,—Polygamy for instance, is to lay yourself open to the charge of Apostacy."

"I am not afraid that any such charge will be brought against me. My views with regard to Polygamy are well known, and my right to entertain them has not been questioned by any one as yet."

"Well, if you live in this valley a year and are allowed the free expression of your opinions on the subject of plural marriage during that time, all I have to say is, your case will be an exception to the history and experience of your brethren. Our leaders have had much trouble to bring the masses of the people, especially the women, to acquiesce in this doctrine, and it is not their policy to allow anything to be said which might unsettle the convictions of those who are, after all, by no means as firmly grounded in the faith as they could wish."

"I don't propose to go about preaching against polygamy, neither do I condemn my brethren who practice it.

"Let every man be fully persuaded in his own mind. If my brother believes it to be his duty to take more wives than one, I am not called to sit in judgment on his conduct. All that I have said and all that I intend to say in relation to polygamy is, that in my own case I am not led either by inclination or conscience, to take another wife."

"Ah," thought Esther, 'we first endure, then pity, then embrace.' How long will it be, I wonder before toleration of polygamy in others will lead to its acceptance as his own duty or privilege," and for the first time she was conscious of a feeling akin to contempt for the man she had honored as well as loved through all the years of their married life. It was only for a moment, however, that she gave way to such a feeling—then her heart made its constant excuse for him, "He is not himself."

"Well might the inspired historian say of a love passing the love of a woman that it was "wonderful." The love that outlives coldness, ingratitude and treachery; that hopes against hope and believes to the last in the loved one, though all the world condemn him, is not usually *man's* love. Here was a woman, proud, sensitive, and counting the marriage tie and the love that makes the soul of the bond the holiest thing on earth, yet pitying and excusing the man who lowered wedlock to the state of a contract that might be abrogated at will—and that the will of the stronger party alone.  If a stranger had ventured to express a sentiment so outrageous, he would have been indignantly ordered from her presence, but while she heard her husband's words with the keenest pain, her heart refused to condemn him.

Little more was said that night upon a subject that was full of bitterness for two of the party at least, and Brother Daniels took his leave without making any further appeals for advice and sympathy in his own trying position.

•

## PART I.—Chapter VII.

OUT IN THE STORM.—WINNIE'S APPEAL FOR THE WANDERER.—RECOGNITION.—LAST PRECIOUS WORDS.

Another month passed. It was now December and raw and chilly winds from the Lake, with an occasional snow-storm sweeping down from the Wasatch peaks, had succeeded the delicious Indian summer that made the valley seem almost like the Garden of Eden.

On one of the bleakest of these wintry days, when the sky was thickly overcast and the snow falling in damp, heavy flakes, Mrs. Wallace sat alone in her little sewing room, busied upon a dress for Winnie. Her fingers moved rapidly, but her thoughts were far from her work. The brightness had gone from her life as well as from the sky, and it required a strong faith to hold fast the assurance that the sun was still shining above the clouds.

The short afternoon was wearing away and darkness was beginning to gather, when she was roused from her gloomy musings by Aunt Eunice, who opened the door leading from the kitchen and asked if,—"Miss Esther would please step dis 'way a minnit."

Laying aside her work, she prepared to obey the summons, thinking that some difficulty had arisen in the preparation of supper, but when she raised her eye to the face of Aunt Eunice, who was standing in the door-way, her faithful servant's look of anxiety and distress betokened more serious trouble than burnt biscuits or muddy coffee. "Miss

Esther," she said in an earnest whisper, "Dere's a poor critter in hyar dat de Lord knows t'would be a sin to send away, but I'm feared Massa Wallace won't see his way clar 'bout lettin her stay. Jes' you come an' ax her to tell what she tole me."

Wondering who could have come to their door in such a storm, she followed Aunt Eunice into the kitchen, and there, crouching in the darkest corner like a hunted animal, was a young girl, bare-footed, bare-headed, her long dark hair damp with the melting snow and her thin cotten garments wet through and clinging to her slender figure.

As Esther entered she turned towards her a pair of wild terrified eyes, but seemingly reassured by the sight of a pitying womanly face she left her place and falling on her knees cried: "

"Don't turn me away, pray don't. You are good, I know. They say you are not a Mormon, and that was the reason why I came here. Nobody else would let me in, and I could not go much farther. You will let me stay won't you? I'll do anything. I'll work for a crust and sleep on the bare floor, and if you turn me off I must freeze to death this bitter night; though I'd rather strave and freeze a thousand times than go back to HIM."

The tone in which she pronounced the last words expressed such dread and loathing that her listener needed no further explanation, yet when Esther asked:

"Go back to whom?" she was hardly prepared to hear in reply the name of one of the highest dignitaries in the Mormon Church.

She would not question the trembling, shivering creature further, but in the kindest words assured her of shelter and protection, and then bidding her sit down by the fire, she went in search of dry garments for her.

Returning with them, she told Aunt Eunice to take the

girl into her bed-room and make her change her wet clothes at once.

"And then," she added, "when you are dry and warm and have eaten your supper, I will hear your story."

It was by this time quite dark, and Aunt Eunice had already fastened the shutters and bolted the door. The storm was increasing in violence and Esther had no fear that any one would follow the girl through it, but in any event she was determined to protect her.

Mr. Wallace had left the city on business in the morning, expecting to be absent a couple of days, and the storm would probably detain him still longer, so she would have ample time to learn the particulars of the girl's history and decide what course to take before his return. Winnie, though she had all of a child's curiosity to know what was going on, remain obediently in her mothers room, where she now sat rocking her doll to sleep, while she waited for mamma and supper, outwardly patient, but thinking in her heart that both were a long time in coming.

Esther entered softly, stood a moment in the doorway watching the childish figure swaying back and forth in the little rocking chair, and listening to the sweet voice that sang, as her mother had sung so often beside her own cradle:

   Holy Angels guard thy bed.

Tears dimmed the mother's eyes as her thoughts reverted to the homeless wanderer in the other room, who perhaps had once been as safely sheltered and as tenderly cared for as her own darling.

"God helping me," she said inwardly, "I will deal with her as I would pray my dear one might be dealt with if left motherless and alone."

"Oh mamma," said Winnie, turning her head and catching sight of her, "I am so glad you have come. Aunt

Eunice said when she lighted the lamp that I must stay here and be a good girl but I have been very lonesome, with nobody but dolly,—but mamma what is the matter? Are you sick?"

"No dear. Wait till Aunt Eunice brings the supper, and I will tell you."

The appearance of the tea-tray diverted Winnie's thoughts for a moment, but from being her mother's companion so much of late, she had learned to watch her moods, and her affectionate heart was quick to note any shadow on the face so dear to her. To-night she could not help seeing that mamma looked troubled, and in her childish way she longed to comfort her, but she asked no further questions.

After they were cozily seated at their own little round table, and Aunt Eunice had poured the tea, Mrs. Wallace said:

"Winnie dear, there is a poor girl in the kitchen who has no home and nowhere to go. She came here in the storm, and wants to stay. Do you think we ought to keep her?"

"Why mamma! of course we ought. Don't you remember the verse you made me learn last Sunday, 'Bring the poor that are cast out to thy house' and if you did'nt have to bring this poor girl, you ought to let her stay when she came herself."

"Thou hast hid these things from the wise and prudent and revealed them unto babes," thought the mother; then she said aloud:

"But suppose she should not be a good girl, would my little daughter like to have her in the house with us?"

"Mamma," said Winnie, raising her serious, earnest eyes to her mother's face, "a long time ago when we lived in New York, you read me a story out of the Testament that I have remembered ever since. It was about a woman who had been very wicked and was sorry for it, and came to the house where Jesus was and began to wash his feet with her tears, and when the people in the house wanted to send her away, Jesus would not let them. Don't you think he meant by that, that if people have been ever so bad, and are sorry, we ought to keep them with us and help them to be good?"

"Yes darling, I do think so, and I don't know that this poor girl has done any thing wrong. I only know what I told you,—that she has nowhere to go and wants to stay with us, but after supper I mean to ask her to tell me about herself."

"Do mamma, and I hope you will think it right to keep her. Just suppose it was me that had to be out on the street in the snow to-night."

In her earnestness Winnie repeated the appeal that had already been made to a mothers heart,—an appeal which, as Esther divined, her father also would find it hard to withstand; and though he might think it a serious matter to risk giving shelter to one who had fled from the house of the High Priest the girl named, he surely could not be deaf to the voice of humanity and the pleadings of his own innocent child. At all events, her own resolution was taken. With or without her husband's consent she would protect the helpless and friendless creature who had sought the shelter of her roof, and leave the result with Him who commanded her to succor the distressed.

When she returned to the kitchen the girl, clad now in warm and comfortable garments and further refreshed by a cup of tea and the food Aunt Eunice urged upon her, looked a different being from the crouching, shivering creature that appealed to her compassion an hour before.

Esther, now that she was able to observe her more closely, thought the face familiar. She had surely seen her before but where? The girl guessing her thoughts said:

"I did not suppose you would recollect me, Mrs. Wallace but I knew you at once. Don't you remember little Bessie Gordon that used to be in your Sunday school class at Easton?"

"Bessie! Is it possible? What could have brought you here. Surely your father and mother did not join the Mormons?"

"No, oh no. All my troubles began by disobeying them and going to hear the Mormon preacher. It is a long story, but you cannot understand how utterly friendless and alone I am unless I tell you all.

"When we left Easton four years ago we moved to Chesterville, and I don't think I have seen you since. Last winter, Elder Harwood, a Mormon missionary, came to our place and many of the people were quite carried away by his preaching. Some of the girls that I knew went to hear him and wanted me to go too. I was certain that father and mother would never consent, so, like a wicked girl as I was, I determined to go without letting them know anything about it.

"The Grays, friends of ours at the other end of the town were among Elder Harwood's converts, though father and mother never suspected it. Mrs. Gray often sent for me to stay over night with her, and I was always allowed to go. She took me to the Mormon meeetings and I saw Elder Harwood at her house.

"I can hardly tell how or why it was that his preaching affected me as it did, but from the first time that I heard him it seemed to me that I had been in the dark all my life before. He talked so much about crucifying every earthly affection and forsaking all for the gospel's sake, that at last I came to believe it my duty to deceive my kind parents and steal away from my home and gather with the Saints at Zion. When I had once given my promise to go, Elder Harwood planned everything for me. The Mormon converts in the place were to start the first of June, but I was to wait a few weeks later that my friends might not suspect anything. When everything was in readiness for my flight, I got permission to pay a week's visit to my aunt who lived a few miles out in the country. I was to go in the stage, and I had to walk a couple of blocks to the place it started from. My father was away at his business and my mother bade me good-bye for the week, little dreaming she would never see me again.

"As soon as I was out of sight of the house, I turned and walked rapidly from the corner where I should have met the stage. I went quite to the outskirts of the town, to a Mormon family who had orders from Harwood to take care of me. They received me very kindly, and kept me concealed till night. The woman said it would be necessary for me to disguise myself in some way, so she made me put on a black dress and cloak, a close bonnet and a thick crape veil. I am quite sure if my father had met me on the street in that dress he would not have known me. When the night express came along, the woman's husband took me to the cars where we found Harwood waiting for me. He traveled with me as far as Buffalo, where he put me in the care of a man and his wife,—Saints on their way to Zion. They brought me through to Florence without stopping, indeed from the moment I stepped on board the cars at Chesterville, I was hurried along so rapidly that I had no time to think about what I had done and we only reached Florence the night before the emigrant company started to cross the plains.

"Thus far, the idea that I was doing something grand and heroic in forsaking home and friends for the Gospel's sake kept me up, but before we had accomplished the first hundred miles of that miserable journey I began to see my conduct in its true light, and I repented bitterly enough of my folly and wickedness:

"I was sick on the way and thought I should die. I would have been glad of that if I had not remembered some dreadful Bible words about disobedient children. I did not want to live but was afraid to die and by the time we reached Salt Lake I thought I did not care what became of me.

"A few days after we got here I was taken sick again. I was stopping with a poor family who did not want to be burdened with me, and they applied to the Apostle from whose house I was driven out this morning. He came to see me and was very kind,—professed a great interest in me, and had me removed at once to his house. There were two women there, both of them his plural wives, though I did'nt know it at the time. I was sick a long while and he was very good to me, and so were the women when he was at home, but when he was away they treated me coolly.

"When I got well enough to be about the house he began to spend a great deal of time with me and finally asked me to marry him. I had learned before this who the women in the house were and also that his first wife was living near. I felt just as badly to have him make such a proposal as I would if any married man at home had talked to me in the same way, and I begged him with tears never to speak of such a thing again. He took my answer very lightly at first, but by and by he began to expostulate and threaten, and at last he told me if I did not marry him he would make me wish I had never been born.

"Sunday,—yesterday, he came to me and told me he would give me a last chance to choose whether I would marry him or meet the punishment that was prepared for the disobedient. I said 'You can kill me if you like but I will never commit such a sin as you ask me to.' Then he talked awfully to me. It makes my blood run cold yet to think of some things he said; and when he was ready to leave the house he took me by the arm and dragged me into a little empty room, where he left me all that day and night.

"Early this morning he came and unlocked the door. 'Well Miss Purity,' he said, ' I hope you will like the fate you have chosen. Last night I had you published in every Ward meeting-house in the city as a vile creature whose shameless conduct could no longer be endured by the Saints, and all the people are forbidden to receive you into their houses or to give you so much as a crust of bread or a cup of water. In an hour's time you will find yourself on the street, stripped of everything except the rags in which I found you. You can try your new life for a while, and when you are ready to come to me and acknowledge your sin on your knees, perhaps I may take you back.'

"Without waiting for any reply he turned and called to the women, who I suppose had been listening in the passage. They came, one of them carrying on her arm the clothes I wore when I fell sick. I should have told you before that the few things I brought with me from home disappeared during my illness on the plains, so that when I reached Salt Lake I was entirely destitute.

"'Take this girl,' said the Apostle, 'and see that when she goes from here she carries nothing away which is not her own.' With these words he left the room, and the women ordered me to take off my shoes and stockings and exchange my clothes for those they brought me. While I was doing this they called me the vilest names and loaded me with reproaches and abuse. Then they took hold of me, one on each side and led me out of the house, bidding me never dare to show my face there again.

"I had eaten nothing since noon of the day before and I was still weak from my sickness, but I found no one willing to take me in or give me a morsel of bread. I was refused food and shelter so often that I had no courage to ask for either again, and many times during the day I thought I must lie down in the street and die. At last I remembered you. I heard your name mentioned often while we were crossing the plains, but never imagined it was the friend who used to be so kind to me when I was a little girl.

After we reached Salt Lake I heard people talk of Brother Wallace and his wife, who was not a Mormon, and to-day I thought if I could reach your door, you perhaps, would not not turn me away."

"I will not, my poor child, of that you may rest assured; but could you not find a single friend among those who came here from your own town?"

"Mrs. Gray died on the plains, and her husband has taken two wives since he came to Salt Lake. I knew it would do no good to go to him for help, and the other families that came from our place are scattered in different parts of the Territory. Two of them remained in Salt Lake I was told, but I could not find them and perhaps they would have been like all the the rest afraid to receive me."

"Well Bessie, I will try to take the same care of you that I would like your mother to take of my little girl, if she found her wandering in the streets, and as I think you need rest now more than anything else, I will let Aunt Eunice make a bed for you in her room, and you must get to sleep as soon as you can. And remember, there is One who will watch over you far better than I can if you will ask him."

"Oh Mrs. Wallace, do you think He would hear me after I have been so wicked? I have'nt dared to pray for a long time. I know I have broken my father's heart and maybe killed my poor mother, and it don't seem to me as though God would ever forgive me."

"Bessie, if it had been your mother's door instead of

mine that you had come to to-night, do you think she would have put you out into the storm again?"

"Oh no! no! she would have hurried me in by the fire and pulled off my wet clothes, and cried over me and pitied me—oh how she would have pitied me and loved me. Oh mother! mother!" and with this bitter cry the poor child broke down and wept and sobbed with a violence that alarmed her kind friend, who reproached herself for opening an unhealed wound.

"Don't, Bessie dear," she said tenderly, "your mother would not like to see you cry so and make yourself ill again. I only wanted you to remember that the Heavenly Father you have been afraid to pray to loves you a thousand times better than even your mother does. If you will tell Him all your troubles to-night and ask Him to take care of you and comfort your father and mother, He will hear you and do more than you ask. Come now, let me see you safely in bed at once and don't try to talk any more until to-morrow."

Bessie rose obediently and striving to check her sobs followed Mrs. Wallace into the room prepared for her. For the first time since the unhappy day when she fled from her home, she laid her tired head on a pillow smoothed by loving hands, and calmed and reassured by the kindness of an earthly friend, ventured to pour all her griefs into the listening ear of the Friend above.

When morning dawned on the little household the snow was still falling, and throughout the day the streets in the neighborhood were deserted, none seeming to care to venture abroad in the storm.

Bessie looking pale and ill, but wearing an air of greater quiet and content than might have been expected, sat in the little parlor of her kind entertainer, answering questions with regard to her recent experiences, and giving a fuller account of herself than she was able to the night before. She said that Elder Harwood furnished the people in whose charge he placed her with money to defray her expenses to Utah, and promised to take her under his own care when he arrived in Salt Lake, but so far as she could learn he had not returned yet.

" And now," said the girl with a shudder, " I never want to see him again. He has deceived me cruelly, tempted me to forsake father and mother and home, and if he should find me here he would want to take care of me in the same way as the man who drove me out into the storm to perish yesterday."

"You need not see him again" said Mrs. Wallace soothingly. "If he has not crossed the plains yet, it is not likely that he will do so before spring, and by that time,—who knows—you and I may find a way to get back to New York."

Bessie shook her head sadly.

"You may get away from here," she said ; " I will pray every night on my knees that you may ; but I will never live to see my home again; I am sure of that. The most I can ask or hope for is that after I am dead, word may be sent to my parents in some way to end their suspense about my fate."

"Have you not written to them since you came here ?"

"I have never been allowed to, and I don't think that letters from any persons who might be suspected of sending out an unfavorable report are ever permitted to leave the Territory. I learned enough while in the house in which I spent the last six weeks to make me certain that the mails are very closely watched."

"In spite of that watch however, we will find some way to communicate with your friends. Don't you think they must at least suspect that you went off with the Mormons? "

"No. Elder Harwood's converts started West, as I told you, three weeks before I did, and no one else in the place knew that I had ever attended a Mormon meeting. Harwood himself took good care not to be seen in Chesterville after they left, and I am quite sure my meeting with him on the night train, that carried me away, was not noticed by any one; I don't remember seeing a person that I knew on the street the day I left, and besides, I knew that father and mother would not begin to feel anxious about me or think of making any inquires until the end of the week, when they would be expecting me home from Aunt Mary's."

"Well I do not despair of being able in some way, to send letters to them and to my own friends at home. I will make the trial at any rate, and meantime you will be as safe here as under your own mother's roof."

Before night, Bessie began to show the effects of the inhuman treatment she had received. The fever from which she had barely recovered when she was turned out into the storm, returned with increased violence, and by noon of the next day she was tossing and raving in wild delirium. Mr. Wallace reached home a few hours later and listened with the utmost astonishment to the story his wife had to tell.

Pretty little Bessie Gordon, when a child, was a great favorite with him as with Esther, and her parents were counted among his warmest friends. He was even more severe than his wife in his condemnation of the brutality that had driven her into the street to die, and announced his intention of laying the whole matter before "President Young" at once. This however, Esther persuaded him not to do, at least while Bessie lay sick and no inquiries were made for her.

Two more days passed, developing the most alarming symptoms in the poor girl's illness. Aunt Eunice exhausted her skill as a nurse in the sufferer's behalf, and Wallace and his wife tried every remedy of which they had any knowledge, but the fever continued unabated until the ninth day.

During all this time no inquiries were made as to who was lying sick in their house. Indeed the weather was such that very few of their neighbors came to their door, and if Bessie had been tracked there they did not know it.

Mrs. Wallace felt assured now that her husband would join her in taking any measures necessary for the girl's safety, but another and greater power was about to step between her and her persecutors.

Death, the friend so often feared as a foe, drew near at last. The fire that burned so fiercely in her veins died out, and white and wasted and weaker than an infant, but conscious, Bessie lay back among her pillows waiting the hour of her release. The friends who had cared for her so tenderly stood around her, and Esther bent her ear to catch the last whispered word: "Jesus saves sinners—saves me.—Tell mother."—Here the faint, fluttering breath ceased, and the tired wanderer sank to rest;—a rest that none might break.

> "Good night! Now cometh quiet sleep,
> And tears that fall like gentle rain;
> Good night! Oh holy, blest and deep,
> The rest that follows pain."

# IN THE TOILS:
## OR
### MARTYRS OF THE LATTER DAYS.
## PART II.

## PART II.—CHAPTER I.

AMANDA JOSEPHINE; HER ASPIRATIONS AND TRIBULATIONS.—"THE DEAREST MOTHER ON EARTH."—THE HEROISM OF DAILY LIFE.

> "I care not, Fortune, what you me deny,
> You cannot rob me of free Nature's grace,
> You cannot shut the windows of the sky
> Through which Aurora shows her brightening face."

The winter was over and gone in the Promised Land. March had come; not the stormy March of those regions where it is a spring month only in the almanac, but a time of soft skies and warm breezes, of swelling buds and opening blossoms.

There was nothing pale or wintry in the sunlight that was thrown back from the glittering peaks of the Wasatch to flood the valleys below. The brown earth, freshly turned by the settler's plow, felt its warmth; the birds, that were building their nests in the willows along the streams, greeted it with a chorus of cheerful song, and the shyest of the early wild flowers crept out of their hiding places into the golden glow.

As far as climate is concerned, Utah surely has whereof to boast and Esther Wallace, leaning from her window that opened toward the sunrise, and drinking in the fresh breath of the early morning, felt for a little while almost in love with her new home.

The winter had passed very quietly with our friends.

The Priesthood, under whose ban Esther, not without reason, supposed herself to be, made no open demonstrations of hostility. Perhaps they hoped in time to convert her and secure her fortune, which rumor exaggerated to four times its real amount. At all events she met with corteous treatment from the Saints and, if they persisted in urging celestial marriage upon her husband as a present duty, she did not know it.

He on his part appeared less absorbed in the mysteries of the Latter Day Gospel than during the first months succeeding their arrival in Utah. After his favorite books were unpacked and the little sitting-room made to do double duty as a library, he spent much of his time at home, and on stormy winter days when they gathered around their cheerful fire, Esther with her sewing, Winnie on a cushion at her mother's feet, and the "darling papa" on the other side of the hearth-rug reading aloud, they presented a perfect picture of a happy and united family.

On such days the year that had brought Esther so much sorrow appeared like a dream, and she could almost fancy that they were back again in the dear old home.

Her husband seldom spoke of anything pertaining to his religious experiences, and she sometimes thought he was beginning to see how grossly he had been deceived by the "messenger from Heaven," through whose instrumentality he was led to forsake home and friends for an inheritance among the Saints.

Elder Harwood was still East, and in his absence Wallace was without a guide in the tangled paths he was seeking to follow. Left to himself, it seemed possible that he might give up the vain atttempt to reconcile the teachings of the new Gospel with his own sense of right. Lately, however, the brethren around them had begun to visit at their house more frequently, and there was no lack of counsel as to what Brother Wallace should and should not do.

During the winter, Esther nourished a secret hope that they might get away from Utah before the end of the year, but this she was now forced to give up. The project of building another house, of which her husband said so little that she thought he had abandoned it, was revived and on the spring morning with which this chapter opens workmen were busy about the foundations.

The house was planned on an ample scale. "Large enough for a family like mine," our old friend Bishop Williams observed, and Esther could not help noticing that this time her husband failed to resent the remark or treat it as an ill-timed jest. The new building was an object of interest to others besides Bishop Williams. Its style and dimensions were so far in advance of those around it, that the good Saints, very like the world's people in this particular, conceived a sudden respect for the man who could afford such a residence.

Almost any day half a dozen neighbors of the sort who take a cheerful interest in other people's affairs, might be seen leaning over the fence or congregated within making friendly suggestions about the work.

It was a noticeable fact, however, that the brethren alone had such an amount of leisure to devote to their neighbors' business. The sisters seldom left their own premises. Household duties and the care of their numerous children occupied most of their time, and the spring brought them additional work, in the shape of planting and watering their gardens.

The Saints, it is well known, go back to the the good old times for their social and domestic models, and as a general thing improve upon the copy

Rebecca and Rachel drawing water for the flocks they tended, Ruth gleaning in the harvest field, and other pastoral pictures of those days, have laid hold upon their imaginations and are reproduced by them in Utah, with variations suited to their circumstances.

Even at this date the traveler in the modern Zion will be reminded of scenes he has witnessed in the Orient. He will see women herding cattle and sheep on the range, planting the tilled fields, digging ditches for the water that is to irrigate their crops, and later in the season gathering in the harvest.

The writer hereof recollects one venerable patriarch who was rich in flocks and herds, and blessed likewise with eight dutiful and affectionate wives. In the valleys of Southern Utah the grass is green throughout the year. and through summer's heat and winter's storm those eight loyal women watched and tended their master's flocks. Their's was no hireling service. They received no wages except the consciousness of duty well performed and their children, growing up around them, were taught to follow in their footsteps. No wonder the patriarch's riches increased until he became the greatest man in all those valleys.

Another wealthy brother, being asked the reason of his unusual prosperity, made answer:

"I married four active strong-armed Danish girls the first year I came here. My wives have cultivated my farm, herded my stock, taken my grain and fruit to market, and earned enough besides to build my houses and barns."

Thus it will be seen that the Latter Day Saints have solved the problem of cheap labor and defined the sphere of woman at the same time.

But to return to our story.

As the new building progressed, there was quite a little army of workmen to board, and some one had to be hired to assist Aunt Eunice in the the kitchen, but domestic help proved a scarce commodity in Zion.

The matrimonial market was brisk, and absorbed most of the girls above the age of fourteen. There was quite a large number of single women in the train which came in the previous autumn, but most of these were sealed to waiting Saints in different parts of the Territory, soon after their arrival.

However, after a week of failures, Wallace came home on Saturday night, tired, but triumphant, and announced that he had secured the services of a sister Saint who was not only an embodiment of all the Christian graces, but a perfect mistress of housekeeping in all its branches.

Aunt Eunice received the intelligence with a scornful toss and sniff. She had had her trials before now with "white trash" in the kitchen, and gave it as her deliberate opinion that:

"Gabriel hisself could'nt put up with sich goins on."

After a little questioning, it transpired that Wallace had not seen the paragon he described, but Bishop Williams had engaged her for them and assured him that she would be on hand bright and early Monday morning.

Monday came, but not the model servant. Tuesday dawned and passed and Aunt Eunice, with grim satisfaction repeated: "Did'nt I tole yer so?" but Wednesday brought the long expected damsel.

She was short and stout, sandy haired, freckled, and a trifle cross-eyed, but then beauty was not in the bond. When shown into the sitting-room, she settled herself comfortably in the nearest chair, deposited her band-box on the carpet and began fanning herself with her sun-bonnet, remarking, "Its powerful warm walkin'."

"I suppose so," assented Mrs. Wallace. "Are you the girl that Bishop Williams engaged for us?"

"Yes sister."

"Have you brought a recommendation from your last place?"

"How?"

"I mean, did the lady you worked for last send you to Bishop Williams?"

"No, I never worked out before."

"Where are you from?"

"Iowy."

"What is your name?"

"Amanda Josephine Harker."

"Well Amanda, can you cook. wash, and iron?"

"I reckon."

"What wages, do you expect?"

"Well, Sister Styles, she would'nt promise me more'n a dollar a week, but Bishop Williams, he said as how you folks up here could afford to give a dollar and a half. I sp'ose I could 'a married old man Styles in a month, but good land! I don't want no sech truck as him. He's seventy if he's a day, and too stingy to give his wives enough to eat."

"Not a very kind husband certainly, in that case, but we were talking about wages. If I give you a dollar and a half a week I shall expect you to do all the washing besides helping with the cooking and keeping the kitchen clean."

"You need'nt be a grain uneasy sister. I calculate the washin' there is about this house won't be a circumstance to what I've ben used to, and as far as keepin' the kitchen clean, my mother always said a body might eat off a floor her girls had scrubbed."

As Amanda Josephine paused a moment to take breath, the master of the house entered the room in search of a paper.

"Why how *do* you do, brother Wallace?" exclaimed the

young lady rising with alacrity and holding out a hand of formidable proportions.

Wallace, considerably embarrassed by the salutation, took the offered hand mechanically and was rewarded by a grip and shake that nearly dislocated his arm. Esther smothered a laugh with difficulty, while her husband, having effected his release from the grasp of the gushing Amanda and found the paper he came for, retreated in good order.

American ladies are apt to complain that servants in this country never know their place, but Mrs. Brown of Fifth Avenue is at least spared the consciousness that Sarah Jane in the kitchen aspires to the position of Mrs. Brown, No. 2.

Mrs. Wallace would have risked the dread possibility of such aspirations on the part of Miss Amanda Josephine Harker, if she could only have been sure of that amiable young persons qualifications as cook and laundress.

As it was, there seemed room for doubt, but she must have help of some sort, and so Amanda was engaged for a week on trial, and duly installed in the kitchen.

The work expected of her she said was, "jest nothin' at all," and from the manner in which she performed it, her word seemed likely to be made good.

But who meantime shall describe the tribulations of Aunt Eunice?

"Sure's you're born Miss Esther," she said the next day "its gwine to to take more'n Massa Job's patience, to put up with dat ar' 'Mandy. Dis morin' I wor 'bleeged to go fur de meat de berry fust thing so I had to trust 'Mandy with the dishes. I tole her an' showed her pertikler 'bout everthing an' when I come home ef dat critter warn't a washin' de chany cups in de hand-basin an' a dryin' em on her dirty apron, an' when I axed her whar she wor brung up that she did'nt know no better, she jest answers as bold as brass, "Hity-tity! 'Pears to me some folks is more nice than wise."

"Well Auntie we must be patient with her this week; Perhaps you had better set her to scrubbing the floor. She seems strong enough to do that well."

Aunt Eunice did as requested, and the scrubbing seemed more in Miss Amanda's line, but she had a soul above drudgery, and aspired to something that would afford a better field for the display of her talents. She wanted to show "Sister Wallace" that she could get up a better dinner than any she had ever eaten, but no opportunity for carrying out her wish occured until Saturday, when Aunt Eunice was laid up with a sick headache, into which she had been fairly worried by the trials of the week.

Mrs. Wallace had some misgivings about the dinner, and remained in the kitchen herself superintending and helping until the vegetables were prepared and the meat was in the oven.

An hour later when she opened the kitchen door to see how Amanda was getting on, she was assailed by a powerful odor of burning meat. The stove was red hot the room full of smoke, and no one in sight. She drew the roast from the oven, a blackened coal, and after opening the windows went in search of her handmaiden, whom she found leaning over the railing of the back porch singing:

"I never knew what joy was,
  Till I became a Mormon."

"Amanda," she called a little sharply, "why don't you stay in the kitchen and attend to your cooking? The meat is all burned up and the dinner spoiled."

The fair Miss Harker left her post at this summons and returned leisurely to the kitchen.

"Where are your vegetables Amanda?" was the next question. "I don't see them on the stove."

"Well now if I hain't forgot to put 'em over. Here they are in the pantry; who'd a thought though that the meat would burn so quick."

It was late when the dinner finally appeared on the table, but it looked well enough, and the tried and worried housekeeper hoped it might be eatable.

Grace was said, the coffee poured and Mr. Wallace raised his cup to his lips but set it down again in haste.

"What is the matter my dear?" his wife asked a little apprehensively.

"This coffee is sweetened with salt, or else it was made with water from the lake."

"I scalded the coffee-pot and put in the coffee myself but perhaps our Amanda has added something at the suggestion of her own genius. I will go and see."

An examination of the coffee-pot showed it to be half filled with some foreign substance.

"What have you put in here Amanda?" asked her mistress.

"Nothin' but some fish to settle the coffee. Did'nt you tell me to?"

And thereupon Miss Harker drew from the pot a piece of dried codfish the size of one of her own delicate hands.

"You will have to keep the word of wisdom, and drink water to-day," Mrs. Wallace said as she took her place at the table, "Amanda has improved upon my instructions a little, and settled the coffee with half a codfish"

The next morning, to the great relief of the suffering household, Aunt Eunice was able to return to the kitchen, and they all ate and drank without fear; but Monday brought fresh trials. Miss Harker, at her own request, was stationed at the wash-tub and the manner in which she rubbed out the clothes, certainly did credit to her muscular development, but before noon, Aunt Eunice made her appearance in the sitting-room with evil tidings written on her face.

"My heart's jest broke Miss Esther," she said. "All de white cloes in the wash is clean ruined. I left em in de rense water so'st I could go an' hang up de flannels, tellin dat 'Mandy not to tech em 'em an' and what does she do but go an' empty all de bluein' in de box on 'em. Ef she don't go 'fore long, dere won't be nuffin left in dis house."

Mrs. Wallace administered what consolation she could and again counselled patience, as there remained only one more day of the week of trial.

On Tuesday evening she called Amanda into the sitting-room, and after paying her a week's wages told her she might go the next day, as they would not need her any longer.

Miss Harker's face reddened till it rivalled her hair, and her voice took an unusually high key as she demanded to see Brother Wallace.

"He is not at home. Had you anything particular to say to him?"

"Pertickiler! I should think so! It was him that sent for me and sent for me to stay. My mother did'nt bring up her girls to work out, and I would'nt a demeaned myself to slave in your kitchen for no dollar and a half a week if Brother Williams had'nt told me that Brother Wallace was a lookin' for a second wife and I was the one he was a lookin' for. A nice thing it would be to send me off when he's away; but I don't go, not till I see him."

"Miss Harker," said Esther in the blandest manner, "if you wish to speak to my husband about marrying him, I have'nt the least objection, but if that was his object in sending for you, he will certainly call on you at your own home, and I must really insist upon your going there to-night instead of to-morrow. The evening is pleasant and it is not far to walk."

Amanda, seeing that her late mistress was quite in earnest, abandoned the strong position she had taken, and after a few sulky mutterings gathered up her worldly effects and departed. She had not been gone half an hour, when Wallace returned.

Esther, with as much gravity as she could command under the circumstances, related her final interview with the damsel who proposed to bestow on him the boon of her fair hand.

"It was too bad of Bishop Williams to make the whole family the victims of his practical joke," said Wallace, laughing a little but coloring and looking annoyed. "He ought to be obliged to eat of the young woman's cooking and to replace the articles she has broken and destroyed."

"Well," returned Esther "we will have to pass by the offense I suppose, after the manner of the good boy who always forgave his school-fellows for striking him if they were bigger than he was. And now arises the question, what is to be done next? Aunt Eunice won't take any more 'white trash' under her wing;—that is settled—and the hard fact remains that there is only one pair of hands to do the work of two."

"I'm sure *I* don't know what to do. I exhausted my resources before."

Wallace was about as helpful in domestic emergencies as men generally are, and having disposed of his own responsibility in the matter with this final remark, he took his hat and went out to look after his horses.

"I've half a mind to let them all go without dinner to-morrow," was Esther's first thought in her vexation, but better counsel prevailed and after sleeping over the matter she decided to start out herself in search of help.

Her first call was on Mrs. Nye. Her neighbor laughed heartily over the history of her experience with Amanda Josephine.

"The young lady is no stranger to me," she said, "we hired her for a little while when I was sick last summer, but she left in disgust at the end of the second week because Mr. Nye did not propose to her."

"She told me she had never worked out before.'

"Very likely. Amanda has her dignity to maintain, and won't compromise herself by the admission that she is or has been a servant, and I may as well tell you that it will be useless to look for help of a different type here. Miss Harker is a fair specimen of the unmarried girls remaining in Salt Lake."

"I did not think of trying to get another girl in the house. If I can only find some one to do my washing and ironing, Aunt Eunice and I can manage the rest."

Mrs. Nye, after reflecting a few minutes said: "I think I know just the person you want; that is if you can send your work to her. She could not leave her children to come to you."

"It will suit me just as well to have her do the work at her own house, and if you will tell me where to find her I will engage her at once; or perhaps you can go with me."

"I cannot leave home this morning very well, but I can give you such directions that you will have no difficulty in finding the place."

"Mrs. Eustace St. Clair, corner of South Temple and Tenth streets."

Esther read aloud the address Mrs Nye had written down, adding:

"Rather a grand name for a washerwoman, is it not?"

"When she took that name she little dreamed what her

future would be," was the answer; "Mrs. St. Clair is the wife of one of the richest men here, but because she refuses to share his heart and home with wife No. 2 she is banished to a log cabin in the outskirts of the town, and left to support herself and her children in any way she can."

"Why does she submit to such treatment? If her husband has property, he can surely be compelled to support his family."

"My dear Mrs. Wallace, who or what is to compel him? As I told you before, there is no law here except the will of Brigham Young, and it is his will that a wife who rebels against her husband's plural marriages shall be severely punished."

"A pleasant state of affairs truly for wives. I had supposed Utah to be within the limits of the United States."

"So we all supposed when we came here, but the attitude of the Government toward us don't seem to bear out the supposition. We might as well be subjects of the King of Dahomy, so far as the protection of our rights or the redress of our wrongs are concerned."

"The women, you mean."

"Well yes, I was thinking of the women when I spoke, but when it comes to a conflict with the ruling power, the same remark applies to the men. Let your husband or mine dare to disobey counsel, and he would soon find that the laws of the United States afforded him no protection; but for my part I don't waste much pity on the men. They come here of their own free will, and most of them with a full understanding of what they call the principles of Mormonism, and as they have sown, so let them reap."

Esther could have found it in her heart to respond Amen, had not her own husband been among the number of those who made this voluntary surrender of their liberties. She would have liked to learn a little more definitely what

Mrs. Nye thought would be the consequence to him of disobeying counsel, but she shrank from asking directly, and as it was growing late she bade her neighbor good morning, and started out to find Mrs. Eustace St. Clair.

It was a long walk, quite to the outskirts of the town, as Mrs. Nye had said, but the weather and the scenery were delightful enough to make her wish it still longer. Salt Lake valley, under those soft skies and bathed in the bright sunshine of Spring, look fair and placid enough to be the very home of peace and good will to men. The cottages she passed were half hidden in blossoming trees, and farther on ·

"Mountain grasses low and sweet,
Grew in the middle of every street."

There might be crushed hopes and blighted lives in the homes behind the flowery screen that bordered either side of the way, but no sob of grief or cry of pain troubled the fragrant air. It was difficult to imagine such a tragedy as the one of which she had just heard, in the midst of scenes so fair and peaceful; difficult to believe the beautiful city of the Saints, as it lay before her eyes, the theater of such crimes against God and humanity.

But even while these thoughts were passing through her mind, she came in sight of the home of the betrayed and deserted wife.

It was a cabin, nothing more; with walls of unhewed logs, a slab roof, a door of rough, unpainted boards, and but four squares of glass in the single window that lighted the interior.

Plainly, the house was the abode of poverty as well as of sorrow, but rude as it was there was nothing repulsive in the aspect of the place. On either side of the door, climbing vines were trained over the rough logs, a few flowers blossomed in a box under the window, and the tiny grass plot between the door and the road-side was free from the slightest speck of litter.

Two little boys, rosy and bright-eyed enough to make amends for their patched clothing, were playing near the house. They drew back shyly at the sight of a stranger, but when she spoke to them, both caps were taken off in a moment. "Their mother is a lady, that is certain," was Esther's mental comment. Then she asked:

"Does Mrs. St. Clair live here?"

"Yes ma'am," said the one who constituted himself spokesman, "She is our mother, but she is not at home just now."

"I would like to see her. Do you think she will be gone long?"

"I don't know but Robbie can tell. Please wait a minute till I go in and see if Robbie is awake."

Opening the door softly, the little fellow tip-toed into the room and came out again directly, saying:

"Robbie thinks mamma will be home in an hour, and says will you please come in."

Entering in response to this invitation, Mrs. Wallace was greeted by a faint, but very sweet voice, saying:

"I am sorry my mother is not at home. Will you sit down and wait for her?"

Looking about for the owner of the voice (for at first sight the room appeared empty), she perceived a small, curtained bed in the farther corner, and as she crossed the floor, a white, wasted hand put aside the curtains, and disclosed to view the face of a boy perhaps fifteen years old, who was sitting up in the bed supported by pillows.

It was a very pale face, with thin cheeks, hollow temples, and a look of patient suffering in the large blue eyes that spoke of weary days and nights of pain.

A pair of crutches, resting against the pillows, told the remainder of the story.

"The poor mother!" thought Esther, her own heart deeply touched, "She has this sorrow too, to bear."

She seated herself beside the bed, and taking one of the thin hands tenderly in her own said:

"I would not have disturbed you if I had known you were sick. Your little brother said you were sleeping just now."

"No. Mamma told me when she went away I must try and sleep, because I had such a bad night, but I could not, though the pain was nearly gone."

"Poor boy! You suffer very much then?"

"Sometimes I do, but there are days when I am very comfortable. The nights are the worst."

Then seeing Mrs Wallace glance toward the crutches, he added:

"Yes, I am a cripple. I have never walked since we came to Salt Lake, but on my good days, as I call them, I can move about the room very well,"

"You were lame then when you came here?"

"Yes. I was hurt when we were crossing the plains. Mother said if I had been where I could have had a doctor and good care, I would be well now, but God would'nt have let me get hurt there, if it was'nt best for me to be lame."

"Do you think it is better for you to lie here and suffer than to be well and strong?"

"It must be, because God is our father, and He gives us what is best for us if we love Him."

"Who taught you that?"

"My mother. When I was quite a little boy, I was sick and had to take very bitter medicine. I begged mamma to give me something that did not taste so bad, but she said 'my son, the bitter medicine is the best,' and afterwards when she talked to me about how much God loved us, she said He gave us sickness and trouble because he loved us, just as she gave me bitter medicine."

His listeners eyes filled with tears as she made answer:

" That is a very beautiful faith, my dear boy, but some of us, when trouble is heavy forget that it is sent in love."

"And that makes it a great deal harder to bear;" Robbie added, " I know for I don't always remember. Lately I have suffered more because"—a faint color straining his pale cheeks—"because we are very poor now, and mother can't always get the medicine I need, and when I have nothing to quiet the pain, I often lie awake whole nights, and the nights are so long. It seems as though morning would never come, and I forget that God loves me."

Then as if struck by a sudden thought, he said earnestly:

"You won't tell mother what I have said will you? I try to make her think I can do without the medicine, and it would break her heart if she knew how much I want it. I keep very still nights so she will not find out that I am awake."

"No, my poor child, I will not tell your mother," Esther answered deeply moved " I have a little girl of my own at home, and I know how mothers feel when their children suffer."

"And my mother cares so much more for us than she does for herself. She is the dearest mother in the world. Oh you don't know how good."

Robbie and his guest were so absorbed in conversation, that neither heard the sound of approaching footsteps, until a shadow darkened the doorway, and Esther, looking up, saw a tall, shabbily dressed woman standing on the threshold.

"Oh mother!" Exclaimed Robbie " I am so glad you

have come. Here is a lady who has been waiting a good while to see you."

"I am sorry to have kept you waiting." Mrs. St. Clair said, turning towards her visitor, "I seldom leave home, but this morning I was compelled to go to another part of the town, and have been absent much longer than I intended."

She spoke in a musical, richly modulated voice, but with a slightly foreign accent. Her bearing was graceful and dignified, and her language and manners alike contrasted strangely with the rude cabin that was her home. In age she might have been between thirty-five and forty. Her face bore traces of rare beauty, but its bloom had faded, and there were deep lines of care in her forehead. The eyes were beautiful still, and of the deepest, darkest blue like her boy's.

There was a look in their depths, like that of one who has done with life and hope; but when her glance rested upon the patient sufferer on the low bed, a smile of unutterable tenderness lighted up the sad eyes, and transfigured the whole face. She might have said with poor Marion Earl:

> I'm dead, you see and if,
> The mother in me has survived the rest,
> Why, that's God's miracle.

Men talk of the courage needed to face death; it is nothing compared with the courage needed to face life sometimes.

Beside the life that this woman had taken up and dared to live for her children's sake, the rock of the Inquisition was a bed of roses, and yet we think and speak as though they who embraced the fagot and the stake, and went through fire up to God, were the only martyrs.

Some such thoughts passed through Esther's mind, as she

studied the mother's face while she bent over her boy and talked to him in low caressing tones. There was such a depth and intensity of love in every look and word, such a resolute putting aside of self and of her own sorrows, that she might minister to her suffering child, no wonder that Robbie thought her the best mother on on earth.

Esther had come to the place prepared to pity the deserted wife. She now felt more disposed to reverence the mother who showed so much of "Love's divine self-abnegation."

The morning was passing, and she had not spoken of the business that brought her there.

If, as Mrs. Nye said, Mrs. St. Clair was compelled to earn her own and her children's bread as best she could, the proposal she had to make might be very acceptable. Robbie admitted that they were very poor now, and every thing in and about the house bore witness to the fact.

The single room, with its bare floor and scant furniture, though as neat and orderly as hands could make it, was cheerless enough. The little boys playing outside were barefoot, and the mother's dress of faded cotton was sadly worn.

Esther longed to help them out of her abundance, but she could not offer alms to this refined and cultivated woman, who was in all respects her equal. Work, however, she could offer.

Too thoroughly sensible herself to be ashamed of any honest employment, she judged rightly that Mrs. St. Clair would be glad to do anything that would bring food to her children.

When she told her errand, and added to the liberal price she named the stipulation that all the work should be done by Mrs. St. Clair at home, there was a sudden light in Robbie's eyes which was reflected on his mother's face, and her offer was accepted with an eagerness that showed painfully how great their necessities were.

Before she left, with a thoughtfulness and delicacy which did credit alike to her head and heart, she insisted upon paying for the first week's work in advance, on the plea that it would be safer to give the money to Mrs. St. Clair herself, than to trust it to the boy who would bring the clothes.

If she had known that there was not a morsel of food in the poor cabin for the children, and that the mother's long walk that morning was undertaken in the vain hope of getting a few pounds of flour from a rich Saint who owed her for work, she would have been still more grateful for the Providence which led her steps thither; for Esther Wallace, good, true and noble woman, and better still earnest disciple of Him who went about doing good, counted it far more blessed to give than to receive.

And could she have looked into the cabin a few minutes after the door closed behind her, and have seen the mother on her knees at Robbie's bedside, giving thanks that her children were spared another day of hunger, she would have been a thousand times repaid.

## PART II.—Chapter II.

THERESA ST. CLAIR.—THE STORY OF HER LIFE.

> To weary hearts, to mourning homes,
> God's meekest angel gently comes.
> No power has he to banish pain,
> Or give us back our lost again,
> And yet in tenderest love, our dear
> And Heavenly Father sends Him here.
> —*Whittier.*

The lessons of that one morning were worth a thousand homilies on patience and resignation.

All that day, and for many days afterward, Esther's mind was filled with the image of the pale boy, bearing the sharpest pain in silence through the long hours of the night, that the knowledge of his sufferings might not be added to his mother's burdens, and the heroic mother, hiding her crushed heart and blighted hopes from her children, and draining the bitter cup held to her lips with a smile for their sake.

As she contemplated this picture, her own trials dwindled into insignificance and she wondered that she had even murmured at her lot.

Her husband was still all her own, her child healthy and happy, and they were surrounded with every comfort that wealth could bestow.

To her, as to most persons born and reared in luxury, poverty alone would have been a very sore trial; and here was a woman as delicately nurtured as herself, earning scant food and clothing for her children by the coarsest and hardest labor, and when work and wages failed, forced to see her sick boy suffer unrelieved, and her little ones want bread.

"But they shall not want again," was Esther's mental resolve when she reached home, that morning, nor did they while it was in her power to help them.

Mrs. St. Clair was skilled in embroidery and fine needle-work, and her new friend added employment of this sort to that already furnished, and insisted on fixing the price herself, which she did at such liberal figures that not only the necessaries of life, but comforts to which they had long been strangers found their way to the inmates of the log cabin. Besides this on all her visits, she carried some delicacy to the sick boy and smilingly claiming to be a better doctor than any one else in Salt Lake. She searched the medicine case she brought from the States for remedies for him, and had the satisfaction of seeing him improve under her treatment. Robbie's gratitude and admiration were unbounded. In his eyes Mrs. Wallace was second only to his mother, and the cordial of her kind words and ready sympathy helped him as much as the medicine she brought.

Mrs. St. Clair too found herself looking forward almost as anxiously as Robbie to the days on which Esther was expected, and little by little she began to speak of herself and her life in Utah.

She had lived in Salt Lake seven years, and four years out of the seven, her home had been in the cabin in which her friend found her, with sickness and want for daily guests'

Death, too, had been there, and taken the youngest of the flock to a home where "they hunger no more, neither thirst any more, neither is there any more pain."

There were three children remaining: Robbie and the two little boys, twins, about eight years old, and for their sakes the mother found strength to live and suffer.

"Death would be such a boon," she said in one of her talks with Esther, "but my children have no one but me, and for their sakes I pray to live. I would pray the same if life were tenfold more bitter. I tremble to think I may be taken from them, or, worse still, they may be taken from me."

"If the dear heavenly Father takes them," Esther answered gently, "it will be well with them. He took my baby from my arms to His own, and, bitter as the parting was, I would not call it back."

"No more would I. Three of my little ones have gone to God, and I thank him every day that they are safely housed from such storms as have beat upon me. If he should call for my children that remain, I would give them up into His hands without a murmur. That is not what I fear, but whenever I do anything against counsel I am threatened with separation from my children by those who have the will and the power to carry out the threat.

"I may be allowed to keep my little boys, but I have good reasons to fear that Robbie will be taken from me before long. He will have a small fortune in his own right when he comes of age—twenty thousand dollars left him, by his uncle. As this money is in the hands of trustees back in our old home, it is out of the reach of the grasping priesthood just now, but they mean to have it all in the end. As soon as Robbie is twenty-one they think they can force him to sign an instrument conveying the property to his father or to the church, and they want him in their power before the time arrives."

"I would not distress myself about that now, if I were you," said Esther. "The evil day is far off, and may never come at all. Robbie is only a child, and much may happen before he is twenty-one."

"He is a great deal older than he looks. He will be

seventeen in June, and I can hardly hope they will let me keep him two years longer; but I won't think of it. I can't think of it and keep my reason. My poor, patient boy, who has suffered so much, to fall into such cruel hands at last!"

Her eyes were bright and tearless now, and there was a hard, determined look on her face—a look that Esther had never seen there before.

"I have borne all things, forgiven all things, as I trust my God forgives me," she said. "I do not love the man whose name I bear. The Eustace St. Clair I loved once, the husband of my youth, the father of my children, died long ago. The Eustace St. Clair of to-day, false, treacherous and cruel, an adulterer, and in heart a murderer, is nothing to me, but if I do not love him, neither do I hate him. I have prayed that mercy and not vengeance might overtake him, but if he takes my suffering boy from me, to be tortured as I know those wretches would torture him, let him look well to himself."

Then in a softer tone she added: "Poor Robbie! he does not dream there is any such fate in store for him. He thinks his mother can help and protect him under any circumstances."

This conversation took place as they were walking along the unfrequented street leading to Mrs. St. Clair's home, but lonely as the place was, it was hardly safe to say so much aloud, and she seemed to recollect this, for she stopped abruptly and began to speak on in different subjects, but as they drew near the house she said in a low tone:

"I have written down the story of my life, for my children to read after I am gone. I want to teach them to hate this accursed system—accursed of God and man—and they will hate it when they learn what it has done for their mother.

"I am going to give the papers to you, to be kept until

called for. They will be safer in your hands than mine just now."

The two little boys were out at their play, and when they entered the house they found Robbie asleep.

"Don't say anything to him of this" his mother whispered, "not for the present at least."

Then crossing the room softly she knelt down beside a small trunk at the foot of his bed, and unlocking it took out a manuscript, and placed it in Esther's hands.

"Am I to read this?" she asked as she received it.

"Yes, if you wish, and God grant you a better fate than mine."

Her strong self-control was giving way and her friend, thinking she would be better alone pressed her hand silently and took her leave carrying with her the manuscrip containing the record of sorrows that might' one day be her own. When she reached home, she put the papers carefully away, feeling that she had no right to speak of their contents to her husband even, and, alas that it should be so. There were many things besides her friend's history, about which she could not speak to him now. He was kind as ever, and she could not doubt his love for her, but the fatal delusion that had mastered him was a barrier to confidence on all matters in which the church was in any way concerned. When evening came, Wallace went out to one of the frequent meetings at which his presence was required, and Esther, after putting Winnie to bed, locked the door, and taking down the manuscript, began to read:

### Theresa St. Clair's Story.

I am of German birth, and though my parents brought me to America when quite young, I have always retained a memory of the dear Fatherland. I do not know who or what my people were in their own country, for they never spoke of their past to me, but they must have had wealth, for I remember a large house surrounded by gardens in which fountains were playing and birds singing.

Indoors were velvet sofas and silk hangings, pictures and statues, and many beautiful and costly things that I thought little about then, but missed afterwards in our new home.

I never knew why we left Germany, but have supposed since I have been old enough to reflect about it, that my father was involved in some of the polittcal troubles of those times. I only know that for days he was away, and my mother looked very sad and wept a great deal. When we left, it was in the night and we went away very hurriedly leaving every thing in the house just as it was. My mother's brother went with us and, my old nurse Bettina. I did not see my father until after we were on ship-board.

When we reached this country, we settled in Baltimore, and our home there though not like the dear German home was very pleasant, but I think my mother's heart was broken when she left the Fatherland, for she drooped and faded from the hour that we set foot on the shores of the New World, and in little more than a year she died.

My father soon followed her, and I was left to my uncle's care. He was a grave, silent man, who had never married, and lived alone with his books, mingling very little with the world, but he had a kind heart, and a very tender love for his dead sister's child. We lived in the home that my father had chosen, with Bettina to keep the house for us, and there, after the first violence of my childish grief abated, I spent many tranquil and happy years.

My uncle took great pains with my education, and in the fondness of his heart used to predict a brilliant future for me.

Dear kind unworldly Uncle Rupert! He little knew what

dangers beset the path of a motherless girl like me. I wonder sometimes whether he knows now of the fate of the child he watched over so tenderly. I hope not, for it seems to me I would be unhappy in Heaven, if I could look down on the sorrows of those I loved.

I was eighteen when I first saw Eustace St. Clair. He was a lawyer, and had charge of business for my uucle which brought him often to our house. We lived very retired, and I had met few gentlemen except the grave, elderly men, my uncle's friends, who spent an occasional evening with us.

Certainly, I knew no one to compare with this Adonis, whose silver tongue added to the charm of his handsome face. I loved him before I knew the meaning of love — watched eagerly for his coming and was restless and ill at ease when he was away, without dreaming why.

And here, let me do him justice, he loved me truly in those days I believe, and meant to keep the vows he made.

We were married in six months from the time of our first meeting, with my uncle's hearty approval, for Eustace had won his heart too and I was not to be taken away from him.

We were all to live together in the old home, and Heaven was to come down to earth, so I thought.

"I look back now with a strange kind of pity on the fond, foolish girl who used to nurse such fancies.

If she had only died then, loving, trusting, and happy.

In the first year of our marriage, Robbie was born. How I loved my baby! How fast my happy heart beat when his little head lay in my bosom! How the touch of the soft baby hands thrilled me through and through.

How happy we all were, Eustace and I and dear Uncle Rupert; but there was a lurking shadow at our fireside, of whose presence I never dreamed.

Uncle had inherited the germs of a fatal disease, and knew himself that his days were numbered, but he hid the knowledge from us, and I was too much absorbed in husband and child, too selfish in my new-found joy, to note the failing strength of one who had been both father and mother to me.

When the blow fell, it found me all unprepared. It was when Robbie began to take his first uncertain steps, and lisp our names, that Death came over our threshold. My grief was real and bitter, and mingled too with self-reproach, but I had Eustace and my boy, and time softened my sorrow into a tender and reverent memory. Then another child came; a little blue-eyed girl, as fair as a lily, but she only staid with us three short months.

My wounded mother-heart clung to Robbie with double love after she was taken, but I trembled lest he should go too, and began to ask myself what sin I was cherishing that brought such sore punishment on me.

When still another child was born, I held it to my heart with a wild dread of loss, and prayed, oh how earnestly! that I might keep it, but in vain. Before the year ended, I sat again beside my baby's empty cradle, asking, "why hast Thou dealt thus with me."

I must be in the wrong way so I reasoned, and these sharp strokes were to turn me back. Then out of the depths of my sorrow, I cried for light, and promised to follow whithersoever the Divine Hand should lead.

That was the beginning of my aspirations after a higher, purer life than any I had ever known,—aspirations that have ended—oh God! *where* and *how* have they ended.

While I was in this frame of mind Eustace came home one day with news of a meeting to be held near us by a stranger, of whose doctrines he knew little, but whose zeal and eloquence he said, were drawing multitudes to hear him.

Hitherto my husband's indifference to religion had caused me much anxiety, and I was glad of the interest he manifested in the wonderful preacher and gave a ready consent to go with him to the meeting.

That night I saw and heard for the first time a Latter Day Saint. And that night paved the way for long years of hopeless misery and unavailing remorse; and yet, why do I say remorse?

I was seeking the truth with all my heart, and though the lie I received for the truth has wrecked my life, and the lives of my children, God will not count my mistake a crime.

When Satan comes as an angel of light, is it any wonder that mere mortals are deceived?

The preacher, to whose eloquent words we listened that night, seemed to us all he claimed to be; the apostle of a new dispensation. Had he decried or rejected the written word of God, I at least would have shrunk from him with horror, but he did nothing of the kind.

True, his interpretations of the familiar language of the Scriptures were novel and startling, but only so, I thought, because the Spirit showed him a depth of meaning in the word which I and others like me had failed to apprehend.

I went home that night prepared to believe that God was speaking again to the world through an inspired Prophet, who could answer the perplexing questions that filled my soul.

It would be difficult to trace and explain the successive steps by which we were led to embrace the Latter-Day gospel, but there is one fact which I wish to record distinctly:

The doctrines presented to us then and there differed as widely as day and night from that which we were asked to accept after we reached Utah.

I never heard one word of the Spiritual Wife system, of

Blood Atonement, or of the absolute temporal power exercised by the Mormon Prophet.

These and many other hideous and repulsive features of the new religion were most carefully concealed from the converts, who were lured onward by interpretations of prophecy that made the second coming of Christ appear near at hand, and by highly wrought pictures of the happy valleys wherein the Saints were already gathered, waiting for their Lord.

Almost as soon as we were baptized into this faith, the missionary began to urge us to sell all we had and go with him to Zion, but Eustace hesitated and waited. His faith in the new gospel was not as strong as mine, and he wanted to be very sure that the Lord called him to go, before he would consent to give up his prosperous business, forsake his home, and turn his back upon civilization.

It is the most painful, among many bitter memories, that I continually urged him on, and it was due more to my importunities than to anything else that he finally decided to emigrate.

This was two years after we heard the Mormon Missionary's first sermon. We had been greatly prospered since our marriage, and with my patrimony added to what my husband made in his business, we could call ourselves rich.

I thought of the early Christians, who sold all their possessions and laid the price at the Apostle's feet, and my heart burned to emulate their example, but my husband, less enthusiastic, said he should keep his property in his own hands for the present; still he converted all we had into money, and we took everything with us except the property my uncle Rupert left, which was to be Robbie's when he came of age. My twin boys were only eight months old when we started, and the journey under such circumstances would have looked very formidable to me, if I had not been upborne by the belief that God would lead us as he led his ancient people through the wilderness.

What hopes filled my heart when we were fairly on the way! At last I should see a Prophet of the living God face to face, and hear from his lips an answer to the question my soul had been asking so long.

"Lord what wilt thou have me to do?"

Eustace, though sincere in his acceptance of the new faith, did not share my hopes, but neither had he shared the agonizing conflict preceding them.

"The religious element is wanting in me," he used to say, and even after he embraced Mormonism, he was always afraid of believing too much.

For my own part, I was almost lifted above my earthly surroundings by the faith that animated me. God, who sees all hearts, knows that my motives were pure. I asked nothing, sought nothing but conformity to the Divine will, and I was going to ally myself to a people who had suffered the loss of all things in obedience to that will.

The first shock to my faith was my meeting with this chosen people. We traveled by ourselves as far as the Missouri river where we joined a company of Saints with whom we were to cross the plains.

I will never forget the first day I spent among them. I could hardly believe my eyes and ears.

Were these the people chosen out of the world to show forth the glory of the coming kingdom of Christ? Were these Saints, these men with sensual faces, leering looks, and speaking not only the language of the world, but of a lower, coarser world than I had ever known? And the women, some of them pale, spiritless, and wearing the look of slaves, crushed to the earth by their burdens and their chains, others bold, loud-voiced, and talking glibly of the principles they had embraced: Did I wish to be like them?

I dared not hint my thoughts to Eustace but he was less reticent regarding his own, and freely expressed to me his disappointment and disgust, adding:

"It is too late now to turn back, and we must make the best of our foolish venture. Perhaps I can find some sort of business in this Eden of yours that will be profitable and pay me in a measure for the sacrifice I have made."

I could say nothing, for the journey was of my own planning. I could only hope against hope that all would be well when we reached Zion.

I even took myself to task for thinking so hardly of my fellow-travelers. Our Lord surely came to save the forlorn, the ignorant and the degraded, and these had been drawn to Zion because they needed Him. If I had but faith and patience to wait, I might yet witness a miracle of transformation wrought in those coarse and vile natures, when His hands were laid upon them.

So not losing my faith in God, and trying to hold fast my faith in Mormonism, I journeyed with husband and children across the desert in that strange company—a sad pilgrimage, and rendered doubly so by daily recurring developments of the character and purpose of those whose lead we were following.

It was on the dreariest and most desolate portion of our route that my boy met with the accident which doomed him to a lifetime of suffering, and then indeed it seemed that my cup of sorrow and self-reproach was full; but he, dear child, never murmured, and comforted me when I should have comforted him.

He was so sure the dear Heavenly Father would bring good out of all this suffering, and make all end well, that my own faith and courage came back to me.

At length our journey ended, and Zion was in sight. I had ceased by this time to expect much, and so my disappointment was not great. It was only the third year since the settlement of the valley, and Eustace said, considering the shortness of the time and the nature of the country, the settlers had done wonders.

We pitched our tent and began to build our cabin with the rest in a cheerful and hopeful spirit, resolved to make the best of every thing. and but for Robbie's affliction I should have been almost content.

The great object of the journey however, remained unaccomplished. I had not yet seen the Prophet of the Lord face to face. He was not at home when we arrived, and we were told he might be absent six weeks. Strangely enough, this was a relief to me, for I dreaded the meeting with the Prophet as much as I had once desired it, dreaded it as the final blow to my faith in the Latter-day gospel; but while we waited his return, that blow came from another quarter.

While on our journey I had only mingled with my fellow-travellers when compelled to do so, and this will account for the fact that I reached Salt Lake in absolute ignorance of the practice of polygamy.

True, I had heard something about "Spiritual wives," and "celestial marriage," but I never dreamed of the system of concubinage and wholesale adultery to which these terms referred.

When I found that our nearest neighbor (a bishop, by the way,) had three women living under his roof, all of whom had borne children to him, and each of whom he called "wife," a wave of indignation and horror swept away the last vestige of belief in the false teachings to which I had listened.

I did not need now to be assured that the Prophet was an impostor and when I saw him for the first time, as he arose to speak to an assemblage of his people, his true character was as plain to me as it is to-day.

His sermon, on the occasion referred to, consisted chiefly of coarse and vindictive denunciations of all peoples and governments outside of the "Kindom of God" as he denominated his own rule.

His closing remarks were addressed to his followers, whom he berated for various short-comings. The women, some of whom it seems had grown restive under the double tyranny of their masters and the church, came in for their share of invective, clothed in such language that I glanced round involuntarily, wondering how men with sisters and wives could sit still and listen to it, but none of the brethren showed the least sign of discomposure.

I would have risen and left the place, but my husband laid a detaining hand on my arm.

"Wait" he whispered "we must not make ourselves conspicuous by going out now. It might not be safe."

When we reached home, I asked him what he meant.

"Just this," he answered, "while we are in Rome, we must not fight against Roman ways. I can't say that the sermon this morning was very much to my taste, but since we are here and obliged to stay, I am not going to render myself obnoxious to the ruling powers."

"But you don't believe that man to be a Prophet, and you are convinced as well as I that we have been grossly deceived, and that Mormonism is an imposture from beginning to end. Is it not so?"

"Don't cross-question me," he answered lightly. "It is one of your own sages who says:

"Die Wahrheit und die Rosa sind schoen; beide aber, haben Dornen."

Surely, Eustace was changing.

The religious element might have been wanting in him always as he said, but heretofore I had given him credit for clear perceptions of right and wrong, a keen sense of honor, and courage enough to be true to his convictions.

As month after month passed away in our new home, the change became more apparent. Still a tender husband and kind father, he was in all other respects, so unlike himself that his friends of earlier days would not have recognized him.

He was much in the company of the Mormon leaders, and obviously a favorite with them, and I charged the transformation to their influence. He affected great faith in their teachings, of which I knew he did not believe a word,—and indeed I think few of them believed what they taught themselves. Those were sad years, when I was compelled to watch the gradual deterioration of the noble nature which had won and kept my love.

Outwardly all went well with us; we built a comfortable house which was much better furnished than those of our neighbors. The property we brought with us increased, for Eustace was quite in earnest about making money out of our settlement in Zion, and he succeeded.

All of us except Robbie had excellent health, and even he was much better than we could have hoped.

Thus more than two years passed away before the storm broke upon me that wrecked my life.

Up to this time, but little had been said in our home about the cruel and horrible system that degraded the women around us below the level of slaves.

I did not go out much, still I could not help seeing something of Polygamy but knowing how powerless I was to help its wretched victims, I tried to shut my eyes and ears.

If ever I spoke to Eustace about it, he answered with a jest, usually adding:

"Why should we trouble ourselves about that which does not concern us? It will be time enough for you to take those matters to heart when you are personally involved."

In the third year after our arrival in Utah, I hired a girl by the name of Lydia Ellis to live with us. She was English and rather more intelligent than most persons of her class; handsome too, as my neighbors observed, when commenting on my folly in taking such a girl into the house, but Lydia's crisp curls, bright eyes and red cheeks, gave me no disquiet.

She was neat and capable and lightened my house-keeping cares greatly. She was kind to the children also, and I congratulated myself on having secured her services as I was now in delicate health, and needed some one upon whom I could rely.

As the months passed and my hour of trial drew near, I was often very ill, and so depressed that I wondered at myself. All my courage seemed to have deserted me, and I chided myself for the sad, tear-stained face which I thought made home unpleasant to my husband, for at this time, when I felt the need of his love so much, he was away from me more than he had ever been before in our whole married life.

He was very busy, he said, and even when with me he was absent-minded and pre-occupied.

I missed the petting tenderness with which he always treated me when ill, and the little attentions that mean so much to a woman, though a man might count them trifles.

Eustace was changed, greatly changed. I did not try to hide that from myself, but not the faintest suspicion of what was in his mind had dawned upon me, when one evening he came into my room and locked the door, saying he wished to speak to me without being interrupted.

He was very pale, and there was a look in his eyes that made my heart stand still with a vague terror;—and yet I never dreamed of what was coming.

"Theresa," he began at length, "I have tried to be a good husband to you; I think you will own that few women have been treated with more tenderness. That I have loved you, you know, but my love for you has been a snare to me. It has drawn me from the path of duty, and made me insensible to higher obligations."

I had risen as he spoke and stood before him breathless, trembling and bewildered.

"Eustace," I gasped, "what does all this mean? Are you mad."

"No," he answered, "I was never saner, but I have made up my mind to live my religion at any cost, and fulfill all the duties it imposes, and as soon as you are able to go with us to the Endowment House, I am to be sealed to Lydia Ellis for time and eternity."

I heard the dreadful words only as a drowning man hears the roaring of the waters about his head. Strength and consciousness were fast leaving me. The last thing I remembered was a throe of intense bodily pain. Then a great gulf of darkness swallowed me up and I knew no more.

When I came to myself, I was lying on my bed and an old woman, bent and wrinkled but with a kind, motherly face, sat beside me.

A taper burned dimly on the farther side of the room, a little stand by the pillow was covered with cups and bottle and the odor of some powerful drug prevaded the apartment.

I tried to move, but found I could not even raise my hand to my head. The old nurse rose and bent over me.

"What is the matter?" I asked and my own voice sounded strange to me, it was so hoarse and weak.

"You have been very sick, poor dear, but you are better now. You must not try to talk."

Then putting a cup to my lips, she told me to drink and and try to sleep.

I obeyed, but though too weak to move I was wakeful, and lay watching the woman's face, wondering vaguely who she was and how she came there. In a little while I heard a faint wail from the crib near my bed, and saw the nurse take up a tiny bundle. Up to this moment I remembered nothing, not even my condition, but the cry that reached my ears roused me as from a dream.

Slowly my benumbed faculties awoke to life, and I began to recall the latest events of which I had been conscious, but the day on which I was taken ill was yet a blank.

I must know more, and disregarding the nurse's injunction I spoke again:

"Is that my baby? Bring it here and let me see it."

"It's your baby, sure enough, and little we all thought that its mother would live to see its face. You knew nothing for three days before the baby came, and it's now three days since, but we will have you well soon if you try to rest and don't fret."

Why should I fret, I thought, but I only said "Give me the baby, and I will go to sleep."

The old woman hesitated a moment, but finally placed it in my arms; poor powerless arms, too weak to clasp my child, as they were too weak to hold and shield her in after days.

But the baby's face, nestled against my breast, brought a sense of content, and in a little while we both slept. I awoke in the early hours of the morning, feeling much better and stronger, and began to ask for my husband and the boys, but the nurse again begged me not to talk, and said if I wanted to get well I must see no one for the present.

Two or three days went by in this manner, and then I

begged so earnestly at least to see Robbie, that his chair was wheeled into my room, but he was not allowed to stay and talk with me.

In the afternoon, Eustace came, but he only stood at my bedside long enough to ask if I was better, and then after saying a few words to the nurse, left the room. I wondered at this, but supposed it must be on account of the perfect quiet that was necessary to my recovery. Of my last interview with him, and the words that struck me down senseless at his feet, I had absolutely no recollection.

After the lapse of a week or more, I found myself so much stronger that the nurse consented to bolster me up in bed. As I looked round the disordered room, I asked:

"Where is Lydia? She might come in and help you put things to rights."

The old woman gave me a pitying glance, but did not reply at once; finally she said·

"I thought you would not like to have Lydia come in."

"Why not?" I asked, but before she could answer I saw as in a flash of lightning my husband's face as it appeared on the dreadful night that had been a blank to me until now, and heard him saying "I am to be sealed to Lydia Ellis for time and eternity."

Everything in the room swam round me, but I did not faint nor cry out. A strength that surely was not my own sustained body and soul. I looked down on my baby sleeping beside me, and on the porch outside I heard the pattering feet of my little boys.

My children needed me. Henceforth they would have only their mother. I must not die.

I did not die but gained strength steadily, day by day. My husband made occasional visits to my rooms, and inquired formally after my health, and I answered always with composed face and voice that I was improving, and hoped soon to be well.

I never saw him alone until my health was quite restored; then I sent for him and he obeyed the summons.

The whole of that interview I cannot trust myself to relate. I heard without surprise that the "sealing" of which he had spoken was consummated, and that Lydia Ellis occupied the place which had been mine for fifteen years. I heard too a homily upon wifely obedience, and an exhortation to accept of the doctrine of plural marriage and thereby make my own salvation sure.

What reply I gave it is needless to record. I wasted no breath in reproaches or complaints, nor did I ask anything except that out of my own money, which Eustace had in his hands, a home might be provided elsewhere for me and my children.

This he at first positively refused, and when I said that I should leave his house before another sunset, whether he provided a home for me or not, he told me I might go when and where I would, but the children should stay with him.

I had never dreamed that he would dare to utter such a threat even, and the possibility that he might do as he said maddened me.

I remember catching up a knife that lay on the table, with a wild impulse to put an end to his life or mine, but the Saint who had witnessed my tortures thus far with the admirable calmness that must have distinguished the Spanish Inquisitors while their victims were on the rack, coolly disarmed me, and said with a sardonic smile:

"On the whole, I think I will let you go. These little domestic scenes, though interesting at first, become wearisome by repetition, and I perhaps might in time become a fault-finding husband,—a thing that I abhor. So if you please, you may prepare to move tomorrow into a house of my selection, you and the children.

"They may remain with you for the present, and possibly the knowledge that I can take them from you any day or hour may help to subdue your impetuosity;—the only fault you have, my dear."

What refinements of cruelty can be practiced upon a mother! With my children in his power, Eustace could torture me at will,—could exact any pledge, any sacrifice from me.

And just here lies the secret of the power of the Mormon Priesthood over the women who loathe their teachings and would welcome death in any shape rather than the slavery to which they are doomed, if other lives were not bound up in theirs.

I was helpless and did as the helpless must;—submitted to any fate. I was allowed to pack my trunk with a few articles of clothing for myself and the children, a little bedding and furniture was loaded into the wagon that waited to receive us and I and my little ones were driven away from what had been our home.

It was a sad and bitter going out into the world, but infinitely preferable to remaining in the house of the man who had ceased to be my husband, and when our scanty furniture was set up in the cabin to which we were taken, and a fire lighted in the hearth, a sense of security and peace, a feeling that was almost happiness, came over me. I had my children and for the present, at least, there was none to molest or make us afraid under the humble roof that sheltered us.

Robbie was the only one able to understand the change that had come over our lives, and he, with a faith and patience that shamed me, bore everything without a murmur, and talked cheerfully of our Heavenly Father's love, and of the good days he had yet in store for us.

For a few months we lived in this way, without the added sufferings of hunger or cold.

Eustace provided us with the necessaries of life during the winter, but in the spring his attentions began to slacken, and at last there were days when the children wanted food.

My own money was all in his hands, as I have said, and my children's hunger drove me to beg help of him.

Sometimes my requests were granted, sometimes disregarded.

I tried to earn something to keep us from want, but work was hard to get and poorly paid.

At length my baby fell sick,—my little girl who came to me in the darkest hour of my life.

She was never strong, and had known the pangs of hunger like the rest of us. It was hard, God only knows how hard to see the pitiful, patient look in those baby eyes when her lips sought her mother's breast in vain.

Hunger for me meant hunger for my darling, and there were days when I wonder I did not go mad, as I searched my empty cupboard vainly for a crust of bread.

What wonder that my baby pined away until I saw the seal of death upon her face!

The last day of her life, we had food in the house, but no light as the night drew on, not even firelight, for I could not leave my dying child to gather the sage-bush that made our summer fuel.

A little after sunset, I saw Eustace coming up the street.

He would stop surely, I thought, for he knew the child was sick,—but no, he passed right on.

In my desperation, I laid my baby on the bed and rushed after him.

"Eustace," I cried, "the baby is dying and I have no light in the house. Are you going to leave us so?"

He never paused or turned his head, and I went back to my children, feeling that I had made my last appeal to him.

That night!—Can I ever forget it, even when I see my baby in the paradise of God?

It was a cloudy summer night, moonless and intensely dark. My little boy slept and Robbie alone shared my sorrowful vigil.

The baby did not suffer, at least I thought not, and for that I thanked the Father of mercies; she was passing away quietly and painlessly.

It must have been still early in the evening, when I found I could no longer discern a pulsation in the tiny wrist I held in my hand, or hear the faint, fluttering breath, when I placed my ear to her lips.

My baby was dead, and my first thought was to thank God that she was spared such sorrows as her mother had endured.

But oh! the long hours I sat with my dead child in my arms, waiting for daylight.

In that awful darkness, I composed as best I could the waxen limbs, and pressed down the lids over the blue eyes, whose piteous, appealing looks would never pierce my heart again.

My baby, my darling! She had gone where they hunger no more; where the tears are wiped from all faces.

The loving, merciful Father of all, had taken my worse than fatherless little one, to his own tender arms.

I thanked Him for that; I thank Him still—and yet how I have longed to see my baby's face once more.

When she is restored to me in the paradise of God shall

I forget the anguish of giving her up without one last look?

The night seemed endless. There was nothing to mark the hours that dragged so slowly past.

I sat beside Robbie's bed until the deathly chill from the little form in my arms penetrated my flesh and seemed to reach my heart.

Would daylight never come? Yes, thank God! the first faint streaks of dawn began to show themselves in the East.

Blessed light! And yet the first sight it showed me was the lifeless face of my darling.

As the morning advanced, our nearest neighbors, rough but kindly people, came in, and when they saw our situation offered to go for Eustace at once.

I said nothing and thinking me too much absorbed in my sorrow to speak, they dispatched one of their number to bring him, while the others remained to perform such kind offices as they were able to.

When Eustace came, bringing with him some of the brethren, he acted the part of an affectionate and bereaved parent to perfection. He even shed tears over the little one murdered by his own cruelty and and neglect, and in tones of sorrowful reproach asked "Why, my dear wife, why did you not send for me before?"

If there had been one lingering spark of love in my heart for him, it died out then. From that hour, I have thought of him only with loathing. He lives in the pleasant house that was my home once, and Lydia shares it with him, but the knowledge of his love for her does not now give me a single jealous pang.

A child has been born to them, and I heard of it without emotion.

My dead and buried love cannot cause me to suffer as living love did.

There is no hope for me in this world, none. The mountain ranges that surround these valleys are the walls of my prison-house. I cannot escape.

Death is the only angel that can open the door for me and loose my bonds, and for his coming I must not pray, because my life belongs to my children. When they cease to need me I believe deliverance will come. Until then I do not ask it.

If my sorrows shall be the means of teaching my sons to abhor the false and cruel faith that caused them, I will not have suffered in vain. I leave what I have written down to be read by them when they reach manhood, and their mother has found the shelter of the *Grave*.

* * * * * * * * *

## PART II.—Chapter III.

"HELP! HELP!"—WEAVING THE TOILS—BROTHER DANIELS A VICTIM—RESOLVING UPON ESCAPE—HARWOOD'S DESIGNS—THE EMIGRANT TRAIN.

Esther had wiped away many tears, as she perused the record of a noble life, so sadly clouded. As she refolded the papers and restored them to their hiding-place she was tempted to ask:

"Why does God permit a sincere soul to fall into such a pit?"

Theresa St. Clair, she knew, was not the only one to whom Satan had come as an angel of light. There were hundreds in these valleys, whose motives were as pure, whose faith was as sincere as hers, and like her they had been snared to their own destruction.

"And I," she thought, "who came here not because I believed the lying message of a self-styled Apostle, but because I wanted to be true to my marriage vow, and cleave to my husband through good and ill, I am likely to reap my reward with the rest."

She leaned out of the window, and gazed across the moonlit valley, to where the rugged peaks of the Wasatch stood up, dark and frowning, against the clear sky.

Well might poor Theresa St. Clair exclaim:

"They are the walls of my prison-house."

No chained captive, pining in his dungeon, was ever more completely separated from the outer world and cut off from succor, than the helpless women between whom and liberty rose those rocky barriers, with the savage desert behind them.

The picture impressed her painfully. Was not she too a prisoner, with as little prospect of release as any of her fellow-captives?

Even if her husband should lose his faith in Mormonism, there was no hope for them. They were in the custody of jailors who permitted no escapes.

She was still at her window, looking out over the sleeping city, when the little clock on the mantel struck the hour of midnight. Her husband had not yet returned, and she began to feel uneasy at his prolonged absence.

Could anything have happened to him? The meeting he had gone to attend was only four blocks away, and the full moon made the streets as light almost as in the day-time.

She would not have been afraid to venture out herself, everything seemed so quiet; but even while the thought passed through her mind, a sharp cry rang out on the still night air:

"Help! Help!"

It was a woman's voice, and almost in the same moment the startled listener distinguished the words:

"For the love of Heaven spare my life."

Then another half smothered cry, and all was still.

The next minute she saw a man turn the corner and walk rapidly towards her own house. It was her husband, and as she opened the door to admit him, two more men came in sight.

They were running, and as it seemed to her from the direction in which she had heard the cry for help.

Wallace drew his wife one side, almost roughly, and hastily shut and bolted the door. As he did so, she noticed his pale and haggard looks, and with a fresh sense of alarm, she inquired what had happened, and whether he knew the meaning of the cries she had heard.

"If you love me, Esther, don't ask me anything about it," he said, "a wrong-doer has been punished, but it is a matter in which neither you nor I have any right to interfere, and I beg, for your own sake, as well as mine, that if you have heard anything you will not let it be known. I am sorry your light was burning, and hope no one will find out that you were up when I came home."

"Charles," Esther said, speaking slowly and looking steadily at him, "a great wrong has been done, of that I am sure. I heard a woman's voice begging for life, and then a smothered sound, as though a choking hand at her throat stifled her cries. Is it possible that you have witnessed a murder without attempting to rescue the victim?"

"I have witnessed nothing, and I wish to Heaven I had heard nothing, but I warn you again that both of us must hide our knowledge of what has happened to-night. To speak of it would be to court destruction for ourselves, without helping any one else."

"You know then, what those cries meant."

"Esther, do you want to drive me mad? I have told you that a wrong-doer has been punished. There are sins that cannot be atoned without the shedding of blood, and the Priesthood count it their duty to purify Zion by cutting off such sinners from the earth. If they are wrong, I cannot help it, and now I beg that you will say nothing more."

Esther was silent, but in her heart she resolved to know more. In some way she feared that the Priesthood, of whose bloody work she had heard before, had managed to implicate her husband in this night's crime.

The next day, she made an errand to Mrs. Nye's thinking that she might learn something there. She found her neighbor alone, and after a few common-place remarks, asked her directly whether she had heard anything unusual the night before.

"I could not well help hearing," was the answer "as the police, who are the most effective agents of the Priesthood, here in the city, seized Pauline R—, almost at my door."

"Who was she and what had she done?"

"Pauline is the pretty little Jewess whom you may have seen about the city during the spring and summer, selling handkerchiefs and embroideries. She came here last year with her father. They belonged to a company of California emigrants who stopped in Salt Lake a little while, but the old man thought he saw a good opening for his business here, and so remained and professed a great interest in the doctrines of the Saints. He may have been baptized even, though of this I am not sure, but I know he has paid his tithing regularly. I have no idea that he has the least faith in Mormonism. It is a simple matter of business with him, and Pauline, more honest or less prudent than her father, has expressed her real sentiments too freely. Besides this she had been about a good deal in Mormon families, and learned some things that ought not to be told, and that she could not be trusted to keep secret; but I think she precipitated her fate by a bold and strongly-worded refusal to become Elder Warren's third wife.

He is a man who never forgives, and he has influence enough to get those who offend him put out of the way. I knew some days ago that poor little Pauline was doomed, but I could not warn her, and if I could what good would it have done? She was like all the rest of us, snared in a net whose meshes cannot be broken. There is no hope nor help for any woman who don't accept Polygamy as a divine ordinance.

"You say you knew she was doomed, how did you find it out?"

"Oh I heard numbers of the brethren and some of the sisters saying that Pauline had taken to bad ways. That is the first thing they say about a woman here after they have decided that she must die. Then one of the Bishops lamented that all his exhortations had been disregarded by sister Pauline, and said that if they could save her in no other way, it was better for the body to perish than the soul."

"But they did not murder her right here, at your door."

Esther asked this with pale cheek and eyes distended with horror.

"No. They bound and gagged her, and carried her away. I do not know certainly how they disposed of her, but I think she was drowned in the Jordan. If so she is not the first woman who has found a grave in its waters."

"But how came she here at your house?"

"She was not at my house. She was spending the night with a friend of her's in the next block, and about midnight was decoyed into the street by a message that her father had been taken suddenly ill and had sent for her."

"I can't realize that such crimes are committed with impunity—that there is no such thing as a law to punish murder?"

"My dear Mrs. Wallace, we have laws in plenty on the statute books of the Territory. The only trouble is, this people live above the law, as their Prophet says. If a man should kill his neighbor without being 'counseled' to do so he might be tried for murder and possibly executed, but killing any one in obedience to counsel isn't murder, it is purifying Zion or destroying the body to save the soul."

"Have you any idea who was concerned in the murder of this girl?"

"I saw those who bound her and carried her away

There were four of them, all members of the police force. Two of the men I know very well; the other two I have often seen on the street, but don't know their names.

"Besides these, there was a man standing at each end of the block, to keep the coast clear, as I suppose."

"How came you to see all this?"

"My room fronts on the street, as you know. I was in bed, but not asleep, and when I heard the first noise, I sprang up and looked out of the window. The full moon made the whole street as light as day, and the men were near enough for me to recognize them. Fortunately for myself, I had no light burning and so was not discovered at the window. Otherwise I might have shared Pauline's fate. The law here is 'mind your own business and ask no questions,' and we are repeatedly told that if we should see any one lying dead beside the way as we walk along the street, we ought to pass on and give ourselves no concern about it."

"But you say you heard Pauline's case talked over some days ago, so it seems her fate could not have been meant to kept secret."

"No. Those who counselled her death don't wish to conceal the fact that her blood has been shed to atone for her sins, as they say, but in view of the possibility that the affair might be inquired into some day, they wish to guard against eye-witnesses, who could testify to the identity of the murderers, and if the Priesthood knew what I have told you to-day, my fate would be sealed. My husband was away from home, and has not returned yet, and I shall not dare to tell him anything about it when he comes."

"He would not betray you?"

"No, certainly not intentionally, but he would be in continual fear that the secret would be discovered, and the distress and anxiety that he could not hide would arouse suspicion."

"Did he know anything about the counsel given to put Pauline out of the way?"

"He heard the the matter talked about, as I did, but I don't think it was decided until last night, when they called a meeting of the brethren and the policemen received their orders."

Esther turned very pale.

This then was the meeting they had summoned her husband to attend. They had made him share their fearful secret, and so far implicated him in their crime. He had not dared to protest, and henceforth his knowledge of the bloody deed would make him their slave.

Mrs. Nye observed her friend's agitation and easily guessed the cause. She had been among the Saints long enough to know that it was the policy of the leaders to implicate their followers in something that would outlaw them, and prevent their return to the world they had left.

Her own husband, she feared, carried more than one guilty secret locked in his breast; and Esther's next words were the echo of her own thoughts.

"I see no hope of escaping from this den of bandits and murderers. All of us, like poor Pauline, know too much."

"That is true enough, but to me it is sometimes the bitterest thought connected with my fate, that my friends at home who know I am held an unwilling captive, have made no effort to rescue me."

"If you have found means to communicate with your friends, you have been more fortunate than I, I have written many times, but have received no reply, and I am led to believe that none of my letters entrusted to the mails have left the Territory."

"I don't suppose they have. The correspondence of suspected persons like ourselves is always taken care of; but I have sent my letters through other channels. Companies of California emigrants pass this way every summer, and as they generally stop a few days in Salt Lake, I have managed to get some of them to carry out letters for me to be mailed in San Francisco. There is a small party expected here this week, and you may have an opportunity of doing the same."

"I hope so. I would like at least to get a letter or a message to the parents of poor Bessie Gordon."

"That is the girl who died at your house last winter? You incurred great risk in giving her shelter, and if you want her parents to know her fate, you must exercise the utmost caution. There is no power here that can save you if you are detected in the attempt to expose the secrets of our prison-house."

"I will be cautious, but I have not given up my faith in God yet. I believe He can deliver us out of the hands of our enemies even here."

"He might help you perhaps, for you have not denied Him, but I dare not ask Him to help me."

"I am sorry you feel so my dear friend. I wish I could show you how wrong you are."

"Oh I am all wrong,—I know that well enough,—and the wrong began the day I consented to cast in my lot with this horde of murderers, but we wont talk about that. Have you seen Brother Daniels lately?"

"No. Why do you ask?"

"Because I am afraid he too has fallen a victim to the doctrine of Blood Atonement. You knew that he had put away Jane, his second wife?"

"I heard something about it a few weeks ago, but I have

not seen him since except in the presence of people in whose hearing I did not like to question him."

"Well, he sent her away last month. He gave her a good house to live in, and made ample provision for her and her children, but he was rash enough or brave enough to tell his real reason for separating from her, which is that he no longer believes in polygamy,—thinks it to be of the devil, in fact, a conclusion that any body might reach by observing its practical workings for a little while."

"Jane takes the separation very much to heart, and is loud in her compaints. She is a weak and silly woman, but has been very fond of Daniels in her way, and very vain of the fact that he treated her just the same as her sister Mary, who is his lawful wife and her superior in every respect. I think Daniels counted the cost fully before he took this step. I know from a word he dropped the last time I saw him, that he realized his danger and there is but too much reason to fear that has met the fate he foreboded. I cannot learn that he has been seen by anybody for ten days past. Mary is sick,—unable to leave her room,—and even poor silly Jane carries a scared face. Daniels is missing, but *Brigham Young knows what has become of him*. I am just as certain of that as though he had told me so himself."

"I hope you are mistaken, but if not, Brother Daniels has done better to die for the truth than to live for the lie that has brought this whole people under a curse."

"I think so too, though I am not brave enough to follow his example. The continued falsehood of my daily life is in itself a punishment too great to bear, and yet I have'nt the courage to tell the truth. I hate the whole abominable system prevailing here, and hate myself for being numbered with such a people, but I dare not say so."

If anything were wanting to complete the dark picture drawn by her fears the night before, the missing touches were supplied for Esther by the recital to which she had listened, and her heart sank like lead in her bosom as she turned her steps homeward. In her husbands' present morbid state of mind, she did not doubt but that his knowledge of the deed of blood weighed upon his conscience like actual guilt. But while his better nature as yet recoiled from the horrid doctrine of Blood Atonement, he held fast his faith in Mormonism as a whole, and since he had been brought to accept polygamy as a Divine ordinance, he might come in time to believe it his duty to obey counsel, even to the shedding of blood.

Her friend's words still rang in her ears—"Snared in a net whose meshes cannot be broken." There was no hope for her husband, none for herself, and,—most bitter thought of all,—none for her child. What would be Winnie's fate if death should deprive her of her mother's protection? Would her father sacrifice her as fathers on every side of them were sacrificing their daughters?

She shuddered, and tried to put away the thought. Her child, her only one, her beautiful darling, it was a cruel deed to bring her here.

"And yet," thought the unhappy mother, "I meant right, God knows I did. Will he forsake me utterly in this time of sorest need?"

Then she recalled the words that gave her strength and comfort at the first. "When thou passest through the waters I will be with thee, and through the floods, they shall not overflow thee. When thou passest through the fire thou shalt not be burned neither shall the flame kindle upon thee."

A calm fell upon her perturbed spirit, as she repeated to herself the unfailing promise of the Mighty One, who alone is able to deliver all who put their trust in Him. Let those who doubt the book in which His promises are written, explain, if they can, why they have comforted the desolate and despairing everywhere and always if they are not, as one has said "God's good tidings spoken afresh in every soul, rather than the mere dying echo of words uttered centuries ago."

Esther did not doubt, but like all of us, she forgot too often the unseen presence of the Divine Helper. As she continued her walk homeward, with a firmer step and a more assured bearing, she turned over in her mind the plans that she had formed and dismissed a score of times during the last twenty-four hours, for escaping from the valley with her child.

Mrs. Nye said that companies of California emigrants stopped here on their way every summer. If so, might it not be possible to get out of the country under their protection? She had money put away safely, double the amount she would need to take her home by the way of California, and she need not therefore excite her husband's suspicions by asking him for so large a sum. The money she brought with her had most of it been in his hands since they came to Salt Lake, and she must leave it behind her if she made good her escape, but she did not give that a second thought. Her flight, supposing flight to be possible would cost her far more than the money she brought to the Territory, for it involved the loss of the lover of her youth, the father of the children, the husband who, notwithstanding the gulf that separated them, was still unspeakably dear to her.

As his face rose up before her, her resolution faltered as it had done many times the night before, while she shaped her plans as he slept peacefully beside her.

Winnie, it is true, was only eight years old, and the evil day might be far off, but she was growing too beautiful for her own safety or her mother's peace of mind; too beautiful to be left here where a young girl with a fair face was like a lamb in the wolf's den. Twice during the past winter, Esther had seen mere children of fourteen, dragged to the Endowment House, in spite of their own terrors and their mother's tears and protestations, to be sealed to hoary-headed members of the Priesthood who had half a score of wives already. Anything was better than to risk such a fate for her own darling, and since she was convinced that her husband was now so completely in the power of the Church that he would not dare to withhold his child, if ordered to sacrifice her; the only hope left to the wife and mother, was that of escaping by flight, and this hope hung on a very slender thread. Many had made the attempt and met their fate at the hands of the Destroying Angels before reaching the borders of the Territory.

Others had been followed two and three hundred miles outside of the Territory and finally overtaken and killed, but a few had succeeded, and their success encouraged her to believe that escape was possible.

At any rate she would try. There were no perils she would not dare,—no hardships she would not endure,—for Winnie's sake.

This was her final resolve as she drew near her home, when raising her eyes, she saw her daughter running to meet her. The little girl's cheeks were flushed and she looked frightened and distressed, as she caught her mother's hand and clung to it for protection.

"Oh mamma," she panted, as soon as she could speak," who do you think is at our house? That dark man that came to see us in New York, and persuaded papa to go to Utah. I was in the room when he came, and papa made me go and give him my hand, and he held me fast and kissed me. I was so afraid of him, I felt as if I should die, I did indeed mamma, and he would not let me go, but held my hand and said I had grown a large girl and he smoothed my hair and said how pretty I was, and that he meant to ask papa for me by and by; and he knew papa would give me to him; and papa looked,—oh I can't tell you how he looked, but he was as pale as he used to be when he was sick, and he never said one word. I ran out of doors as soon as he let go my hand. I can't help it if papa does punish me, for I could not stay in the house another minute."

"Hush dear; speak lower. Your papa will not punish you."

"And you won't let him give me away to that dreadful man?"

"No, never."

Esther spoke with an assurance that surprised herself, as she held the small, trembling hand that lay in her own with a firm clasp. She would save her child. She could save her. Maternal love made her strong enough to face the whole Mormon priesthood, and in her heart she defied them She would watch over Winnie night and day until the hour came, as it surely would come, when they could fly from this accursed spot. They might perish by the way, but death would be a thousand times better than such a life as they must look forward to if they remained.

Harwood's words which any where else would have been taken as harmless pleasantry, had only too much meaning in them when spoken here.

Esther remembered with a shiver of fear and loathing the way in which his baleful eyes were fixed on her beautiful child as well as on herself when she last saw him. He had been their evil genius from the first. No one else could have influenced Wallace as he had, and now his power over him would be greater than ever.

"If Harwood should demand me as well as Winnie would

Charles dare to refuse him I wonder?" she asked herself bitterly.

Hitherto she had thought little of herself, or of any possible personal danger. Her fears were for her husband and child, and even now she did not for a moment seriously entertain the thought that the same fate she dreaded for Winnie might befall herself.

And yet, facts had come to her knowledge within the past few weeks that might have aroused her fears. A near neighbor of theirs was sent out on a mission in the spring, and perished mysteriously on his way to the States. It was whispered about that he did not obey counsel, but a clearer explanation of his disappearance was afforded when it came to light that his young and beautiful wife was sealed to one high in authority as soon as he was out of the Territory.

It was plain that a wife had no more assurance of safety than any one else, if she was coveted by one of the rulers of the people, and Esther Wallace, in the prime of her glorious beauty, might well have trembled for herself.

As they walked homeward together hand in hand, the mother and daughter formed as perfect a picture as any ever painted. Winnie's childish loveliness, her flowing, brown curls, violet eyes and dimpled cheek and chin never appeared so bewitching as when contrasted with the graver beauty of her mother's face. Both were too fair to look upon for their own safety. Well may Esther pray that He who walked beside his children in the fiery furnace would walk with them to-day. While perils of which she was conscious, lay before them perils of which she knew nothing were thickening around them. Women as pure, children as innocent, were being sacrificed day after day to the Moloch set up in these valleys. A man 'cruel as death, remorseless as the grave, reigned over the people and in his hands they were as he himself declared, as clay in the hands of the potter. Families were broken up, homes made desolate, husbands robbed of their wives and parents of their children, to furnish victims for the unclean altar he had reared.

Will Esther and her child escape, or will they share the fate of those around them? We shall see.

When Mrs. Wallace and Winnie reached home, they found the unwelcome guest still there, though they had turned aside and taken a long walk to avoid meeting him.

He greeted Esther with the assured manner of an old acquaintance, and congratulated her on her safe arrival in Zion.

He was as bland, as courteous and smooth-spoken as ever, but his assumption of familiar and friendly relations with the whole family augured ill, for it showed that he *dared* to be familiar while knowing that to all, except the head of the house, his visits were most unwelcome. Esther, in spite of her dread and detestation of him, felt compelled to receive him with civility as her husband's guest, and forced herself, though with difficulty, to go through the forms of courtesy in returning his salutation and answering his questions. She might not have succeeded so well in the attempt, if she had not caught an appealing look from her husband;—a look that said plainly, "I am in his power, for my sake do not offend him."

After a few common-place remarks, Harwood said:

"This meeting with old friends gives me the greatest pleasure, but I regret to tell you that I have come to the Territory as the bearer of evil tidings. It is no secret of course that the people of the world, and more especially the American people, are unfriendly to us. It is now as it was in the beginning,—'I have chosen you out of the world therefore the world hateth you.' We have done nothing to deserve the ill will shown us; on the contrary, we have borne our injuries in silence, and when they have persecuted us in one city we have fled to another. We hoped, when we were driven from our home in Illinois, that we would have rest for a season.

To find this rest we penetrated into the heart of the desert, and made ourselves homes where none had courage to go before us. We thought that in this savage wilderness there would be nothing to tempt the cupidity of our enemies, and that they would hesitate to follow us so far to gratify their malice, but it seems we have made a mistake and at this very hour troops sent by the authorities at Washington are on their way, to destroy our homes and drive us again into the desert, or if we resist, to shed our blood on the soil which we have redeemed from desolation and made to blossom as the rose."

"I hope you may be misinformed," Wallace ventured to observe. "It seems hardly creditible that the Government should invade a peaceful Territory with troops without any pretext whatever."

"Oh! a pretext is not wanting, it never is, when the children of this world wish to harass the children of light. Eighteen centuries ago a blameless man was hounded to death with the cry 'We found this fellow perverting the nation, and forbidding to give tribute to Cæsar,' and to-day this people are accused of treason, and why? Because forsooth President Young has said what preachers all over the United States say every Sabbath in the year, without let or hindrance;—that the laws of God are above the laws of man and should be obeyed in preference to them."

"And troops are to be sent here to chastise us for this?"

"Yes the thing was planned secretly, and I only learned of it the last moment. I have traveled night and day to give President Young timely warning."

"And what does he propose to do about it?"

"We don't know as yet. If I were asked for counsel, I should say: 'Don't be driven any farther. Stand here and die if needs be, like men, but don't fly like frigthened sheep.' That would be the counsel of flesh and blood at any rate, but our president waits for Divine direction, and if, it is revealed to him that we should not resist this most unrighteous invasion, then there will be nothing left us but flight; but mark my words! If we are compelled to leave this city, we will make a Moscow of it. Before the homes that we have reared shall again become the prey of our enemies, we will burn every building and destroy every green thing, and leave behind us only the desert that we found at the first."

Wallace at these words glanced involuntarily through the open window towards the new house, now nearly finished.

Harwood, observing the looks said:

"It seems hard to you, no doubt, Brother Wallace, to think of putting the torch to that house that you have just built at such a great cost, but those who would share the final triumph of the Saints must share their present sacrifices. I am very sorry however that you must lose so much, and if you will allow me to say so, I think it was a little unwise to put so much money into a building."

"Perhaps it was, but I thought as you did that the Saints had found a resting place at last. None of us are above the possibility of making mistakes yet it seems."

There was the slightest possible touch of sarcasm in Wallace's voice, but the Elder did not appear to preceive it.

"Well never mind," he answered, "we who forsake what we have here, shall receive a thousand fold in the world to come, whether it be houses or lands, husbands or wives sons or daughters,—and now good night and good bye for I have urgent business which I have been near forgetting in the pleasure of meeting you all again, I may not see you again until the day of battle or flight, whichever the Lord orders, and meantime I shall be in places of danger, so pray for me."

He held out a hand to each in turn;—a hand taken most unwillingly by two of them at least, — smoothed Winnie's bright curls again as he passed out, saying, "the Lord bless the child," and was gone.

Wallace drew a long breath of relief as the gate closed behind him.

From some cause, it was evident that he did not now regard Brother Harwood just as he had done when he received him as a messenger from heaven, but he was none the less in his power.

Esther would have given much to learn what had passed between them before she came home, but she knew it was idle to expect any confidences from her husband on that subject. Neither did she expect he would tell her in what light he viewed the coming of the troops, but she thought nevertheless that she detected a glean of hope in his eye when Harwood first spoke.

It might be that he too was revolving in his mind the possibility of escape;—but no,—his faith in Mormonism was too deeply rooted to be destroyed at once. She must wait, for years it might be, for such a consummation.

Then after all, supposing that Harwood told the truth and that United States troops were really on their way to the Territory, would any of the disaffected be able to profit by their coming? The talk about making a Moscow of the city was most likely mere bluster, but it would be quite consistent with the usual practice of the Mormon leaders to send the women and children away, before the troops arrived, together with such of the brethren as they could not rely on fully.

Yet in spite of all this, the mere fact that the government thought it worth while to investigate, and if need be punish the conduct of the Mormon leaders, was a hopeful sign for Esther and her fellow captors. If federal troops were sent to Utah, they surely would not return without making some effort to accomplish the object for which they came, and through them the authorities at Washington could not fail to learn of the crimes of the Mormon priesthood, and the wretched state of their victims.

If the truth could but be known, they could have help at once;—so thought many who held to the simple faith that governments are instituted among men to protect the rights of the governed and punish wrong-doers. How great the mistake they made, the history of after years will tell.

The rumor that the troops were coming spread rapidly, and among the few who dared trust each other with their hopes of escape, there were secret and hurried conferences as to what it was best to do, or rather what was practicable. The first idea that presented itself, and the only one that finally appeared tenable, was to let their situation be known to the officer in command before he reached the territory.

But who would be the bearer of the message. The risk was great, but a volunteer was found in the person of a young man named Harris, who, though brought up in the Mormon Church, hated the Priesthood with a perfect hatred; and he had cause. While yet a boy he had seen his aged mother turned out of doors to beg or starve because she resisted the introduction of a plural wife into the household, and his sister sold into polygamy by her father and sealed to a wretch whose brutal treatment caused her death. Later, his betrothed wife was taken from him and given to an elder in the church and his own life threatened because he dared to remonstrate.

He had nothing to live for, he said, and there was no one left to mourn for him if he perished. Besides, he knew every foot of the country, every stream and canyon, and could succeed in the venture if success were possible to any one.

He would carry only a verbal message. If overtaken and searched no scrap of writing would be found to compromse anyone else. He had learned caution in a bitter school, and all of them felt that he could be trusted when the time should come to make the attempt, but as yet nothing definite was known of the whereabouts of the troops, or when they might be expected to reach the Territory.

The Mormon leaders were without doubt fully informed, but in private conversation and in their public addresses as they told the people whatever happened to suit their own purpose best, so that there was no hope of learning the facts through them.

Meantime, those who cherished a hope that deliverance was coming could only communicate with each other under the greatest difficulties. If half a dozen of them had met at one place, upon any pretext, suspicion would have been at once aroused, and the spies of the church would have been kept so constantly on their track that there could be no move made by them, which would not be reported at once at headquarters. As might be expected, those who laid plans for escaping from the tyranny of the Priesthood were mostly women, but there were a number of men, some of whom had been driven to desperation by the wrongs inflicted upon them, while others, who had embraced Mormonism in good faith and from pure motives, had renounced the imposture in their hearts as soon as their eyes were opened by their experiences in Zion.

In the latter class, honest, impetuous Brother Daniels

might have been included, but the weeks were lengthening into months, and still there were no tidings from him.

His wife had risen from her sick bed, the shadow of her former self. Whether she knew the worst concerning his fate, or whether she only feared it, none could tell. To the few who ventured to question her about his absence she gave no answer except that she had not heard from him.

What mortal terror sealed her lips, could only be guessed by those who pitied her grief, but were powerless as she herself was to cope with the tyranny that held them all in its iron grasp.

"Dead men tell no tales," had long been a favorite maxim with those in power, and their crimes were most easily hidden by burying witness and victim in the same grave.

The summer was passing, and rumors of the threatened invasion abounded, but nothing more definite was known on the subject in August than in June. The Mormon leaders made it a text for endless tirades against the Government, and there was much loud talking about what " this people" would do in case the authorities at Washington dared to lay a finger on them, but no one seemed to know on what the reports they heard were based.

Meanwhile, another rumor began to circulate concerning the coming of a very large emigrant train bound for California. It was said that many persons in this train were from Missouri, and had helped to drive the Mormons from the State, and hints were thrown out that they meant to make trouble for the Saints as they passed through the Territory.

So much was said to their prejudice before they arrived, that a strong feeling against them prevailed among the people when they finally entered the city, but there was nothing in their conduct during the few days they remained to justify the reports that had been so industriously circulated. Nearly all the men in the train had families with them, and everything in their appearance and manners indicated that they belonged to the better class of society. Some of those who had been looking forward to the coming of United States troops as affording a possible opportunity of escape from the Territory, visited the camp of the emigrants in the hope of hearing favorable news, or of inducing the leaders of the company to aid them in some way.

Among these was Mrs. Wallace, whose situation was every day becoming more intolerable. Her husband, while in a measure convinced that he had been grossly deceived by Elder Harwood, was nevertheless unwilling to give up his faith in what those around him designated "the principles of Mormonism." Just what this expression meant, he perhaps could not have defined any more clearly than his brethren, but like them, when confronted with damaging facts in the history of Mormonism, he took refuge in the assertion that its principles were true.

Esther could not make up her mind how much he doubted, or how much he still believed, but she saw plainly that he was more than ever in the power of the Priesthood, and that he lived in continual fear of incurring the displeasure of *the Church*—a myth behind which could be found only the one man who held the keys of power.

She was at a loss to account for the feeling, sometimes amounting to abject terror, which seemed to govern him of late. In his present state of mind, he doubtless regarded himself as being in some sense an accomplice in the murder of the poor little Jewess, and the fearful oaths he had taken in the Endowment House fettered him, but it seemed as though there must have been some still stronger influence brought to bear upon him to bring his naturally strong and courageous spirit into such a state of absolute subjection.

And if he felt his chains, it was equally evident that his masters felt their power, and took pleasure in exercising it.

Their new house in which Esther had promised herself as much comfort as it was possible to take in such a country, appeared to belong less to them than to the Mormon leaders, who came and went in the most unceremonious manner invited themselves to dinner or supper with a freedom that would have astonished her, if she could have been astonished at anything, and talked to her husband and herself in a way that would have warranted their being ordered out of doors in any civilized community.

Wallace writhed under these inflictions; of that his wife was certain, but he dared not give the slightest sign of what he felt. Esther planned her visit to the emigrants' camp without consulting him, and went without his knowledge, for she wanted him to be able to give his inquisitors a truthful answer to that effect, when they should call him to account, as she knew they would.

When she reached the camp, she was agreeably surprised to find a class of persons as different from the rude pioneers she had expected to meet as from the bandit horde the Mormon leaders had warned the people against. The emigrants were men of wealth, judging from their equipments, and their wives were refined and Christian ladies.

There were a large number of children in the camp of all ages, from the babe in arms to boys and girls in their teens. Among the latter, Esther noticed particularly a beautiful dark-eyed girl of twelve or thirteen, whose face called up a memory of some one who had been connected with her past life, though she could not tell when or where.

The longer she studied the face, the more the likeness impressed her, until finally she called the young girl to her and asked her name.

"Esther Cleveland," was the answer.

"Esther! Why that is my name," Mrs. Wallace said. "Do you know for whom you were named?"

"For mamma's cousin who lives at the North. I have never seen her, but mamma used to love her dearly when she was a little girl, and wanted me called after her." A light broke upon Esther's mind at those words, and with it a hope that made her heart beat fast. The girl's face was the face of her cousin, Margaret Pryor, as she last saw it nearly twenty years ago.

Margaret was the daughter of the Robert Pryor mentioned in the former part of this narrative, and at the death of her own mother she was consigned to the care of Esther's parents, and remained with them a number of years. To the little Esther, she had been an elder sister, her protector always, and the confidant of her childish troubles. If Margaret were here, she would dare to tell her the whole painful truth, and let her know why she must leave her husband and fly from the home that was no longer a place of peace or safety.

Margaret would help her, if any one could, and with something of the same feeling of reliance with which she used to go to her in childhood, she sought her now.

Her cousin's unbounded astonishment at finding the beautiful and gifted Esther Pryor, the little "Queen Esther" of her chidhood, among the Mormons, soon gave way to indignant pity as she listened to her story.

"You shall not spend another night under that roof or within the reach of those wretches," were her first words when Esther finished her recital. "I will go with you at once and bring your child and good old Aunt Eunice to the camp."

"No, no," Esther interposed hastily, "that would defeat all my plans of escape, and involve not only you but this whole company, in the greatest danger. You don't know the people we have to deal with. My only hope is to get away from the city before you start, and join you beyond the limits of the Territory. We have an acquaintance living on a farm fifty miles away, with whose family we have exchanged one or two visits. Mr. Wallace has already proposed that Winnie and I should spend a part of August there, as he thinks we are both suffering from the effects of the hot weather. He does not expect to go with us, but I am to take Aunt Eunice and a boy who works for us. This boy I have taken care of through a severe illness—saved his life, he says, and I can depend on his attachment and fidelity. Now hear what I propose to do.

"I have money put away for just such an emergency, and it will not be difficult to conceal provisions enough in the carriage to last us a couple of weeks. To-night I will tell Mr. Wallace I have decided to take Winnie out to Henly's, and think we had best start to-morrow. Early in the evening I will send Aunt Eunice out to make some purchases and she must manage to see you. You can find out before that time just what route your party intends to take, and then I can make arrangements for joining you. My husband will not expect me home in two or three weeks, and will not be surprised if he does not hear from me in that time, as I could have no opportunity of sending him a letter except by some of the farmers, who are likely to be too busy this month to go to town.

"I know where to find a guide who will meet me at a safe distance from the city, and conduct me to you by a route that will expose us to the fewest chances of capture."

"You don't mean to say that after all the precautions you are going to take, there will yet be a chance for the Mormons to capture you and bring you back?"

Esther smiled faintly:

"I have lived among the Mormons less than a year, but that is long enough for me to find out that the chances are almost all against me. I am willing however to run all risks, while there remains a possibility of making good my eseape. If I had only myself to think of I should remain with my husband and endure whatever might befall me, but I have no right to neglect an opportunity of getting Winnie away from here."

"I should think not! And I'll tell you what it is Esther, I believe, as I said at first, you had better come right to us, and go with us openly. We are a strong party;—all the men are well armed, and I know if we are followed and attacked we can fight our way out of the Territory, for these miserable Mormons are just as cowardly as they are wicked."

Esther again shook her head sadly:

"It would be madness to attempt any such thing," she said, "The Mormons are far stronger than you think, and not lacking in courage; at least not here on their own soil. The very children are trained to the use of fire-arms, and mere boys of twelve and fourteen mount their horses and take their guns to accompany older persons on expeditions full of difficulty and danger. I hope most earnestly that nothing will happen to involve you in trouble with the people of the Territory, for they are none too well disposed toward you now."

"Still somehow, I can't feel afraid of them. They don't look so very formidable, and I think I could trust my husband alone to defend me against a score of them."

Alas! If the beautiful woman who spoke so proudly and confidently of the one in whose strong right arm she trusted could have looked into the future, she would have prayed to fall into any other hands rather than those of this people of whom she 'could not feel afraid;'—but no foreshadowing of the doom awaiting her loved ones, no presentiment of her own dreadful fate, oppressed her, and when she took leave of her cousin for the night, it was with the anticipation of carrying her and her child away without difficulty from the place that was so hateful to her.

Soon after sunset Esther, after giving Aunt Eunice all necessary instructions dispatched her to the camp of the emigrants according to agreement. In about an hour she returned, overflowing with wrath.

"I'se done tried my best Miss Esther," she said, "but dem ar good-fer-nothin' perlice is a watchin' ebery street an' corner. Fust I took de straight road to de camp an' wor walkin' along peaceable like, when one o' dose yer critters wheels round in front o' me an' says, 'you can't go there.'"

"'Go whar?' says I.

"'Why to the camp.'

"'I'se boun' to go jess dar,' says I, 'cause one o' dem ladies sold me a shawl, an' I'se gwine to fotch it.'

"I hope de Lord won't count notin' agin me fur tellin' sech a lie, 'cause I could'nt think o' nothin' else.

"'You go long,' he says, 'I'll see about the shawl.'

"Well den, I goes back an' comes up another street, but it war'nt no sort o' use, Dey stopped me agen an' when I begins to tell about de shawl I'd paid fur, one of 'em says:—'I know her, its that Wallace's nigger, and I know she's a lying,' and den he lifted his club an' says, 'You start yourself home—mighty quick too.'

"Sech a triflin' low-lived critter, to talk about Wallace's niggar! Let me ketch him roun' dis place, an' ef I don't heave a pot o' bilin' water on him, it 'll be 'cause he makes hisself skeerse mighty suddent."

Aunt Eunice puased for breath here and wiped the perspiration from her streaming face, Her mistress had not heard her last words. After the first throb of fear lest her plans were known, she remembered having heard that the police guarded the camp of the strangers at night. She wondered that she had not thought of this before. In the morning, she would send Aunt Eunice again. She could contrive some plausible errand, and as people were coming and going at all hours during the day, it was not likely she would be stopped. She had spoken to her husband about going to Henly's, and he approved the plan but said she must wait another day as he would be obliged to use the horses in the morning himself.

This gave her a little more time for preparation and a single day could not make mnch difference in the carrying out of her project.

It may be thought that these last hours she expected to spend under the same roof with her husband, would be filled with the bitter anguish that must attend the sundering of the tie that bound their lives together. She had feared herself that when the day of trial came, the pain of the final parting would be more than she could bear, but to her own surprise she felt a greater calmness of spirit than she had known for months.

The severest struggle had been when she first resolved to attempt an escape. Now her mind was made up, the cost fully counted and nothing could turn her back.

She slept as quietly that night as captives have been said to sleep the night before mounting the scaffold, and awoke the next morning as strong in her purpose as ever. Her husband ordered the horses and drove away after an early breakfast, and as soon as he was out of sight Aunt Eunice started the second time for the camp, and Esther set about such preparations as she had to make for her journey.

## PART II.—Chapter iv.

DISAPPOINTMENT—"JEM" AND HIS DISCOVERIES—BAFFLED ESCAPE—THE NAUVOO LEGION CALLED INTO SERVICE—DOMESTIC FELICITY IN A SAINT'S HOUSEHOLD.

Busy, and absorbed in painful thought, it seemed to her that scarcely twenty minutes had elapsed when she heard the gate open and shut, and directly afterwards Aunt Eunice whom she was not expecting for an hour at least, came into the room and closed the door carefully behind her.

" Dey's gone Miss Esther " she said in a cautious whisper.

"Gone? Who? Where?

'Sh, honey. Mebbe dat Harwood's a listenin' for I 'clar for't I blebe he's de debbil.

" Nobody stopped me dis mornin' an' I hurried straight along to de Square, but when I gits dar, what does yer spose I see? Why nuffin'. Not a tent, not a waggin' not a livin' soul. Peared like de yarth had opened an' swallered up de hull camp. I was so dumbfounded dat you might a knocked me down with a feather, an I stood dar' a starin' five minutes, mebbe more, when I felt suthin tech me on de shoulder. I turned roun' an dar stood dat Harwood, a grinnin' an a showin his white teeth. 'Too late Auntie' he says, un den he tole me to take his *complemens* to my misses an' say dat de train started with de fust streak o' light this mornin'. He wor sorry, he said for his fren's to be disappointed, but sech things would happen. I wor so tuk back

I never answered a word an' he turned an' walked away."

Esther listened to all this 'dumbfounded' as Aunt Eunice declared herself to be. What did it mean? What *could* it mean?

One thing at least seemed certain. Her plans were known to Harwood, though how he became possessed of such knowledge was a mystery, but what had become of the emigrants?

The day before they had no thought of going so soon, that she knew, and if anything had occurred to make it necessary for them to leave in haste, why did not her cousin Margaret send her word? To these perplexing questions no reply presented itself, but to the question, what is to be done now, her courage and resolution supplied an answer.

She would spend the day in effort to learn the probable route of the emigrants and if successful would still try to carry out her plan of joining them.

Jem, the boy who was to drive the horses for her, was at work in the garden. She had other employment for him today, and called him into the house to give him his instructions. As he will figure in our story to a considerable extend in future, he deserves more than a passing notice here.

Jem was a waif, without parents or kindred that he knew of. He said he "'sposed he must a' had a father or mother or something o' that sort but never hearn tell about 'em."

His first recollections were of the poor house where he was kicked and cuffed and starved so regularly and systemaically, that in his own words he "got used ter it all and never 'spected nothin' else."

His next home was with a hard-fisted old Pennsylvania farmer, to whom he was bound out. Here he was beaten oftener, but not so badly starved, and he took the same philosophical view of his circumstances as before. A couple of years after he came into the family his master was converted to Mormonism and emigrated to Utah, taking Jem along. Like other good Saints, the farmer soon espoused a second wife and Jem was assigned to this lady's service; and now for the first time he began to take less cheerful views of life.

His mistress was a vixen whose tongue and temper soon made her spouse repent his hasty bargain. He kept away from her as much as posible, and having no one but Jem on whom to pour on her wrath, a double portion of abuse fell to his share.

His work began before daylight and did not end until long after dark. He was fed on scraps that a decent dog would have refused, and there were many days that he was whipped oftener than he was fed. Jem's constitution was pretty well hardened by exposure and rough usage, but a frame of iron could not long endure such treatment as he was receiving. Mrs. Wallace often passed him in her daily walks, and the ragged, emaciated figure and wan face so stirred her sympathies that she inquired into his case, and persuaded her husband to buy his time of his master.

Jem's good days were dawning, but for a while it seemed that they had come too late. He was sick for weeks after he was removed to his new master's house, but Mrs. Wallace nursed him like a mother and brought him back to health. It was the first time the poor boy had ever breathed an atmosphere of kindness; the first time he had been treated like a human being, and his gratitude and devotion to his benefactress, awkwardly enough expressed, were the first signs of the new life to which he was slowly awakening.

Mrs. Wallace knew she could count on his fidelity under any circumstances, and she knew likewise that the keen wit hidden under his stolid exterior would serve her well in the present emergency.

But we have left Jem a long while standing, cap in hand, in the doorway.

"Come in Jem," said his mistress, "and shut the door."

The lad obeyed and waited silently for further orders.

"Jem, have you been to the emigrants' camp on the square this week?"

"Yes 'm."

"Were you there last night?"

"No ma'am. I was goin' down jist dark, but th' p'leece stopped me."

"Did you go near enough to see that the camp was there yet?"

"Yes 'm, but you know the Square is fenced on three sides. On the open side it looked as if they was takin' down tents and loadin' up wagons, but I didn't have a chance to see much, for the p'leece was sharp on the boys and druv us all back."

"Well Jem, the emigrants went away this morning,—and now listen to me. I want you to go on the street and find out if you can, why they left so soon and what road they have taken. Don't ask any questions, but try and hear what people are saying. You can do that without seeming to listen."

"All right Mrs. Wallace. I'll do my best."

"I know you will. Go now, and come back as soon as you have any news for me."

Jem slipped out of the room as noiselessly as he had entered.

Outside the door, he stopped to take down a bag of marbles from a nail, and with these in his hand he sauntered idly along the sidewalk, until he came to the principal street.

The police, most of whom he knew by sight, though they wore no uniform, stood in little knots at the corners, and a few men were gathered about the shops and stores. There was little stir on the street—indeed a sleepy quiet prevailed there most of the time except on market days.

"Hillo," said Jem, slapping the first boy he met on the shoulder, "got any marbles? I've got three dozen in this 'ere bag and I'll bet you what you dare that I kin win yours if you want to play."

"I 'haint no marbles," answered the other a little sulkily, "Dad never buys me nothin'. I wanted to go a fishin' this mornin' but he would'nt git me any hooks."

"Well, I'll lend you a dozen marbles to begin with and we'll see who'll beat."

The boys knelt on the sidewalk and were presently to all appearance absorbed in their game, but Jem kept his ears open, though his eyes were fixed on the marbles. He had selected a spot within three feet of a group of policemen, and not a single word spoken by them escaped him.

"You see Brother Burt," said one in a low, cautious tone, "they found out they had to obey orders. Some of the men did a little tall talking but it was no use. We *persuaded* them without much trouble, when they made sure that we would send twenty men to their one to start them if they did'nt march of their own accord."

"Yes, I guess they've changed their minds by this time about the poor Mormon devils. Should'nt wonder if they see some more changes between this and St. George."

At this moment the man addressed as Burt turned his head, and observed the proximity of the two boys.

"Get out of this you young whelps" he said raising his club threateningly. "What do you mean by blocking up the sidewalk. Clear, I say," at the same time giving the marbles a kick.

"There now" whimpered Jem, "my chiny alley is lost in the ditch."

"I'll throw you in after it if you don't strike for home in double quick. And you too," to the other boy "if you hang around here."

The boy started on a run without waiting for a second bidding, while Jem, hastily cramming his remaining marbles into the bag, disappeared around opposite the corner.

On the next block, a woman was leaning over the fence, talking earnestly with another who was at work in the garden. Jem walked that way, throwing up and catching his bag of marbles as he went, apparently oblivious of everything else. At the fence corner, he dropped down on the bank of the ditch and began to build a dam across it.

Jem's ears were sharp but at first, he could distinguish nothing of the conversation between the two women, and finding they paid no attention to him he moved nearer.

"I don't care," The one outside the fence was saying, "I don't believe the stories about them. We live as near the Square as anybody and they never disturbed us."

"Well, there must have been something wrong," the other answered, or they would'nt have been ordered away. It seemed though, like it would have been a good thing for them to stay awhile. We all needed the money they was o free to spend."

"Yes; but have'nt you heard that it's forbid now to trade with them? Brother Smith has gone South ahead of the train, to warn all the people in the settlements not to have any deal with the emigrants."

"That does seem a little hard, but it don't become us to question what's done by them that's set over us. I've seen before now what comes of disobeying counsel, and I'm glad I did'nt sell them chickens they wanted last night; though to be sure they offered a big price, and my children 'aint got a shoe to their feet for the winter."

"You're a fool then. Counsel or no counsel, I would'nt let my children go barefoot in the snow."

" 'Sh. I'm afraid Mariar, that you'll git into trouble some day by talking so free. Nobody knows who might be listening."

"Mariar" seemingly heeded the caution, for her reply was inaudible to the listener on the bank, and concluding he had heard all he would be likely to hear, Jem slipped out of sight and took a roundabout way home.

He made a faithful report to his mistress, and Esther gathered from it a tolerably clear idea of what must have taken place. The emigrants, driven out of the City in haste, and prevented from communicating with any one, had taken the direct route through to Los Angeles in Southern California. This was not their original purpose, but doubtless the same power that compelled them to break up their camp a week sooner than they intended, had likewise forced them to change their route, and if they were preceded by carriers to warn the people against them, they were of course followed by spies who would report whether the orders given were obeyed or not.

The difficuties in the way of joining them unperceived were increased tenfold, but she could not bring herself to abandon her plan altogether.

Mechanically she continued her preparations for flight, and long before nightfall they were finished. She wondered at herself—at the strange calmness that possessed her in view of parting from her husband, and encountering dangers that might appall the stoutest heart.

Sometimes it seemed as though she must be living in a dream, and she half expected to wake up and find herself in her old home. The feeling, of which all of us have been conscious at some period in our lives, that her suroundings and even her own acts were unreal, was strong upon her during all the hours of that day and night.

Wallace returned about dark, looking unusually worn and dispirited. He was moody and silent, answered his wife's questions in monosyllables, and when Winnie ventured to climb on his knee, repulsed her so roughly that the sensitive child burst into tears.

He was up before daylight the next morning, hurrying the preparations for their journey.

"They will give you good quarters at Henly's," he said; "and I shall probably be out of town much of the time on business, so don't be in haste to get back."

He took leave of his wife and child kindly, but there was a strange, though suppressed eagerness to get them away, that Esther could not help perceiving, and that she understood only too well afterwards.

The sun was just coming in sight above the mountains— when they started, and she ordered Jem to drive fast while it was cool. She hoped to reach a cross road about ten miles out of town, before many of the people along the way were stirring. This road led south through a section of country, so little traveled and so thinly settled, that she thought it would be possible to make a day's journey in that direction without interruption.

But before half the distance to the crossing was accomplished, they heard the clatter of hoofs behind them, and turning their heads they saw a horseman enveloped in a cloud of dust, riding rapidly toward them.

"Its dat Harwood," exclaimed Aunt Eunice as the dust cleared a little.

Esther's heart almost stood still for a moment, It was indeed Harwood, and for whatever he was following them it certainly was for no good. He overtook them in a few minutes, and reining his panting horse close beside the carriage, lifted his hat to its occupants.

"My dear Mrs. Wallace," he said in the bland tone that she had learned to detest so heartily, "how fortunate that I happened to have a little business out at Henly's to-day. It would be quite unsafe for you to make the journey alone, and if Brother Wallace had lived in this country as long as I have, he would not think of allowing you to do so. I called at your house just after you started, and learning from him that you had taken no one with you, I rode on as fast as possible to offer my services."

To all this Esther vouchsafed not a syllable of reply. She saw clearly enough that her plans were known and defeated, but by whom? Had her husband suspected anything? Did he know of her interview with her cousin?

She was not likely to find out before her return home and perhaps not then. Mrs. Nye was right. They were all snared in a net whose meshes could not be broken. Was escape impossible? It seemed so, since like the bird in the snare of the fowler, all her efforts only served to tighen the cords that bound her.

As she remain determinedly silent, Harwood, after a few ineffectual attempts to draw Winnie into conversation, fell back a little and suffered them to continue their journey unmolested.

Jem drove rapidly until they came in sight of the cross-road. His mistress had acquainted him with her plans as far as she judged it necessary, but he did not quite understand what was expected of him under the present aspect of affairs.

"Drive on to Henly's Jem." Mrs. Wallace said in answer to his look of inquiry. They passed the crossing without slacking the speed of the horses, but neither Esther or Aunt Eunice could forbear a look in the direction which they had hoped might prove a way of escape. As the carriage sped on, Aunt Eunice clasped her hands and muttered half aloud, "No use. De debbil helps his own," but her mistress made no sign.

It was past noon when they reached Henly's. The occupants of the carriage were hospitably received by Mrs. Henly and her daughters, but Esther detected on their faces a look of surprise not unmingled with fear when Harwood rode up.

"The men are all at work on the west farm," Mrs. Henly said in answer to his inquiry for her husband, "but you can put your horse in the stable or picket him in the pasture just as you like."

"Thank you. I will put him in the stable then, and give him some grain, for I have a long ride before me yet."

"He is going away then," thought Esther as she followed her hostess into the house, and there was an inexpressible sense of relief in the prospect of being rid of his presence.

The Henlys were old residents, that is to say they entered the valley with the first settlers, nearly ten years before. They owned two good farms, raised abundant crops, were rich in cattle and horses and lived much more comfortably than most of their neighbors, but alas for the peace of the household there was a second wife domiciled at the "West Farm."

Mrs. Henly was a comely matron of fifty. Her daughters, red-cheeked, flaxen-haired lasses in their teens, bustled about to prepare dinner for the guests, while the mother entertained them in the "square room." Everything about the furniture and arrangement of this room told of the New England home in which the good housewife was reared, and perhaps it was the same New England training which rendered it impossible for her to be "reconciled," as she said to the plural establishment on the west farm.

Dinner was soon on the table, but to Esther's surprise Harwood was not present when they sat down. He asked for a slice of bread and a glass of milk, one of the girls said, and then hurried away to the other farm to see their father.

"I wonder what he's after this time," she added; "No good I'll warrant."

The mother made a warning gesture, and the girl stopped.

Esther thought is best to take no notice of the remark. Harwood did not seem to be a favorite with the family, but it might not be wise to express her own opinion about him, or to let it be known that his coming in their company was other than accident.

It was late in the afternoon when Harwood returned. He seemed in a great hurry and not very well pleased about something, and as soon as his horse could be saddled he mounted and rode back in the direction of the city.

This information Jem communicated through Aunt Eunice. Harwood did not come into the house before starting. He told the girls he had dinner at the other farm, and would need all his time for the ride back to the city.

"He has not gone there then," was Esther's mental comment.

If he was really going back to the city, he would not have taken trouble to say so.

Did his movements concern her? Would he watch the route she still meant to take, if possible, in order to join the emigrants? She would have given much for an answer to these questions, but since she was not likely to obtain it from any source, she resolved to lay her plans and attempt to carry them out without any reference to Harwood.

"I will be no worse off if I fail," she thought "and I will make at least one more effort."

Harris was the guide on whom she depended to conduct her through the Territory, by a route which he had assured was so little traveled as to be comparatively safe for her. He was to wait that day on the cross-road mentioned before, and if they did not come he was to return to the city after nightfall and remain there until he received further orders.

She must contrive some plausible errand for Jem, and send him back to the city in the morning; meantime she could do nothing, but wait and endeavor to disarm suspicion, if any existed in the minds of her entertainers.

Henly came home to supper, accompanied by one of his two sons.

"Where's George, father?" asked the oldest girl.

"Had to send him to the range after a horse" the old man answered rather shortly: "One of the horses fell lame to-day."

At the supper table, Henly tried to act the part of host affably, but he was plainly anxious and ill at ease. Before they left the table, Esther, in pursuance of the plan she had formed, asked if one of the girls could be spared to help them unpack their things.

"The girls are busy" Mrs. Henly answered, "but I will go with you myself and help you."

They went up stairs together, and as soon as they were alone in the chamber, the hostess surprised her guest by softly closing the door and slipping the bolt.

"Mrs. Wallace," she said in a hurried and agitated whisper, "thank God that I have found a chance to speak to you to-night, for if you should do what you are thinking of doing to morrow, it would cost you all your lives, listen: That Harwood came here for no good, as my Mary said.

He followed you from the city because he knew you were trying to get away, and he has given orders to have you closely watched here. If you should succeed in getting away from this place, it would be only to fall into the hands of some of his spies and,—dear Mrs. Wallace you don't know this people yet. It would be too good a chance of putting you out of the way for them to miss, and as for your little girl, Harwood says she has property and is worth saving. I almost wonder that he did'nt let you go right on to-day and fall into some of the traps he had set for you; but nobody can tell just what his plans are.

"Lord have mercy on us!" Clasping her hands with a sudden despairing gesture, " when such devils as he is have the power on their side, what can poor weak women do?"

Esther listened to all this with colorless cheeks, clenched hands and set teeth. A spirit of fierce defiance possessed her for the moment. She would dare the worst that Harwood could do. She could but die, and it was a thousand times better to die now than to live in the power of such wretches. But her child! For the first time she felt the full force of poor Theresa St. Clair's words, "What refinements of cruelty can be practiced upon a mother!"

If she made the desperate venture she had proposed, and fell into the hands of the church spies, they would kill her and Aunt Eunice, but Winnie, as Harwood said, was "worth saving."

No, she must not throw her life away, and leave her child helpless and alone in such hands. For the present, all hope of escape was cut off, and the future she dared not contemplate. She sank into a chair, overcome by a sudden deadly faintness. For the first time, her strength and courage seemed deserting her, and Mrs. Henly's next words sounded like the voice of the Tempter appealing to her in this hour of mortal weakness.

"It's no use, Mrs. Wallace, I thought at first that I could make a stand for my rights and fight my way through, and hundreds of women here have thought the same, but we've all had to give up. We're in the power of them, that don't stop at anything; that would tear the baby from its mother's breast and kill it before her eyes, if they could not conquer her in any other way. I don't believe in Mormonism any more than you do. I did once, but Iv'e seen too much wickedness here to have any faith left. But I don't let any one know what I think. I always talk as though I held to all the principles yet, and you will have to do the same; act as though you were contented with your lot and be baptized.

"You must give up trying to fight against what can't be helped for your child's sake if not for your own."

Esther made no reply to this in words, indeed she was too stunned and bewildered to comprehend the half that was said, and Mrs. Henly went on.

"Harwood ordered my son George to take his horse and gun and start south to-day, and his father had to let him go. He don't dare to say a word, though he knows well enough the boy is sent on a bad errand. The Nauvoo Legion has been called out to follow the emigrant train; I only hope it is for nothing worse than to capture their stock."

The last words roused Esther and gave a new direction to her fears.

"Why, what worse errand do you think they might be sent on?" she asked.

"They *might* be ordered not to let any of the company get out of the Territory alive, but I don't think it is as bad as that. They say it is a large train, and all the men are well armed so I hope they may get through with no greater harm than losing some of their property."

Footsteps were now heard on the stairway and Mrs. Henly unbolted the door and began arranging the room for the night.

Winnie came bounding up the stairs and into the room, followed by one of the Henly girls, "I've been helping milk the cows mamma," she said, "and I've had such a splendid time. I hope we are going to stay a good while, for I like it ever so much better here than in town."

"We will stay a couple of weeks, if Mrs. Henly does not get tired of us," was the answer, and the hostess, much relieved by the words, added:

"You will stay I hope until you get such red cheeks as my girls have. We will do our best to take good care of you and your mother."

Aunt Eunice now came up, and Mrs. Henly wished her guests good-night and left them to their rest;—and here for the present we will leave them also and return to Harwood.

Esther made a mistake in supposing that he spoke of returning to the city only to mislead his listeners.

For once he meant what he said, and about nine o'clock in the evening he dismounted from his horse at Wallace's gate. Entering with the manner of one not to be denied, he walked up so the front door and rapped with his riding whip.

"Who is there?" asked Wallace from within.

"Open quickly" was the answer, given in imperative tones. "There is no time to lose."

Wallace recognized the voice and obeyed, though judging from the expression of his face the guest he admitted was far from welcome.

Harwood closed the door behind him, and Wallace

remained standing in the hall-way with the lamp in his hand.

The two men regarded each other a moment in silence. Harwood was the first to speak.

"You are ready to start I suppose," he said.

"No."

"And why not pray? Orders such as you have received are not given to be trifled with as you should know by this time."

"I want to be assured first that no harm is intended to these people."

"You want to be assured! It is rather late in the day for you to begin to question what is done by those who are set over you in the Lord, or to have conscientious scruples about obeying their counsel. You should have thought of these things sooner."

Harwood bent his keen, gray eyes on the man before him, and Wallace quailed under the look. Whatever hidden meaning was couched in these last words, he understood them well enough, for his head sunk upon his breast and every spark of courage died out of his face and mien.

"I am in your power" he said in smoother tones. "Do with me what you will."

"Now you begin to talk reasonably," though I must say you have a peculiar mode of expressing yourself. I am going to change my jaded horse for a fresh one and I will be back in half an hour,—time enough for you to get ready; and remember, the orders are, to march armed and equipped as the law directs."

Half an hour later two men on horseback rode rapidly down the street leading from Wallace's house to what was known as the State road. Here they halted a few minutes, and while they waited two or three small squads of mounted men came in sight from different directions and joined them.

Harwood gave some orders in an undertone to one of the horseman, and then turning to Wallace said:

"These brethren are to be your traveling companions. They know the route and have all necessary instructions with regard to the duty expected of them. I part company with you here. I have orders to remain in Salt Lake for the present."

So saying, he wheeled his horse and galloped back in the direction from which they had come.

Wallace's new companions took the road, riding two abreast. One who seemed to be the leader, directed Wallace, to fall into the place beside him. After this there were few words spoken. The night was dark, the road solitary; no sign of life was visible at the few farmhouses they passed; not even the baying of a watch-dog broke the oppressive silence.

Once during the night, they halted at a cross-road and after a few minutes waiting, were joined by about a dozen men similarly mounted and armed.

As the day began to dawn, the leader ordered them to break rank and separate into companies of twos and threes. They were now approaching a small settlement, and some of these detached squads halted here while the others rode forward.

Wallace and the leader were among the latter. Both were well mounted and they were by this time half a mile in advance of any of the others. During the night, Wallace absorbed in his own bitter thoughts, had shown as little disposition to converse as his taciturn companion, and since daylight revealed the hard, determined face of the man beside him, he felt still less inclined to exchange a word with him. He was apparently about thirty-five years old, of medium height, but broad shouldered and very strongly built. His dress was the ordinary gray homespun, worn by most of the settlers, and furnished no indication of either the military or ecclesiastical rank of the wearer, though from the fact that during the ride he was addressed by some of the company as "Elder" and by others as "Colonel," Wallace concluded that he must be an officer in the Nauvoo Legion as well as in the church.

Thus far he had spoken to no one except to give some necessary orders, and now although riding side by side with Wallace and apart from the others, he maintained the same impenetrable reserve. But the cold eye, the cruel mouth with the square, heavy under jaw forming a physiognomy altogether repelling, told their own story of the man's nature, even if they revealed nothing of his mission.

About seven o'clock they rode up to the door of a comfortable looking farm-house.

"We stop here," said Colonel Ricks, for this was the name by which Wallace had heard his companion addressed during the night. We will get something to eat for ourselves and our horses and lie by most of the day."

A frowsy headed girl opened the door, and turning her back on the strangers called to some one within, "Brother Foote you're wanted," and immediately disappeared.

Some minutes elapsed before Brother Foote answered the summons. He had been disturbed at his breakfast, apparently, for he carried a portion of it in his hand, and as he was barefoot, and his toilet in other respects somewhat incomplete it was probable he did not expect visitors so early.

"Oh! it is you Brother Ricks," he said. "I'd got round sooner if I'd a knowed. Light right down," he added hospitably. "The boy's 'll take your horses and the wimmen 'll have your breakfast ready in no time. Come in this way you and brother———"

"Wallace" said the Colonel. "He came down with me from Salt Lake."

"Yes, yes. We've heard of brother Wallace down here. Glad to make his acquaintance." And Brother Foote, shifting the slice of bread he held to the other hand, gave Wallace a fraternal grasp.

The room into which they were ushered seemed to serve a variety of purposes. A loom with a web of cloth in it, nearly filled one end, while a bed still unmade, occupied the other, and a cradle with a sleeping baby in it stood in a corner.

"Jest excuse me a minnit Brother Ricks" said their host "while I see to the horses and speak to the wimmin folks about breakfast."

With this apology, Brother Foote betook himself to the kitchen regions, from whence the savory odor of fried bacon was wafted through the open door of the room occupied by his guests.

"Say Marthy," it was the voice of their entertainer speaking in persuasive tones, "Brother Ricks has stopped here to breakfast, and that rich Brother Wallace you've heerd me tell about is with him."

"I wish to goodness your grand company would bring their victuals along with them. You need'nt think *I'm* agoing to wait on them."

"For shame Marthy;" interposed a third voice in a weak treble, its a duty an' a privilege I consider to offer Brother Foote's company the best in the house. I've jest sot the table in my room and I've cooked a chicken because,—because you know Brother Foote, you said yesterday mebbe you'd take breakfast with me this mornin'."

"He take breakfast with you indeed! I'd like to see him

doing it, when it's his week to stay in my part of the house."

"Dear me, Marthy! If you was the Queen of Sheby you could'nt put on more airs than you hev sence Brother Foote married you; but what was you afore I'd like to know?"

"And what was you, Jane Holman? But I won't waste any more words on you. Brother Foote, you can bring your company in to breakfast in about twenty minutes. That is all the time I ask to set out a better meal than Jane ever thought of."

"Well, well, don't let's have any quarreling when these's strangers in the house. We'll take breakfast with you of course Marthy, and if they stay maybe they'll eat dinner with Jane."

The sudden slamming of a door at this juncture deprived the audience in the front room of the remainder of the conversation, and a few minutes afterwards their host entered smiling and rubbing his hands briskly.

"I guess them horses of yourn is cooled off enough to have their feed now "he said, I was afraid the boys would'nt manage right and I've bin out and tended to 'em myself."

## PART II.—Chapter v.

### THE MOUNTAIN MEADOW MASSACRE.

Nearly three hundred miles south of Great Salt Lake, and not far from the line which divides Utah and Arizona, lies what is well named Mountain Meadows,—a valley thousands of feet above the level of the sea; a grassy park, walled in by the peaks of the Sierras.

The streams which feed the Colorado and Rio Virgin have their source here. Mere rivulets they are, tiny threads of silver, almost hidden by the tall rich grass.

Myriads of wild flowers, wonderfully beautiful in form and coloring, dot the surface of the Meadows and bloom and die unnoted,—for the solitude is seldom broken by human foot-steps.

To the traveler whom chance may lead thither, the mountain valley seems the abode of Silence and Peace; and so it seemed to the company of emigrants, who reached it, tired and travel worn, after their long march through an enemy's country.

The party whose sudden and mysterious disappearance from Salt Lake gave so much anxiety to some who hoped for help from them, had traveled as fast as their tired animals could be urged to go, through the inhospitable Territory in which they found themselves, and early in September arrived at the Meadows where they hoped to rest and recruit themselves before starting to cross the Desert.

It seemed to them, as they entered the narrow defile

leading into the park, that they had at length found a haven of safety, and they pitched their camp and lay down to sleep that night with thankful hearts. The next day passed quietly and with no foreboding of danger on the part of the emigrants. When night fell again, they prepared for rest without taking any precaution save such as had been their custom throughout the journey. Two men only were left on watch, one at the camp, and one where their animals were corralled, a few hundred yards away.

The hours of the night wore on. The stars that rose over the valley when they lay down to rest, looked from mid-heaven upon the sleeping company,—mothers with their babes nestled in their arms, children breathing softly in unbroken slumber of youth and health, and strong men wrapped in oblivion of the day's fatiguing cares.

Midnight and all is well!

But in the nearest settlements might be heard the stealthy tread of armed assassins, and half-suppressed sounds of warlike preparations.

The Nauvoo Legion, obedient to "orders from head-quarters," have surrounded the unsuspecting emigrants, and while they sleep, the plot for their destruction is maturing.

A portion of the Legion painted and disguised as Indians, have been sent on in company with savages less cruel than themselves to attack the train. The remaining companies of the Mormon militia have other orders.

As the first glimmer of dawn appeared in the sky, the guard at the emigrants camp discerned dark forms moving on the hill-sides around them. Fearing, he scarce knew what, he aroused his comrades.

"Indians," was the word passed from lip to lip, as the figures showed more plainly in the growing light.

Before the sun rose the scattering forms in sights had

increased to scores, and as an attack was plainly intended, a barricade was hastily formed with the wagons of the company, and manned by husbands and fathers, who knew that on the issue of the fight depended the safety of the lives dearest to them.

Their hurried preparations for defence were scarcely concluded, when the sharp crack of rifles and the whizzing of bullets announced that the battle had begun.

It was already only too plain that their assailants greatly outnumbered them, and from savages, as they supposed them to be, no quarter was expected. It was a fight against desperate odds, but love stronger than death nerved their arms and strengthened their hearts.

Let the father who reads these pages by his own fireside, with the bright heads of his little children clustering round him. ask himself against how great odds *he* could fight, if a cruel and lingering death menaced his darlings.

Let him take his youngest born on his knee and while the soft, baby eyes are uplifted to his, let him measure, if he can, the anguish of those fathers who turned from a last look at just such faces, to meet the fierce onset of their murderous foes.

All day long the unequal battle raged. At nightfall the fire from the attacking party slackened, but the light from piles of burning brushwood showed that they still surrounded the emigrant's camp on every side.

Before sunrise, a murderous rain of bullets commenced. and again continued till nightfall.

Access to the springs and streams of water was now cut off, and the horrors of death from thirst stared them in the face, but they fought with desperate courage, and when the sun went down the second day, still held their position, and kept the foe at bay.

The morning of the third day found them worn, exhausted,

tortured by burning thirst, but with hearts as undaunted as ever.

Late in the afternoon, the steady firing of the besiegers ceased, and when they looked out to ascertain the cause, they saw, oh joy! a body of white men entering the valley, their leader bearing a flag of truce.

Be it remembered, the emigrants had never doubted that those who attacked them were Indians, and the sight of white men, coming, as they believed, to their rescue, was welcome as a vision of angels.

Unbounded rejoicing now took the place of despair. Mothers, who during all those dreadful days had knelt with their babes in their arms and besieged heaven with agonized prayers, began to pour out thanksgivings with a rain of grateful tears. Strong men, who had kept up the desperate fight without wavering for a moment, broke down at the prospect of deliverance and wept like children.

In answer to the flag of truce, a little girl was dressed in white and placed on one of the wagons.

In view of what followed, this act was full of unutterable pathos

Truly, they had decked a lamb for sacrifice.

The white men, as they approached the camp, proved to be a detachment of Mormon militia headed by their officers, who were likewise the Bishops of the surrounding settlements.

After a brief parley with these officers the beleagured emigrants, seeing no other hope of saving their wives, accept the terms, which they proposed. These were, that they should surrender all their possessions to the "Indians," stack their arms, and march out of the valley under the protection of the militia.

After making this surrender, they were divided into three companies. The men went first, under the escort of a detachment of the Nauvoo Legion. The women and children followed at some distance, and a wagon containing the wounded brought up the rear.

And now comes the blackest page in this chapter of treachery and murder; a page that the most callous historian might shrink from recording.

At a given signal from the officer in command, the unarmed men, who were being marched out under guard were shot down like dogs, and when the last one lay dead or dying on the bloody sod, the slaughter of the women and children and the butchery of the wounded began.

* * * * * * * * *

The closing atrocities of that day of blood may not be written nor told.

When the sun set that night upon the reddened and trampled Meadows, one hundred and twenty corpses strewed the ground. The men lay where they fell, in pools of stiffening gore. The bodies of the women and children were scattered over the hillside, toward which they fled in their frantic fear. Away to the north of the camp, half hidden by a clump of bushes, lay Margaret Cleveland and her daughter, still clapsed in each others arms. A merciful bullet, from the gun of the nearest savage, had passed through the body of the child and entered the mother's heart, sparing both a more horrible fate.

As the veil of night and silence fell upon the awful scene, the murderers, encamped just outside the valley, gathered up the money and jewels taken from their victims and delivered them to the officer, in command. Among those who come on this business was one who asked to speak apart with the Colonel. "Brother Dame" he said, "I wish you'd tell me what to do with that white-livered chap that was send down from Salt Lake. He fainted away at the first smell of blood, and was brought from the Meadows in my wagon. He's a layin' there now, sick with a fever or somethin' worse, it seems like, and ravin' about 'murder' and all that. Sech kid-glove gentry air no manner o' count when there's rough work on hand. I wonder who was fool enough to send him."

"That's none of you business," was the curt rejoinder, "I will go and see him. Lead on."

It was a walk of nearly a quarter of a mile from the "Colonel's" headquarters to the camp-fire of his subordinate, where lying in a covered farm wagon, Charles Wallace alternately raved in delirium, or moaned in a stupor that was not deep enough to shut out the awful sights which had burned themselves in upon his brain.

"He talks altogether too much for a sick man. Shouldn't wonder if I was obliged to give him something to make him sleep soundly" said the Colonel grimly.

Then after a few minutes' reflection he added:

"Stay, I have thought of a plan. There is nobody here to be disturbed by his talk to-night, and in the morning you can take him to Bill Stewart's ranch down the river. His woman there is Danish and won't understand a word that may be said. I will send Bill down himself some time to-morrow, and under his care our fine gentlemen will do well enough. How long has he been with you?"

"Since yesterday. I was in the same squad with him when we got our orders to go and help the emigrants? He seemed mighty uneasy, and asked a heap of questions about the errand we had been sent on. . Brother Allen told him the Injuns was usin' up the emigrants, and we was goin' to try and save them. I did'nt say anything, for I wa'ant asked to, and besides I make it a pint to let folks do their own lyin'."

"You've got altogether too free a tongue, Brother Jim. Mind that it don't get you into trouble some day."

"Oh as to that I always have a care where I do my talkin'.

"Well as I was sayin', this new recruit, Wallace I believe they call him, was uncommon perticklar to know why we had been ordered out, and I don't think he felt just satisfied when them chaps stacked their arms, but he kept his place in the ranks till he heard the word 'fire,' and then his gun dropped from his hands. Five minutes after, when the smoke cleared so's to show what the shot had done, he dropped too, and rolled almost under my feet.

"I picked him up, (there wa'ant more heft to him than a girl), and dragged him out of the way, and after it was all over, old man Davis helped carry him to one of the wagons, I had'nt any orders to do it, but seein' he was in Colonel Rick's company and they made somethin' of him, I sposed they'd want him looked after. They put him in my wagon after they got to my camp."

"Well, all you have to do is to obey orders. Take care of him yourself to-night and don't stop anywhere on your way to Stewart's to-morrow."

With these words the "Colonel" turned away, leaving Wallace in the hands in which he found him; and here for the present we will leave him also, and go back a couple of months to the night on which poor Pauline met her fate.

It will be remembered that on the evening referred to Wallace received a summons to attend a meeting of the brethren, to be held at the house of the Ward Bishop. This was no uncommon occurrence, and at such meetings hitherto, no business of very great importance had been transacted.

On this particular night, Wallace went as usual without knowing or caring particularly why he was sent for. When he arrived he found the room well filled with men, most of whom were strangers to him. Several persons whom he knew to belong to the police force were also present, occupying the seats next the door.

There was a little talking in a subdued tone, and in answer to a question from Wallace, the Bishop said they were waiting for the brother who was to speak to them.

Wallace sat with his back to the door and did not notice when it was opened, or hear the sound of footsteps, until the Bishop, turning round, offered his hand to some one who had entered, saying, " good evening, Brother Harwood."

Raising his eyes with a start, he encountered the fixed gaze of the man whom he supposed to be hundreds of miles away. Somehow, this unexpected meeting with the returned missionary gave the convert less pleasure than might be supposed;—he was even conscious of a shiver of dread and repulsion, when the new-comer grasped his hand, with great seeming cordiality, and inquired after his family.

By this time, several other brethren had gathered round, and Harwood, after exchanging greetings with them, asked the Bishop to open the meeting with prayer.

Then rising, and speaking in a low voice, scarcely above a whisper but so distinctly that no one could lose a word, he said:

"Brethren when the Lord gave us these valleys of the mountains for an inheritance, he commanded us not to suffer sin among us. If we disobey this command, we lose all he has given us.

"Do you ask how we are to keep it? Why, as his people of old kept it;—by cutting off sinners from the earth. If we find one among us who will not keep the law and will not be admonished, it is better for that one to die than for the whole people to perish.

"It is to decide the fate of such a one that we are met to-night."

For half an hour he continued talking in the same strain,

withholding the name of the doomed one until the last sentence, but when he pronounced the final words:

"All of you whose mind it is that Pauline R,—should be cut off for her sins, raise your right hand,"—it was evident that he knew his audience, for every hand was raised. Wallace sat directly before the speaker, whose baleful eyes, fixed on him with mesmeric power, seemed to paralyze his faculties and control his will. When the fatal words were spoken that doomed a fellow creature to death, his hand was raised with the others, but dropped immediately by his side.

Staring straight before him, conscious of nothing but the glittering eyes that held him, he heard, without comprehending the next words, addressed to the policemen.

"Brethren do your duty."

There was a little stir near the door, as the men spoken to, passed out, then the voice of the leader was heard again.

"Let us pray."

And in awful though possibly unconscious mockery of the Being whose laws they were breaking, the Bishop, again prayed for a blessing on the night's work.

It was not until the meeting broke up and he found himself alone, with the cool breeze from the mountains blowing in his face, that Wallace awoke as from a frightful dream, and began to realize what he had done.

"I am a murderer," he said half aloud;—and he held up his hands in the moonlight, as though expecting to find the stain of blood on them.

With his brain in a whirl, feeling every moment as though he should go mad, and yet conscious of the necessity of silence and watchfulness over himself he turned his steps homeward.

In the midst of his mental confusion and bewilderment,

one thought was only too clear. He was accessory to the murder of the unhappy girl who was perhaps already in the hands of her assassins;—and even while he was striving to banish the dreadful picture conjured up by his tortured brain, her cry for help rang out on the still midnight air.

Fairly stopping his ears, he hurried from the spot to his own door, there to be met, as we have seen, by his wife's accusing question: "Is it possible that you have witnessed a murder without raising a hand to save the victim?"

He passed the following week in a state bordering on insanity, and finally settled down into a state of mind which if he had been forced to describe, he would have expressed somewhat in this manner:

"I am not a free agent. I came here consenting to subject my reason to my faith. I have no right to reason about this matter. If the girl was guilty as alleged, it is not for me to say that the Priesthood had no right to decree her punishment. I will leave the responsibility where it belongs—with those who planned the deed." Full of contradictions as this attempt at self-justification may appear, it is a fair sample of the defence made by Wallace's fellow-believers who have been guilty of actual crime; and these may be numbered by thousands.

Still, in spite of all his efforts to silence reason and conscience, he could not wholly put away the awful feeling of blood-guiltiness which haunted him at first.

Besides this there was the fear, always present with him now, that he might be called at any day to assist in some other deed of darkness, and the consciousness that he would not dare to disobey such a call.

No wonder then that after the experience of the past two months, the little which he saw of the bloody tragedy of Mountain Meadows was sufficient to strike him down senseless at the feet of the murderers who called him "Brother!"

## PART II.—Chap. VI.

AT THE FARM-HOUSE—THE RETURN—TERRIBLE REVELATIONS.

It is time now to return to Mrs. Wallace and Winnie, whom we left at the Henly farm-house.

The two weeks named at first as the limit of their stay passed, but as the weather still continued very hot, Esther now that all present hopes of getting safely out of the Territory seemed cut off, decided not to return to the city until the last of September. As yet, they had heard nothing from Wallace, but his wife felt no anxiety on his account, believing him to have gone, as he had led her to suppose, to some of the northern settlements. Another week passed quietly at the farm-house. Winnie was growing so rosy and strong that her mother felt well repaid for bringing her away from the town. All the members of the Henly household seemed intent on making their visitor's stay a pleasant one, but the head of the family, though cordial to his guests, appeared restless and ill at ease. The eldest son, George, who was summoned away by Harwood, had not yet returned, and once or twice Esther happened to overhear his sisters wondering at his long stay. On both occasions, they were sharply reprimanded by their father for troubling themselves about what did not concern them, and told that their brother was old enough to take care of himself. The mother, since the first evening's conversation with Mrs. Wallace, had not spoken of her boy, though it was evident from her manner that she was not altogether free from anxiety about him.

Toward the end of the third week, Mr. Henly rode into town and remained away a couple of days. When he returned he brought Mrs. Wallace a message which he said was left with her tenants who occupied the small house and took care of the place in her absence. It was to the effect that Wallace had joined a party going north, to look for land suitable for a town-site, and that he might not be home before the middle of October.

It is scarcely necessary to say that this message was of Harwood's coining. It certainly did credit to his inventive genius.

Esther however, received the word brought her in good faith.

Henly told her it was sent by a brother just in from the north; and to the natural inquiry why her husband had not also sent a letter, he replied that the party met Brother Allen on his way to town, and he could not stop for a letter to be written.

Brother Henly also brought his family tidings, probably quite as truthful as the above, with regard to George's whereabouts.

The boy, he said had got back as far as Salt Lake, and as he wanted to stay in the City a few weeks, he had given him permission to do so.

Meanwhile, no word had reached the farm-house with regard to the fate of the emigrant train, and Esther, finding the suspense unbearable, ventured to seek a private interview with Mrs. Henly, for the purpose of asking what she knew or suspected.

"They say no news is good news," was the matron's reply to her anxious questions.

"If anything very bad had happened them, it would be

whispered about among those who were thought trustworthy, but I am quite certain that not a word has reached this settlement. It is most probable that the Indians have been employed to run off their stock, and that the emigrants have made their way out of the Territory, glad to get off with only the loss of a few cattle and horses."

"But George? If he has been South he must know all about it."

"I dare say he does, and that is the reason his father keeps him away from home for the present. He won't come back till the affair has blown over."

"Then you feel quite sure that nothing worse has happened to the emigrants than the loss of some of their property?"

"That is what I think, but if there has been any serious trouble we will know something about it soon, though we may never find out the whole truth."

This conversation took place three or four days after Henly's return from the City. It was not reassuring, and Mrs. Wallace decided to start for home the following Monday, thinking that in Salt Lake she might hear something which would relieve the painful anxiety she felt regarding the fate of her cousin.

The day of their return to their home in town was almost the counterpart of that on which they entered the valley, just one year ago;—the same golden light bathing the earth, the same soft haze resting on the mountain-tops.

Autumn flowers still blossomed in the little garden, and the trees bent under their weight of ripened fruit. Very fair, very peaceful everything looked, but to Esther, whose heart was filled with gloomy forebodings, all this outward loveliness was but as the flowers blooming above a grave. Here she had buried hope and happiness; here was the grave of all she had cherished most;—here too, was the pit into which the fair child by her side might fall some day.

The tenant of the little house came bustling forward on their approach, with the keys in her hand,

"We're very glad to see you all home again," she said heartily. "I took the privilege of opening the house and airing the rooms this morning, thinking you might come to-day,—but where is brother Wallace?"

"Still at the north, I suppose. We have not heard from him since we got his message through you."

"His message! Why Sister Wallace we have'nt heard a word from him since he left the keys with us, and that was the night after you went away."

For one moment Esther felt as though she should fall, and caught at the railing of the porch. She had never fainted in her life, but the steady nerves and strong self-control which had withstood so many shocks were weakening.

In the single minutes following the discovery that the message which set her mind at rest about her husband was a lie, a flood of direful apprehensions swept over her.

Had he too been put out of the way? Perhaps his body was even now lying in some canyon, food for the wolves. All the horrible stories she had heard during the past six months came rushing into her mind, and for the time her fear for her husband's safety swallowed up all other fear and anxieties.

She tried to recall what he had said when she left home but could remember nothing which would afford a clue to his whereabouts. It was possible, however, that the tenant might know something with regard to the parties in whose company he left, or the route he was to take; so as soon as she could collect her thoughts, she bade Winnie to stay with Aunt Eunice, and turning to 'Sister Mead,' said:

"I will go over to your house and rest a few minutes and you can tell me how things have gone since we have been away."

Sister Mead was a widow with one son, who was just then at work in the farthest part of the lot, so the two women were quite alone when they entered the house and sat down.

"Mrs. Mead," said Esther, "more than a week ago, Mr. Henly brought me a message which he said was from you. He told me that a Mr. Allen, coming in from the northern settlements, stopped here and left word that my husband had joined a party who were looking for a town-site, and that he would not be home until the middle of October. You say you have heard nothing, and I don't know what to think."

"No more do I Sister Wallace. As I told you, the last I saw or heard of your husband was the night after you left. He was away all day, but came home about sundown. My boy put up his horse and I offered to get his supper, but he said no, he should not want anything. Early in the evening somebody rode up to the gate and stopped. I looked out, naturally, but it was so dark I could'nt see who it was till he knocked at the door and it was opened. Then for a minute the light shone full on his face."

"And you knew him?"

"I dont know his name, but it was that tall, dark man who has been at your house so much during the summer."

"Did my husband go away with HIM?" Involuntarily, Esther pronounced the last word in a tone which betrayed her fear and detestation of the man who had such a strange power for evil over those who gave themselves up to his guidance.

Mrs. Mead looked up surprised.

"I can't say for sure that they went together, but I suppose so. I saw the man's face for just a minute, as I said, while he was standing in the doorway. Then he went in but came out again soon. About ten minutes afterwards Brother Wallace came over here and asked John to saddle his horse and bring him round to the gate. He told me he was obliged to go out of town on business and might be away until you came home, so he would leave the place in my care. He did not say where he was going, and I did'nt ask, but John said he waited at the gate till another man on horseback came up and they rode away together."

"Have you seen that man since the night Mr. Wallace went away?"

"Yes, I saw him about two weeks afterwards and again this week, but as he is a stranger to me I did not think of speaking to him."

"And you have heard nothing whatever from my husband."

"No, nothing." Then observing Esther's pallor and agitation she added in a lower tone:

"But I can tell you what I think. Quite a number of men from this city were sent south just after those emigrants were here. It was said that as they were a very lawless company they would be likely to make trouble on their way, and I heard that the militia were ordered out to watch them. Since then, my daughter has been up from Lehi, and she says she thought she saw Brother Wallace in company with Brother Ricks and about a dozen men from Salt' Lake, who rode through the settlement going South."

"Was it your daughter Mary who used to live across the street?"

"Yes, and she knows Brother Wallace so well by sight that I don't think she could be mistaken."

"Have any of the men who went south returned to the city do you think?"

"Yes, some of them, but not all. There are at least two men from this ward besides Brother Wallace who have not got home. Then I know of others whose wives have been expecting them for two weeks and have heard nothing from them, but no doubt they will all get safely back soon. It's a long way to the Southern settlements and a good many things might happen to delay them on their journey."

"Did those of the men who have returned bring any word about the emigrant train? Have you heard anything?"

Sister Mead changed color and moved uneasily on her chair. She had a vague recollection of hearing that Mrs. Wallace had relatives on the train. What should she say to her? She was an honest woman in spite of the influences under which she lived, and had still some old-fashioned scruples about telling a direct lie. She *had* heard something;—much more than she was willing to repeat to the woman who sat before her, waiting for her answer with pale face and anxious eyes. The only evasion she could frame sounded weak and shallow enough to herself.

"You know, Sister Wallace that I hardly ever go out, and what news I hear comes through John, who is like all other boys,—repeats a story in such a way that it don't lose anything in telling. John has heard something about a fight between the emigrants and the Indians, but I don't think the news he picks up is very reliable."

"Does John say that any of the emigrants were killed?"

"Some of them I believe. The fight took place a good ways from the settlements and by the time our people got there it was mostly over."

"Our people! The Mormons, you mean. What did they do?"

"Why of course they started out to drive off the Indians; but as I said before, you can't place much dependence on what John has heard."

## In the Toils.

It was plain enough to her questioner that Sister Mead whatever she knew did not mean to tell anything more and with a very heavy heart Esther rose to go.

When in her own room, alone with her fears and distress, she recalled Mrs. Mead's confused looks and evasive answers and found in them almost certain evidence that the worst that could be foreboded had befallen the doomed emigrants. What did Mrs. Henly say? "The Nauvoo Legion might be ordered not to suffer any of them to leave the Territory alive." This seemed too horrible for belief and yet the conviction began to force itself upon her mind that if one had perished all had perished. No one knew better than the Mormon leaders how fatal would be the escape of any of any one who could tell the tale of his comrade's doom. A fight with the Indians! No. There had been no such thing. She remembered well enough having overheard a party of Mormons just from the South say there were not a dozen Indians on the whole route. This was in August while the emigrants were camped at Salt Lake. If harm had befallen the emigrants, white men were responsible for it. Had her husband any knowledge of what had happened? Was the fate of the train in any way connected with his prolonged absence? Her fears supplied one answer to these questions, the remnants of her faith in her husband another. \* \* \* \* \* \*

In after years when she looked back upon the two weeks of torturing anxiety and horrible suspense that followed, she marveled that she kept her reason. It was now October and still no tidings of her husband. Day after day she watched the road leading southward. There was no timber, no rising ground, nothing to break the view, and with a glass she could see every moving object on the highway for many miles. It was near sunset on the fourteenth day since her return. Somehow as night fell upon each day of watching and waiting, the feeling that she must be at her post, the first to meet the absent one, was stronger than ever. To-night, as she lifted her glass to scan the distant horizon, and then dropping it watched the portion of the road leading into town, her mind was carried back to that never-to-be-forgotten night when she stood watching for her husband on the porch of the stone house;—the night that closed upon her last day of happiness and peace. Then without any mental effort this picture was shut out and the far-off home of her girlhood rose up before her. She saw the sun set again behind the groves of Louisiana. She stood at the gate watching and waiting for her father's coming. She heard the sound of wheels on the highway. She roused herself with a start. The picture faded and in its stead she saw the dusty highway leading southward, and the lumbering canvas-covered wagons of the settlers turning off from it into the principal street of the town. It was not for these that she was watching and with a weary sigh she left her post and entered the house, but almost immediately Winnie called out:

"Mamma! There is a wagon stopping at the gate."

Hurrying out she saw one of the heavy covered farm wagons which had just now come into the city. The driver jumped down from his seat as she appeared and extended his hand to some one inside. There was a minute's delay and then the figure of a man wrapped in a long traveling cloak and with a slouched hat concealing his face, became visible at the opening of the canvas. He made one or two ineffectual attempts to descend and was at length fairly lifted to the ground by the driver. By this time the whole family were at the gate, and Esther was the first to receive into her arms, the trembling, emaciated figure that staggered toward her. "Let me help you ma'am," said the driver respectfully, "He's been pretty sick and the ride has shook him up a good deal." The man's kindly offer was accepted and leaning heavily on him and on his wife's shoulder, Charles Wallace re-entered the home he had hardly hoped to see again. His eye brightened for a moment as the door opened to admit him, but before he could be seated in the arm-chair that stood ready for him, he fainted quite away. When consciousness returned his gaze rested first on the face of his wife, who bent over him. "Am I home again? Thank God!" he said feebly, trying to reach out his hand to her.

The man who had brought him still stood in the doorway, but as soon as Wallace showed signs of consciousness, he moved back a step, or two, and saying: "I must be going" strode to the gate and jumping into his wagon drove rapidly off and was soon out of sight.

"'Pears like he's in a powerful hurry" muttered Aunt Eunice " Don't stop for nobody to ax him nuffin."

Wallace who still clung to his wife's hand, without seeming to notice the presence of others in the room, now spoke again. "I have been very sick. I thought I was better, but this ride has tired me so, I'm afraid you will have to let me go to bed."

"Can you walk?" asked Esther.

"Yes, if you will help me. I want you. Nobody else."

Esther signed to the others to leave the room, and Wallace exerted all his strength to walk, with her help, into the next room. He seemed nervously afraid that she would call some one, and to soothe him she told him she needed no assistance, and did indeed manage to get him into his bed alone. He thanked her earnestly as she settled his pillows for him, and then closing his eyes, but still holding her hand, appeared to sleep. For more than an hour she sat thus beside him. Winnie tiptoed softly into the room to see "poor papa." Her loving heart ached a little because he had not spoken to her or seemed to see her, but his sickness excused everything. Mamma whispered to her that she could not leave papa tonight, but Aunt Eunice might send in a cup of tea by and by. "May I stay with you mamma" she asked. "Not now dear"--and though Winnie's face was saddened for a moment, she kissed mamma and went out directly, reasoning in her wise little head upon the need of perfect quiet in papa's sick-room. She loved her father with all the strength of her affectionate nature, and much as she wanted to be with him she would stay away all the time rather than disturb him by a foot-fall even.

Esther, alone, watching beside the sleeping figure that at times seemed scarcely to breathe, was conscious for the time of nothing but her intense solicitude that he might rest long enough to wake refreshed and rational. His sleep appeared to be that of one utterly exhausted and surely he must be the better for it.

Toward midnight the sick man showed signs of disturbance. He began to toss and mutter incoherently and every few minutes threw up his arms with a sharp cry. His wife prepared a quieting drink and tried to induce him to swallow it, but in vain. His ravings became so violent that she was forced to call both Aunt Eunice and Jem to her assistance. Before morning however he quieted down again and sank into a sleep which lasted most of the day, and thus for two weeks alternated between delirium and stupor, without a single rational interval.

Strange to say, there were no inquiries after Brother Wallace during his sickness, and with the exception of Mrs. Mears, who staid with them most of the time and relieved Aunt Eunice of her household cares that she might wait upon her sick master, no one came near them. Toward the end of the second week Jem came in from the street and called Aunt Eunice out on the back porch.

"Auntie," he said, "there's a chap at the gate, with some farm truck, and he wants to see Mrs. Wallace."

"You go 'long", Aunt Eunice answered with some asperity. "What for you 'spose Miss Esther would bodder 'bout sech trash when she can't leabe Massa Wallace for a bressed minnit."

"Better go stay with him yourself then, for that man is so earnest to see the mistress I reckon he's got some word for her."

"Mebbe det's so Jem. You's a wise chile after all. I'll tell Miss Esther sure."

Aunt Eunice knocked softly at the door of the sick-room. "Let me stay a minnit with Massa, honey. Dere's somebody out hyar is 'bliged to see you." As Esther came out the stranger, preceded by Jem, walked in at the kitchen door. He was apparently not much older than Jem himself and wore the ordinary rough, homespun dress of the farmer lads who came in every day to market. As he stood before the lady, twirling his whip in his hands, he seemed more than commonly awkward and ill at ease.

"What do you wish?" Mrs. Wallace asked pleasantly.

"I thought perhaps you might be wanting to buy some winter potatoes"—then glancing at Jem who stood on the walk outside he added in a hurried whisper "I must see you alone, Mrs. Wallace." "Step this way" she answered in the same tone, pointing to an inner room — then aloud — "I will perhaps buy a few bushels, if they are good" and then calling to Jem to go to the barn and look for a large basket, Mrs. Wallace turned from the door and stepping into the next room confronted her strange visitor. The lad removed his hat, and disclosed a face pale in spite of its sunburned tints and boyish blue eyes that were full of trouble and dread. "Mrs Wallace" he began in a low hesitating voice, "I was with your husband at—at the Meadows. I went there as he did without knowing what for. They told us the Indians were killing the emigrants and we must go and help them. I stood beside Brother Wallace when they gave the order to fire. I saw his gun drop from his hands—saw him fall the next minute. I know he never fired a shot or struck a blow and no more did I; nor would I not even if they held a gun to my head to make me do it. And yet I've never had a day's peace or a night's rest since. I never will have until I drop into my grave. Oh it was awful—awful!—and the women and children—Oh me!"

He stopped, shuddering, and covered his eyes with his hands as if to shut out some horrible sight. "The women! The children! What of them?" Esther found strength to put this question, though her senses reeled and the room was turning dark before her.

"Don't ask me. I have said too much already. I only wanted you to know that Brother Wallace was not guilty. I have come a long way to tell you this, and if I'm found out they will kill me too, but I don't care. I've wished myself dead a good many times since then." Without waiting for another word he picked up his whip, replaced his hat, which he pulled low over his eyes, and hurried out to the gate, where Jem who seemed to understand his part in the business, was measuring the potatoes, which were paid for by Aunt Eunice who soon made her appearance and called John from the barn to help carry them into the cellar.

It was well for more than one of the parties concerned that this very commonplace transaction covered the real object of the stranger's visit, for, unknown to the Wallaces, vigilant eyes watched their house night and day and none went in or, came out, unmarked.

Esther looking out from behind her closed blinds, saw the wagon drive away with mingled feelings. The dreadful news of the massacre was only a confirmation of what she had believed for weeks, and the certainty of the emigrants, fate was no worse than the horrible suspense of the past month.

Then she had at least one consolation.  Her husband had no part in the awful crime.  She entered the bed-room softly, and looked at him as he lay asleep.  During the past two weeks his ravings had told much of the story of his mental tortures since the night of poor Pauline's murder. His wife thought she understood now how he loathed the slavery he had brought himself into, and she believed he would welcome death as a deliverance from it.  Was the end near?  It seemed so, as he lay there so ghastly, so wasted and drawing his breath with short quick gasps.

For nearly an hour she sat thus, silently watching him occasionally wetting his lips with a little wine and water.

She noticed at length that his breathing appeared more natural, and placing her hand on his forehead was certain she felt a little moisture.  He was better, surely, and with a beating heart she bent over him, hoping, almost for the the first time, that he might be restored not only to life, but to her.

Another hour passed.  He still seemed to be in a quiet, refreshing sleep.  Esther moved softly about the room, putting things in order.  When she turned to the bed again, she met her husband's eyes, which were open and following her with a look in which there was none of the wildness of the fever.  She spoke to him and he answered rationally, and for the first time asked for Winnie.  The little girl was not far off, for when not allowed in the sick room she kept her post outside the door, unless sent away by her mother into the open air.

Poor child!  She was almost wild with joy when she learned that papa was better and had really asked for her, but with a thoughtfulness beyond her years, she came softly into the room and spoke to him as quietly as though she had talked to him every day.

From this time Wallace improved steadily and rapidly and in less than a week was able to sit up. As he grew stronger his wife thought she perceived a change in him, but one hard to define. It seemed almost as though the memory of the past two years had been swept away from his mind and he had gone back to the old days in the stone house.

He never made the least allusion to his present position and surroundings, but talked freely and naturally upon subjects that used to interest him in his former life.

When, however, he grew so much better as to be able to walk out he became more reserved.

He was kinder than ever to his wife and child and seemed full of solicitude for their comfort, but he talked little and spent much of his time in his study, seldom going anywhere except to the service in the Ward meeting-house on Sunday morning, and his attendance there his wife thought must be compulsory for he went and came in silence and with a face of the deepest gloom.

The winter this year set in early and was unusually stormy;—which perhaps accounted for the fact that they had few visitors.

It was an unspeakable relief to Esther to be spared the almost constant presence of the Ward Bishop, his counsellors, and various other brethren who used to make themselves quite at home at her house, but most of all she felt thankful that the evil face of Elder Harwood never darkened their doors. Incidentally she heard that he had gone to Australia, and she earnestly hoped he might stay there. In his absence Wallace seemed to recover something of his former independence and in many respects their home life was almost as pleasant as before his baleful shadow fell across their pathway.  \* \* \* \* \* \*

More than three months had now elapsed since the emigrant train left Salt Lake, and still nothing was said publicly about its fate. The Deseret *News*, the only paper then published in the Territory, never mentioned the subject. At first Esther looked over its columns every day thinking possibly she might find something which would give a clue, however slight, that if followed might enable her to learn whether any of the doomed emigrants had escaped alive, but as the weeks passed by she gave up the search as hopeless. To-night she picked up the paper from the floor where her husband had dropped it and glancing carelessly over the column which first met her eye, her attention was arrested by the following paragraph:

"MORE INDIAN TROUBLES.

"It seems, as we prophesied long ago, that emigrant travel across the plains to California is to be a never-ending source of trouble with the Indians. Our readers will remember, that quite a large company of emigrants bound for California passed through this City about three months ago, intending to take the Southern route to the Coast. Brethren coming in from the settlements through which they passed brought reports at the time concerning the lawless conduct of these emigrants, mentioning among other things that they had poisoned a spring used by the Indians and also distributed the flesh of a poisoned ox among them. It appears that the savages were so exasperated by this that they followed the emigrants to the southern boundary of the territory surrounded their camp at night and surprised them. From the rumors which have reached us we can only glean enough to make it certain that the emigrants got worsted in the fight. Their stock and considerable other property belonging to them has been seen in the possession of the Indians;—also a number of white children too young to give an account of themselves but supposed to belong to the missing emigrants. At the instance of Brother John D. Lee who has charge of Indian affairs in the South, the children have been ransomed and placed in families where they are kindly cared for. A report has just reached us that an agent sent out by Government will soon be back here to gather up these children and take them back to the States. If this is so, it seems to us that the government should also pay those who have with their private means ransomed the children and taken care of them until the present."

Here was "news" truly. What had inspired the priests who conducted the paper to make this late mention of the fate of the slaughtered emigrants? Since her husband's sickness Esther had remained so closely at home that if rumors of the deed of blood were circulating among the people she would have had no opportunity of hearing them. Now she bethought herself of Mrs. Nye and decided to go there in the morning and talk the matter over. Mrs. Nye was a Bureau of information in herself, as her friend sometimes pleasantly told her. She went out a great deal, and was, if the truth must be owned, rather fond of gossip. If anything out of the usual way happened, Mrs. Nye would hear of it if anybody did. News that circulated in whispers reached her ears through women who, though disaffected like herself were cautious enough to keep their practical opinions from the knowledge of the Priesthood.

It was still early when Mrs. Wallace rapped at Mrs. Nye's door the next morning. The weather was damp and unpleasant and there were few people on the streets but the police, faithful in the performance of their duty as spies would be likely to be on the alert; so Esther made her appearance at her neighbor's house with a bundle of dry-goods in her arms, which, as Mrs. Nye did a little dress-making offered a convenient excuse for her visit.

It no doubt seems incredible to the readers of this narrative that in a Territory of the United States, a little more than a dozen years ago a lady could not make a morning call without being watched and followed by the city police, but the writer wishes it to be distinctly understood that such was the actual fact, and that the pictures of social life in the Mormon capital which these pages present are not overdrawn in the least particular.

When both ladies were seated in Mrs. Nye's upper room a little out of the hearing of anyone who might be listening below, Mrs. Wallace unfolded her copy of the *News* and pointed out to her neighbor the article which prompted her visit.

"I had not seen this" Mrs. Nye said after looking it over "but I can translate it easily enough. Dr. Forney, the Government agent spoken of, is already in the City, and Brother Carrington means to anticipate his inquiries. Also Brigham Young, who is as you know, Superintendent of Indian affairs for this Territory as well as Governor means to turn an honest penny by bringing in a bill for the pretended ransom of the children. You will see that when the affair comes to be investigated he will claim that the brethren who have the children in their care have been paid by him for all expenses incurred."

"You don't think then that the Indians ever had the children?"

"I know just the contrary. You have not been here lately and I have not seen you anywhere where it was safe to speak above one's breath, or I could have told you much. I went South myself as far as Parowan six weeks after the massacre, (for that is what it was,) and I saw some of those very children. They were in Mormon families, and had been since the day their parents were killed."

"Killed by the Indians?"

"No, by white men; by the priests and elders of this accursed Church; by the very men who have their property and their little ones to-day. Listen. In the family in which I stopped there was a beautiful little girl about six years old, the child of one of the murdered emigrants,—ransomed from the Indians,—so they told me. One day when, as it happened, the family were out, a poor woman living next door came in with a shawl which she wanted me to buy. It was a handsome and costly one but she was plainly ignorant of its value, for she offered it to me for less than a quarter of its real worth.

"The little girl was in the room when the shawl was spread out for examination. As soon as she saw it, she clasped her hands and uttered a startled exclamation. The woman did not seem to notice her and as I declined buying, went out to find a purchaser elsewhere.

"As the door closed behind her, the child turned to me with a piteous look.

"'That was my mother's shawl,' she said 'Why did she take it away?'

"'Where is your mother?' I asked.

"'Dead! dead! They killed her and the baby, I saw the blood, Oh, dear!'

"Then beginning to cry, she clung to my dress saying:

"'Dont tell please. At the other place they beat me when I talked about mother, and the man that brought me here said they would whip me nearly to death if I told about father and mother and the boys.'

"'Do they whip you here then?'

"'No, I never say anything and they think I don't remember, but I do. I saw them all killed, and I saw the Indian that killed mother, wash his face at the spring, and he was a white man. He took me home with him. I did'nt want to go, but I was afraid, so afraid. Then the women at his house said she couldn't bear to look at me, and so he brought me here. He had some of mother'sthings but the woman told him to take them away. She said there was blood on them, but there wasn't, they were clean things, out of mothers trunk. This man here, was there with a gun too, I saw him but he dont know it. Oh wont you take me away please? I'll be good always if you will.'

"I tell you, Mrs. Wallace, the poor little thing's pitiful looks and words almost broke my heart. I would have given all I had in the world to take her home with me, but I knew this would not be allowed. I didn't dare hint such a thing even, lest they should suspect that the child had talked with me. I comforted her as well as I could by the promise that she should be taken away soon and I hope Dr. Forney is going to redeem my promise now."

Mrs. Nye told the dreadful story with strong dramatic emphasis, and rendered the child's description of the deed of blood in such a manner that her listener could not repress a cry of horror. Now at the close of the narration she leaned back in her chair with a face so white that Mrs. Nye thought her fainting, and sprang up in quest of restoratives.

"Don't get me anything" she said. " I shall not faint; this is not a time for fainting, but for action. If there is a Government agent here, all the details of this awful crime must be furnished him, that it may be punished as it deserves.

" Dr. Forney can get evidence enough if he goes to work in the right way, but I'm afraid it will be a long time before justice overtakes the murderers. I haven't much faith in a Government that puts Brigham Young at the head of everything here."

Three months later, when with the children which he had

gathered from the different settlements in his care, Dr. Forney returned to Salt Lake, Mrs. Wallace sought and obtained an interview with him, but though she learned that the facts elicited by his inquiries, were such as to fix the guilt of the massacre upon the Mormon leaders, she found him not at all hopeful of being able to interest the authorities at Washington in the matter.

"The fact is Mrs. Wallace," he said, "the people are just now too much occupied with political questions of national importance to give much thought to anything else. Utah is a long ways off, and neither the Territory nor its inhabitants are likely to receive even a small share of public attention. As for the officials at Washington, they are too much exercised over the distribution of the loaves and fishes to find time to look into other affairs.

I shall make a faithful statement of the facts which have come to my knowledge supported by such affidavits, as I have been able to get but I doubt much if anything is done about it."

The next week, having heard that two of the rescued children were staying with Mrs. Cooke, a lady with whom she was slightly acquainted. she called on her, ostensibly to talk about music lessons for Winnie, but really hoping to see the children and possibly exchange a word with them alone.

Mrs. Cooke taught music in Brigham Young's family, and on this account Mrs. Wallace supposed her to be a devout Mormon, but on the present occasion the lady's cordiality toward herself and the freedom with which she spoke of the children and the circumstances under which they were brought to her, changed her opinion somewhat. After a little time the children themselves, came in from an adjoining room. They were boys, the elder apparently between eight and nine, the younger about seven.

After a moment's hesitation, Mrs. Wallace turned to her

hostess and said: "Mrs. Cooke, will you allow me to ask these boys a few questions? I had relatives in that unfortunate company and I may possibly learn something of their fate." A little to her surprise Mrs. Cooke answered: "Ask them anything you please."

Mrs. Wallace called the elder boy to her and said:

"My child, did you know Mrs. Cleveland and her daughter Esther?"

"Yes ma'am."

"Where are they now?"

"Dead, I think."

"What makes you think so?"

"I wasn't very far from them when—when they began to shoot. I heard somebody say 'Run for your lives' and mother and I were running as fast as we could when Mrs. Cleaveland and Esther passed us. She had hold of Esther's hand. They were trying to run away from a man with a knife,—a white man. The Indians were ahead of them and they had guns. Mrs. Cleaveland fell down. She had hold of Esther. I think the Indians shot them both. They put us children in a wagon after the shooting was over, and we staid there while the white men talked with the Indians. I never saw Mrs. Cleaveland or Esther again. I never saw any of the women or the big boys and girls. There wasn't anybody in the wagon bigger than me, except Charley, and he talked about the man that killed his father one night and in the morning they took him away. I've never seen him either since then. They told us he'd gone to live with the Indians."

"Was Charley your brother?"

"No ma'am, they killed my two brothers and father and mother and all our folks."

"Who killed them? The Indians?"

"No.—White men killed them but the Indians helped."

By this time both the children were trembling and crying, overcome by the memory of all they had lost.

"Better go to your own room, my dears," Mrs. Cooke said, and the boys went obediently, trying hard to check their sobs.

When they were gone, Mrs. Cooke turned and faced her visitor.

"This is dreadful, Mrs. Wallace," she said.

"I have no reason to doubt what these children tell me and their story makes it only too clear that white men—Mormons—have committed a crime that savages would shrink from."

"And is it not also apparent that this whole people have aided in covering up the crime?"

"No. For multitudes of our people knew nothing of it; many know nothing of it to this day, but we will not talk about it, talking can do no good now and the whole subject is something too horrible to dwell upon."

After a few words more upon ordinary topics, Mrs. Wallace took her leave, carrying with her the conviction that Mrs. Cooke believed the Mormon leaders responsible for the massacre, and the impression that she would no longer follow such leaders. She learned soon afterwards that Dr. Forney had returned to the States taking the two boys with him, the other children having been previously sent East under a safe escort.

## PART II.—Chapter VII.

TWO YEARS AFTER. — TIGHTENING OF THE TOILS. — THE BLOW SO LONG DELAYED FALLS AT LAST.

We pass now over an interval of two years.

It is spring again in the City of the Saints. The valleys, filled to the brim with bloom and verdure, and bound with a glittering circlet of snowy peaks are more lovely than ever. The air is heavy with the fragrance of a thousand blossoming orchards. The Lake glows like molten gold under the rays of the setting sun and rosy lights and purple shadows clothe the mountains like a monarch's robe. There is nothing to mar the perfect beauty of the picture. No rude sound breaks the almost Sabbath stillness.

The blue waters of the Jordan tell no tales of those who sleep beneath them. There is no crimson stain on the sod of the valley and the mountains give no sign of the bleaching bones hidden in the caverns.

"What a fair mantle to cover so much that is vile!"

This thought was always present to one at least whose eyes rested on the beautiful landscape spread out under May skies.

To-night as on many other nights, Esther Wallace sat on the balcony of her house with her daughter beside her and echoed the longing of the Psalmist: "Oh that I had wings like a dove!"

Had she been alone, for her husband's sake she might

have resigned herself to what seemed her inevitable fate.

But she was not alone.

Winnie, growing more beautiful with every passing year was now nearly twelve and so womanly in appearance that she might have been thought three years older.

The mother's eyes turned from the landscape to rest on the fairer picture at her feet.

Winnie knelt on a cushion with her head resting against her mother's knee. The level rays of the setting sun shone on the rippling waves of her chestnut hair and as the mother looked down it seemed to her that a glory encircled her darling's head.

Long and tenderly her gaze lingered on the kneeling figure and the uplifted face tinged with a sweet seriousness which did not belong to her childish years.

Winnie's violet eyes were fixed on the distant mountain tops as though she too shared the longing that stirred her mother's heart.

A flock of gulls rose slowly from the lake and sailed away eastward. She turned her head and followed their flight with a wistful look. When they were out of sight she sighed audibly.

"What is it my daughter?" asked the mother.

"I have been watching those birds, mamma. It is so easy for them to get away, so hard for us,—and then they don't have to leave anybody behind that they love."

"Dear, have you forgotten who it is that cares for the birds and asks 'Are ye not better than they?'"

"No mamma, I have not forgotton, and that is the only thing that makes it possible to live here. The sun shines and the flowers grow in this dreadful country, and all the little things—the birds, and the squirrels, and rabbits that we see when we walk out on the hills, are taken care of, so God must be here too."

"That reminds me of a hymn my mother used to sing when I was a very little child."

"Sing it to-night mamma."

And in a low sweet voice, and with her eyes raised to the calm heavens, Esther sang:

> Could I be cast where Thou art not,
> That were indeed a dreadful lot,
> But regions none remote I call,
> Secure of finding God in all.
>
> I hold by nothing here below,
> Appoint my journey and I go.
> Though friends forsake and foes deride,
> I feel The good;—feel naught beside.
>
> To me remains nor place nor time,
> My country is in every clime,
> I can be calm and free from care
> On any shore, since God is there.

"That is very beautiful mamma, I only wish we could feel so."

"We might, if we had the faith that comforted and sustained the sorely-tried one who wrote the hymn."

"Who is it mamma?"

"One who lived and died long ago. She was called Madam Guion."

A summons from below here interrupted the conversation, and hand in hand the mother and daughter descended the stairway. In the hall Aunt Eunice met them and handed her mistress a a note. Esther opened it and read:

"MY ONLY FRIEND:
Will you come to me to-night? Robbie is dying.
THERESA St. CLAIR."

She passed the note to Winnie who read it and turned to her with tearful eyes.

"May I go with you mamma?"

"No love. I will stay all night, and you will be better at home,"

"What is it?" asked Wallace, who at the moment entered the hall.

"Mrs. St. Clair has sent for me. Her boy is dying."

"Shall you go?"

"Certainly."

"I will go with you then. It is too far for you to think of going alone, and if you have to stay all night, I will come for you in the morning."

It may be remarked here that ever since the occurrences of two years ago, Wallace seemed nervously afraid of having his wife or Winnie go out alone, even in the day time. He always accompanied them himself if possible and when unavoidably absent made them promise to take Aunt Eunice or Jem with them.

Now as soon as Esther was equipped for her walk he presented himself at the door and giving her his arm rather hurried her steps down the path and along the sidewalk.

"You are going almost too fast for me," she said when at a little distance from their own gate. "Why do you hurry so?"

"Because it is going to be quite dark. The new moon gives a little light now, and I want you to reach Mrs. St. Clair's before it sets."

"I am not afraid of the dark."

"No, perhaps not. But the light is safer nevertheless."

The husband and wife talked little during their rapid walk. Wallace, as we have noted before, had grown to be a reserved, silent man; and to-night Esther's mind was filled with thoughts of her sorrowing friend.

At the door Wallace bade his wife good-night, declining to enter but promising to call for her early in the morning.

Esther rapped softly and the door was opened by Bernard, one of the twins, now grown to be tall boys of twelve.

Mrs. St. Clair sat beside Robbie's bed, supporting him in her arms. At first sight he did not seem like one near death. His fair hair was brushed back from his transparent temples, his blue eyes shone with almost startling brilliancy and there was a bright crimson spot on either cheek.

He smiled as Esther drew near the bed. "I thank you for coming," he said, "you are very good." His voice sounded clear and strong, and she thought it must be as hard for the mother as it was for her to realize that the hand of death was upon him.

"You knew I would come Robbie. Why did you not send for me before?" she asked.

"Mother did not think me any worse than usual until this week, and we have taxed your kindness so much, but I am glad you are here now,—glad for her sake as well as for my own."

"I have come to stay, Robbie, but you must not talk too much."

"That is what I have just said to him."

It was Mrs. St. Clair who now spoke for the first time. She had acknowledged Esther's entrance by a grateful look and a pressure of the hand but when she tried to speak, her voice refused to serve her.

"Mother" and Robbie turned his bright eyes full upon her, "let me talk to-night. I must say all I have to say in a little while."

A spasm of pain passed over the mother's face. She lifted her eyes, full of anguish, towards Heaven, and the cry of burdened hearts through all time found utterance in the unforgotten language of her childhood:

*Lieber Gott, erbarme Dich meiner.*

"Mother, mother, He does have pity. Is it not His pity,

His love, that is lifting me above all pain and sorrow into his blessed rest?"

"Child, I do not grieve because you are going, but because I must stay;" then as her eyes fell upon the two boys who were standing at the foot of the bed, she added remorsefully:

"But I should not wish to go and leave these behind, like lambs in the wolf's den.—I who brought them here."

"Mother!" Robbie raised his head from her arm and looked from one to another with the clear glance of dying eyes—eyes that see through and beyond the mists of earth, "Am I going so very far away? Remember how you used to love the lines in Uncle Rupert's book.

>  *Ich sag' es Jedem das er lebt
>  Und auferstanden ist.
>  Das er in unserer Mitte schwebt
>  Und ewig bei uns ist.*

"And who knows? Maybe the dear God will let me do something for you and the boys when I am gone to Him."

"Oh Robbie." It was Bernard's voice, broken with sobs, that answered. "What can you do for us when we are never to see you any more. You will be gone from the house, gone when we come in to talk to you or bring you something we have found,—gone, and how will we live without you?'

Robbie held out his thin hands to both his brothers.

"Come to me Bernard, and you too Herman.

"How strong your hands are! How warm! They are kind hands too. They have done a great deal for me, and they will work for mother I know.

* An inadequate translation of these beautiful lines of Novalis is given below:

>  I say of each one that he lives;
>  That he is risen;
>  That he moves in our midst
>  And is forever with us.

"Brothers," and Robbie's voice was very tender, " I shall love you just as well when you cannot see me as I do now. I will never forget you. I will watch for you till you come to me, and while I am watching and waiting you must take care of mother. Promise me now that while you live you will try never to do anything that would wound her dear heart."

"We do promise," said both the boys together, their sobs hushed, whi e Robbie still held their hands.

"Now do one thing more for me, like the good boys that you are. Lie down and sleep until mother calls you. I think I can rest awhile, if I know that none of you are grieving for me."

The boys obeyed, and Robbie added, "Mother darling, fix my pillows so that I can lie down, and then let Mrs. Wallace sit beside me while you rest."

When his wish was complied with, Mrs. Wallace took the chair beside him. He motioned his mother to a low seat at the foot of the bed saying, "If you will only sit there and rest your poor tired head on a pillow I can sleep. I would have nothing to trouble me now if you were not so tired and so sorrwful."

The mother did her best to please him. He watched her a few minutes, and then thinking she was really resting, closed his own eyes and in a little while slept.

The hours of the night wore on. The two anxious watchers kept their places, speaking in whispers, and listening to the sleeper's quick, irregular breathing. Gradually the color faded out from his face and a clammy moisture covered his cheeks and forehead.

Esther wiped it away, keeping her finger on his pulse.

The day was beginning to break and still he slept. The mother put back the curtain and let the light fall upon his face. He stirred a little and partially unclosed his eyes.

"Call the boys," Esther said in a quick whisper. The mother roused them and in a moment they stood with her beside the bed. "Robbie" she said aloud. He opened his eyes and fixed them on her face with a clear bright look, then tried to reach out his hands. "My brothers! Where are they?" The boys pressed nearer. "Good bye Bernard. Good bye Herman. I am going to the dear God. Mother, good bye. I see a light. They are coming. Kiss me once before I go."

His lids dropped, his voice failed, and every faint, fluttering breath seemed the last.

All at once he opened his eyes, lifted both hands and cried in a clear, strong voice, "Dear Lord, I come!"

He sank back, his limbs relaxed and the pallor of death settled upon his features. "It is over" said Esther. "Thank God? He is already where the tears are wiped from all faces, where there is no more death neither sorrow nor crying nor any more pain."

The mother did not answer. Her whole soul seemed drawn out in the fixed gaze with which she regarded the dead face of her first-born. The two boys threw themselves across the foot of the bed sobbing loudly.

Esther put her arm around her friend. "Dear, can you not give thanks that all his weary days and nights are ended? That he is saved from the evil to come?"

The last words roused her.

"Yes," she said. "He is out of the power of wicked men I do thank God."

\* \* \* \* \* \* \* \* \* \*

Five years later.

There is little outward change in the principal characters of our story, except such as time always makes. The children have grown to maturity, and the men and women carry a few more scars from the Battle of Life.

Winnie Wallace has blossomed from childhood into womanhood. At seventeen she is taller than her mother and fairer even than the picture that through her life has embodied all her dreams of beauty;—the "Queen Esther" hanging on the parlor wall;—her mother's portrait, painted the year of her marriage.

And the mother,—what of her? She is past her thirty-seventh year, past the noon of life, and though these years and the sorrows they have brought with them have left their traces on cheek and brow, she is still a beautiful, graceful woman with a sweet dignity of manner and an air of command that keeps for her the title earned in her girlhood.

Her husband is more changed. He is only four years her senior, but he looks older. His tall figure is slightly bent and the "golden fleece" about which his wife used to jest in their honeymoon, is turning to silver. There are deep lines of care on his still handsome face, and his eyes, the beautiful violet eyes that Winnie has inherited, no longer meet those of wife and child with the clear, open look of other days. To his family, these changes are less apparent because they have come so gradually and there are other changes in him which they feel less for the same reason.

He is always reserved, often moody, and though he never speaks unkindly to wife or daughter he spends little time in their society even when at home. His study is tacitly understood by the family to be forbidden ground, and there he sits alone, often with locked doors, through the long summer mornings and winter evenings. \* \* \* \* \*

On the particular summer of which we are writing, however, another change occurred which they could not help noticing. He began to spend days and even weeks away from home, " on business," he said, though what the business was he did not explain. He spoke sometimes of going into the country to look at land or look at stock, and once told his wife, he thought of buying a ranche, but his jaded, harrassed looks, when he returned from these trips, were hard to account for in connection with the every day business which was their ostensible object.

A growing uneasiness oppressed his wife as his absences from home became more frequent. She could hardly define what she suspected, but the fear that the Priesthood were drawing him into complicity with some fresh crime haunted her continually.

It was late in September when her husband, returning one day from the country, brought an invitation from the Henlys, with whom they had always maintained friendly relations. Mrs. Henly wished Mrs. Wallace to bring her daughter and spend a week at the farm house, he said, and he seemed quite anxious that they should go—Jem could drive and they must take Aunt Eunice with them.

Mrs. Mead, who was still their tenant, could take care of the house and get his meals for him when at home, but he should probably be out of town a good deal.

Esther, from some cause which she could not explain, felt reluctant to accept the invitation, but Winnie was eager to go and her wishes prevailed.

As on that never-to-be-forgotten morning eight years before, they started early to escape the mid-day sun.

Wallace took an unusually affectionate leave of them, coming back the second time to kiss his wife and daughter good bye and charge Aunt Eunice to take good care of both.

When they reached the end of the street leading out of town, Esther looked back and saw her husband still standing at the gate watching them. With a strange chill, an undefinable presentiment of evil, she continued to look back until a turn in the road hid him from her sight. Never, not even on that other morning when she thought she might be bidding him good-bye for the last time, had she felt such a sinking of the heart. The day was warm, but she shook as if in an ague fit.

Winnie was leaning forward, chatting merrily with Aunt Eunice, and none of the party noticed her agitation. In a few minutes she regained outward self-control, but her heart lay like lead in her bosom all the way, and during their week's stay at Henly's the same feeling continued.

It was an unspeakable relief to her when the time named for their visit expired, and though Winnie begged to stay a little longer and all the family united in urging them to do so, she would not delay her return an hour. Once on the road, a feverish anxiety took the place of the dull pain that oppressed her and she ordered Jem to drive faster, and repeated the order until the horses were urged to their utmost speed.

They reached home early in the afternoon. Mrs. Mead, from her own door saw them drive up and came over with the keys. "I would have had the house open," she said apologetically, "but we did'nt look for you so soon."

" Where is my husband?"

" Brother Wallace? Oh he ain't home. He's been away most of the time since you left, but I've looked after things. You'll find the house all right. Here's the keys. I must run over home now, for I've left some bread in the oven. Jem can call me if I'm wanted."

Sister Mead appeared considerably " flustrated," to use a favorite expression of her own. She never once raised her eyes during the delivery of this rapid monologue, and as soon as the keys were out of her hands she turned and ran towards her own house with a haste which even burning bread could hardly excuse.

Aunt Eunice looked after her muttering:

" Dere's some more debbiltry afoot, sure's I'm standin, hyar. Dat critter means well enuff, an' when she knows 'bout enny ob dere wickedness she can't hide it like she's tole for to do. Wonder what's up dis time? Hopes its nuffin dat's gwine to tech Miss Esther or dat bressed lamb."

Winnie, in spite of her tall stature, was still Aunt Eunice's "lamb," and cared for accordingly She watched her now as she tripped lightly up the stairs, praying in her honest, affectionate heart for her darling's safety, and not until the girl was out of sight did she think of the chaos that might reign in her own dominions in consequence of her week's absence.

Esther, meantime, had gone directly to her own room on the first floor.

As soon as she opened the door, she was conscious of a change. Some familiar articles were out of their places, others were missing entirely, and a general air of confusion and disarrangment pervaded the room. Her first impulse was to call Mrs. Mead and speak to her about the disordered furniture, but as she was crossing the room to do so, her eye fell on a letter lying on the table directed to her in the well-known handwriting of her husband. She took it up and held it a moment unopened. What was it? What could it mean? Again she felt her heart turning to ice in her bosom. All the dread, the nameless fears of the past weeks rushed back upon her. With an effort she broke the seal, and there traced in unsteady characters which showed how the hand that held the pen trembled, she read:

ESTHER:

Wife, I dare not call you, for when you have read these lines you will count me your husband no longer. I have been a slave for years, this you know, but you cannot know the strength of my bonds or the depths of my degradation. In my blindness I took upon myself oaths —oh, such fearful ones—in that accursed Endowment House, and when my eyes were opened I was bound hand and foot for I was already a criminal. My masters made me share in their blood guiltiness.

Guiltiness, knowing that afterwards I could not rebel if I would.

Esther, I have lived by your side year after year, knowing myself unworthy to breathe the same air with you. My very presence was contamination, I ought to of left you long ago. Now, in obedience to those whose command I imbrued my hands in blood, I am about to commit another crime, one that will separate us for ever. I am to be sealed to one chosen for me by those who hold me, body and soul, in their hands. I have only seen the girl once. She is a timid creature who accepts the fate forced upon her as I do,—because she dares not rebel.  \*   \*

I have done what I could to spare you painful meetings. My personal effects have all been removed to the farm I have bought. I shall live there. Your threshold I will never cross without your permission and that I dare not hope for.   \*   \*   \*   \*

Esther, My first, last, only love,—I do not presume to ask forgiveness. of you or of God,— I can do nothing but look back from the hell I have made for myself to the heaven that was ours once. Is it possible for you to pity me? I do not know. I deserve nothing, I ask nothing, only — only, by the memory of the happy years we have spent together, by the memory of that little far-off grave we have both watered with our tears, I pray that my daughter may not learn to hate her wretched father. My sin against her is not like my sin against you and she may not cast me out of her heart altogether. Sometimes, perhaps; you will not refuse to let me see her. This is the only hope I have, Do not take it from me.

CHARLES WALLACE.

She stood as though turned to stone, with the letter still in her hand. The lines glared at her from the page with horrible distinctness.

"I am going mad, God pity me" she said aloud, There were footsteps in the hall, Winnie was looking for her. The door was within reach of her hand. She locked it and shoved the bolt. Winnie knocked gently, calling:

"Let me in, mamma. I've come to help you."

"Not now," she answered and heard her daughter turn from the door;— listened till her footsteps died away. As yet, the hideous secret was her own. Winnie did not know. Oh, if she might never know.

She lighted a candle and held the letter in the flame until

it burned to ashes. The blaze scorched her hand. She smiled as she felt the pain. "How good it would be if I could turn to ashes as easily as that paper" she said aloud. Then the horrible feeling that she was going mad again took possession of her. "I must not, I must not," she cried, "Winnie; my child, my lamb, I must live, I must keep my reason until you are safe. Oh God forsake me not utterly."

When did such a cry ever go up from human lips without reaching the ear and the heart of Infinite Pity? It was heard and answered now. The mists began to clear away from her brain. She sat down and began to think calmly.

The blow, so long delayed had fallen. She knew, all along, that it might come, and yet it was as crushing and paralyzing as though she had never dreamed of it. What was it that he had written?

Will it be believed that of all the fatal letter which now lay before her, a heap of white ashes, the only line that she recalled at first was, "Esther, my first, last, only love."

He had loved her then through all these years. If she had known, might he not have been saved by love? Was she altogether free from blame? Then like the hoarse cry of a drowning man his bitter, despairing words rang in her ears. "I can only look back from the hell I have made for myself to the heaven that was ours once," and for the time pity for him swallowed up every other feeling. The coming years rose up before her; blank, empty years; — years of that hollow mockery that the world calls living when all that makes our life is gone. Would it not be harder for him than for her? Would he not go about like Cain, crying: "My punishment is greater than I can bear?"

Winnie knocked at the door again.

She could not see her yet; could not tell her that she was fatherless and her mother worse than widowed. Poor child!

So young, so tender, so unused to sorrow, the blow would kill her.

Word by word the unhappy father's prayer forced itself upon her mind: "Do not let my daughter hate me." No, she would not.

"He is still her father though he is not my husband," she said half aloud. "Let that be as though I had happily died last week. Winnie shall not hate her father."

Once more she heard her daughter's voice calling in pleading tones, "Mamma, dear mamma, let me in. You looked so tired on the way I fear you are sick."

"Wait a minute, dear," and with the quick instinct of love,—was it love for the father or daughter, or both?—she extinguished the candle, brushed the ashes of the burned letter carefully into the grate, removed her bonnet and shawl, and darkened the room by dropping the blind before she opened the door.

"What is the matter mamma? Everything is out of place said Winnie looking around. "Surely you have not been trying to put the room to rights yourself when you are so tired?"

"No, love. The room will do well enough until morning. I am tired as you say, and if you will bring me a cup of tea I think I will lie down."

"Let me help you undress first."

"No, I would rather have you make the tea. You know I always like it best when you make it yourself."

"Very well mamma, but may'nt I bring you something to eat."

"Yes dear, a little toast," and Winnie turned and went out with the light, quick step that the fond mother loved to watch and listen for, while Esther, glad of the few minutes delay as a condemned criminal of a reprieve, bathed her pallid face, brushed back her hair, changed her traveling dress for a wrapper and seated herself in an easy chair in the darkest corner of the room. How she dreaded the questioning looks of those bright young eyes. How she feared that she should betray herself! For Winnie must not know to-night. Oh, no. Let her sleep in peace one night more, ignorant of the blight that had fallen upon their lives. She had scarcely seated herself when Winnie entered, bringing a tray spread with the whitest damask and holding the tea-service of dainty china brought from their old home. "Now you dear, tired mamma," she said gaily, "You cannot help eating and drinking, I have made everything so nice. Here is the toast, golden brown, just the shade you like, and here is some of the jelly I made myself in the summer, and the tea — oh, I know you will say that is superb."

Esther smiled faintly. Like poor Marian Earle, through all these sorrowful years she had

>   Kept a sort of smile in sight
>   To please the child, like a flower in a cup.

Winnie drew a light-stand beside the chair, placed the tray on it and was about to raise the curtain when her mother stopped her. "Let it be dear," she said, "that west window makes the room too light for sleeping and I am going to lie down as soon as I drink my tea." Winnie obeyed and seated herself at her mother's feet, declining to share the cup of tea and plate of toast upon the plea that she did not wish to spoil her appetite for the good supper Aunt Eunice was getting up. She would not leave the room until she saw her mother safe in bed, and not then until she had exacted a promise from her not to fasten the door. "I'm coming in again after supper," she said, laughing and looking back as she went out with the tray, "so make the most of your time till then."—When the door closed behind her retreating figure, the mother's forced self-control gave way. No tears moistened her burning lids, but dry shivering sobs convulsed her whole frame. She clenched her hands until the nails cut into the flesh. How long she lay there battling with hysterical spasms, she did not know, but the moment she heard Winnie's returning footstep she was recalled to the necessity of mastering herself. With a powerful effort she composed her features, closed her eyes, and lay so quiet, that Winnie, coming softly to the bedside, thought her sleeping and so reported to Aunt Eunice at the door. Esther listened to their whispered conference, heard them plan to make themselves beds in the parlor, within call, in case she wanted anything, and heard the door close finally with the hope of being left alone till morning.

The history of that night will never be written. The stricken heart, alone with God, fought the terrible battle with self and suffering through which so many hundreds were passing all around her, but unlike many others, came off victorious. The morning light found her prostrate in body but calm in spirit. Too weak to rise from her bed, she felt in the depths of her soul the peace of God. Bereft of earthly love and earthly hope, her whole heart was drawn above. She seemed again to hear her dead mother's voice singing softly:

"I feel Thee good;—feel naught beside."

Winnie came to her bedside at sunrise. She had been there once or twice during the night but thinking that her mother slept well had left her to her rest.

"You feel well this morning mother dear." she said cheerfully.

"Quite well, my daughter but not very strong. I think I will not get up quite yet."

"That is right, lie still and I will make your breakfast."

Noon came and still she did not feel quite strong enough

to rise. Thus a couple of days passed. Winnie wondered a little at her father's absence, but would not speak to her mother about it. Aunt Eunice was anxious and worried at heart, but kept a cheerful face. On the third morning Winnie was standing at the gate when two of their neighbor's daughters passed. They were bold, forward girls, who regarded Winnie's beauty and her elegant dress in the light of personal affronts which they were bound to resent. They stopped now on seeing her at the gate, and bade her good morning. She answered them civilly, and Maria, the elder girl, asked, " Is your pa home ? "

"He is not," was the quiet answer.

"S'pose he's staying out to the farm this week with his other wife."

"With *what?*"

"Why, with his second, that was Lizzie Simmons. We hadn't seen her around, but we s'posed your pa 'ud bring her here sometimes. We knew Lizzie. She used to live in our ward."

"I do not understand you," Winnie said, with dignity, turning from them and walking back to the house. Poor child! Her heart was nearly bursting. The girl's coarse words were spoken just in time to give shape to the fears awakened by her mother's sickness and her father's prolonged absence. Now the dreadful fear that what was said *might* be true, kept her from her mother's room and sent her to the kitchen instead. Aunt Eunice listened to her story and shook her head sorrowfully. "Poor lamb! So does yer no 'count white trash 'sult yer 'cause yer auntie wa'ant thar. I don't go for to say as yer pa haint acted very 'sterious an' I'se feared some sech story has got to yer ma in some way, though how I doesn't know, but dare's sumfin I *kin* do, dat Missis Mead knows whar yer pa is I'll be boun' an' I'se gwine straight to make her tell."

"Oh, no, Auntie," Winnie began, but Aunt Eunice was already half-way across the lot, and a minute afterwards she entered Mrs Mead's kitchen door. The good woman was rolling out pie-crust, but stopped to bid her caller good morning.

"Mornin'."

Aunt Eunice answered shortly, "I'se come hyar to ax a question an' I wants a straight answer. Whar's Massa Wallace?"

Sister Mead turned crimson and dropped her rolling-pin.

"Brother Wallace? Why he—he's at the farm."

"Wat's he doin' dar when his place is hyar an' his own wife dunno, no more'n de dead whar he be?"

"Why, business,"

"Don't you go to tell bout bizness. You knows better, Hyar's my missis sick an' low-lived white trash 'sulting Miss Winnie 'bout her pa's second wife. Now you knows de troof an' you's got to tell it."

Aunt Eunice's portly figure blocked up the doorway and her hand was raised threateningly. Poor Sister Mead gasped, looked about helplessly as though seeking a way of escape and finally answered desperately;

"Brother Wallace was sealed to Liza Simmons the day after you left. I helped him pack his things to take to 'the farm. He didn't give me any word for you, and I could'nt tell any more if you was to kill me."

Aunt Eunice dropped her raised arm and walked away without a word. It was only the confirmation of her fears, but the truth, put into plain words, struck her like a thunderbolt. She could not face her mistress or Winnie, so she walked to the barn to gain a little time, and there met Jem, who had heard the news from another quarter and was coming to tell her. She answered him roughly as was her wont when troubled, and turned back to the house. Winnie m..

her in the door-way. "Oh Auntie," she cried, " it is true. I know by your face that it is. Poor mamma! She will die."

"Hush chile, yer ma 'll hear ye. An' don't you go to her with no such scart look."

"I will not, Auntie. I will be quiet, but oh tell me where is papa?"

"What fur you call him dat? What's he now to you or yer poor ma"? Then noticing poor Winnie's white face and quivering lip, she added in a softer tone, "Pore lamb! yer Auntie did'nt mean to be cross. Better go up to yer own room an' pray de Good Lord fur help in time ob trouble. Go, honey. He's de only fren' we's got now." True, Winnie felt it in the depths of her sorrowful young heart, and turned away to hide her trouble from all other eyes, even the most kindly.

An hour later, she came down stairs, fearing her mother might miss her, and call for her. She had tried to wash away the traces of tears from her face and came into her mother's room hoping she would notice nothing, but it is so hard for the young to dissemble;—so hard for them to carry a bright face above an aching heart.

The quick eye of maternal love saw at once the white cheeks and swollen eyelids and the mother's ear detected the quiver in the voice that tried to bid her a cheerful good morning. "What is wrong my darling?" she asked.

The tender question brought an uncontrollable burst of tears. "Oh mamma," she sobbed, "you know as well as I." The moment the words were uttered she would have given anything to recall them, but it was too late. The mother's pale face grew a shade whiter, and for the first time in her life, Winnie saw her faint quite away. The fright and distress this caused made her forget the other trouble entirely for the time. There were plenty of restoratives at hand, and shrinking instinctively from calling any one to witness a sorrow she felt they must both henceforth hide, the young girl did her best to bring her mother back to consciousness unaided. In a little while she had the happiness of seeing her open her eyes. "Mother darling are you better? Oh I am so glad," she cried with the quick revulsion of feeling that of which only youth is capable. "I am better, love. Lock the door and sit down by me."

When Winnie was seated, her mother, holding fast the strong, young hand, as though it was her only stay in life, said slowly:

"My daughter, a great sorrow has a fallen on us, but it need not crush us, for 'The Eternal God is our refuge, and underneath us are the Everlasting Arms.' Life is short, and in a little while this great grief will be to me as though it had never been. You are young and God is good. He will see to it that this trouble does not follow you through life. After to-day we will never speak of it except to Him. All I wish to say about it now is, do not think hardly of your father. He is in the power of wicked men, and they compel him to do as they wish. He loves you the same as ever, and his only hope in life is that you will not turn against him. It would add tenfold to my trouble if I thought you felt bitterly toward him. Promise me now that you will never say a word to wound him."

Winnie bent her head. She could not trust her voice·

"Now, love, go to your own room. I want to be alone."

In the hall outside, Winnie met Aunt Eunice "Massa Wallace is at de gate," she said frowning darkly. "Will you go tell him he does'nt b'long hyar, or mus' I?"

"Neither of us, Auntie," Winnie said firmly. "My mother does not wish any such word said."

"You go 'long an' meet him den. I washes my han's ob all ob it," and Aunt Eunice quickened her steps toward the kitchen and shut the door violently.

"Can't sp'ose fur de life ob me what's come ober Miss Esther," she muttered, " no more sperrit dan a pet kitten. Wish't ole Massa Pryor wor alibe. Ole Massa 'ud make him stan' roun'. Should'nt wonder ef he'd gib him lead fur breakfus', but deary me. Dere's nobody hyar to tuk Mis's Esther's part."

Winnie, meantime, walked rapidly to the gate, fearful that her courage would fail. Was it her father who stood there? She would not have known him except for the familiar dress. His face was haggard and colorless, his cheeks sunken, and his eyes downcast. "Good morning papa," she said, holding out her hand. She had conquered herself so far that only a little tremor in her voice showed what she had passed through.

"Good morning, Winnie. I have heard that your mother is sick. Will you tell me how she is?"

"Better, I think. Will you come in?"

The blood rushed into his pale face. "Does your mother wish it?"—he asked.

"She does not know you are here but I will tell her. Come with me."

"No, Winnie," he said sadly. "I have no right to come one step farther unless your mother sends for me."

Without another word, Winnie turned and hurried into the house. It seemed to the wretched man standing at the gate that she was gone a long time, but in reality it was not more than five minutes before she returned, and saying only: "Come! mamma wishes to see you," led the way into the house and to her mother's room and left him there What words were spoken in that most painful meeting it is not for us to record. We have to do only with what Wallace said as he took his leave:

"It will be safer for you and Winnie, safer for the whole household if I am sometimes seen to come here, and perhaps for Winnie's sake we both ought to forget our own feelings so far. If it is not asking too much I would beg leave dine here sometimes when in town. It will cost you much pain, I know;—I have no right to speak of my own feelings,—but for the sake of one dear to both of us, will you consent to this?"

"For the child's sake." As we have said before, this is the key to much which is otherwise incomprehensible in Utah;— the only explanation of what seems voluntary slavery and degradation on the part of hundreds of women born to a better life. For the sake of Winnie's safety father and mother endured what was equal torture to both, and on every alternate Sabbath, Wallace rode into town and dined with his family, and Mormon gossips spoke of Mrs. Wallace as "reconciled" to her husband's second marriage. Happily for her this gossip never reached her ears. Winnie heard a word or two, sometimes, but wisely kept silence.

## PART II.—Chapter VIII.

THE ABDUCTION OF WINNIE.—SUSPENSE.—GENERAL CONNOR'S AID.—THE RESCUE.—THE RETURN.—AFTER MANY DAYS.

A little more than six months after the events recorded in our last chapter, Wallace on taking his leave of the family after one of his Sunday visits left a folded paper in his wife's hand. As soon as she was alone she opened it and read:

"Watch Winnie carefully. Don't let her go outside the gate alone. Don't leave her at home alone for an hour. A danger that I cannot explain threatens her, and I, alas, cannot protect her."

Here was a new and terrible anxiety. Winnie threatened with a mysterious calamity, which the utmost watchfulness might fail to avert. Months before, Esther had left her own room below stairs to share Winnie's bed. Jem and Aunt Eunice slept on the first floor, and a powerful St. Bernard dog, the strongest ally of the unprotected family, always had his quarters for the night on the rug outside Winnie's door. Mother and daughter went out together in the daytime, taking the dog with them. After dark none of the family except Jem ever left the house.

The reader may again need to be reminded that we are writing history, not fiction. We are portraying one instance among hundreds of the Reign of Terror which endured for a quarter of a century under the shadow of the American flag and which is not altogether abolished in the Year of Grace, One Thousand Eight Hundred and Seventy-Nine.

To return to our story. About ten days after Mrs. Wallace received the warning mentioned above, she was sent for one afternoon to see a child sick with the scarlet fever. The child's mother was a poor widow largely indebted already to Esther's charity, and she thought nothing of being sent for by her in this fresh trouble; so putting on her bonnet hastily and telling Winnie she would be back in a few minutes, she went out leaving Aunt Eunice in charge of the house. It was baking day, and the latter was unusually busy in the kitchen, but mindful of her charge she called to Winnie who was in the front yard.

"Better go in the house, honey."

"In a minute Auntie, I just want to get a few of these early violets."

As Winnie stooped to gather the flowers a light canvas-covered spring wagon drove up and a young man sprang out. He carried a shawl hanging on his arm and held a letter in his hand. "Does Mrs. Wallace live here?" he asked. "She does," was the answer. "Well, I have a letter for her," and he advanced a step or two up the walk leaving the gate open behind him. Winnie went toward him and held out her hand for the letter but as she was in the act of taking it from him, the shawl was thrown over her head, and in less time than it takes to record it, she was lifted from her feet, carried through the gate and forced into the wagon with the help of someone inside. She uttered a single half-stifled cry as the shawl was thrown over her. That cry brought Aunt Eunice from the house just in time to see her lifted into the wagon. The sight paralyzed her for one moment The next, with a wild shriek for help, she darted after the wagon which was already driving away at a furious speed.

Aunt Eunice was past sixty, but love gave wings to her feet, and she ran for more than a block so fast as to keep the wagon in sight. When it disappeared she sank down helplessly and prayed: "Dear Lord Good Lord, let me die now, I'se done let dat lamb be carried off by de wolves right before dese eyes. I can't go back to Miss Esther no more. How kin I stan' up an' hear her ax' whar's my chile.' You knows Lord I can't do dat." Then a vision of her mistress perhaps exposed to the same fate, rose up before her, and she hastened back to the empty house almost expecting to see her "Miss Esther" struggling in the hands of kidnappers.

The gate and the house were open as she had left them but in the neighboring houses every door and window was closed. No one looked out; no notice seemed to have been taken of what had happened.

The counsel of the Priesthood, "mind your own business and ask no questions" was well obeyed in Zion.

Aunt Eunice sat down on the steps of the porch, her ebony face actually gray with anguish and fear. She rocked herself to and fro moaning: " My lamb, My lamb. Oh ef yer pore ole Auntie could only a' died to sabe you. Ef de good Lord would only let me die now an' bring you back."

In the midst of her lamentations Esther came up the walk with hurried steps. " Auntie " she cried as soon as she saw her, "Mrs. Boyd did not send for me. There is something wrong. Where is Winnie?" Aunt Eunice fell on the ground and grovelled at her feet.

"Don't ax me, Miss Esther, don't look at me so, I couldn't sabe her. Dey carried her off right before dese eyes."

" They ! Who ? Speak quickly ! "

I don't know honey. Thar was a wagon an' two men. You hadn't been gone a minnit when I called her to come inter de house. She said yes, an I went back in de kitchen. Den I heerd a kind ob cry an' run out, an' dere was a wagon an two men a liftin' her in. I screeched fur help an' run after de waggin till it wor out ob sight. Oh, Miss Esther, honey you doesn't blame me?"

"No, get up. Some one must go for her father at once. Where is Jem?"

"Ain't back from de blacksmith's yet. No, dere he comes now," as Jem appeared at the side gate, riding one horse and leading the other. His mistress called him to her.

"Jem, take the horse that is saddled and ride at once to the farm. Tell Mr. Wallace that Winnie is gone. Carried off. Dont speak,"—as Jem endeavored to express his astonishment, — "and don't stop at the farm. Go from there to Camp Douglass. Tell General Connor I wish to see him at once on important business."*

Jem waited for no second bidding. Leaving the other horse loose in the yard, he sprang into the saddle and was out of sight.

The two women in the solitary house, left to the watching and waiting that falls to woman's lot through hours of intolerable anguish and suspense, could do nothing but pray that help might come quickly.

The sun was but two hours high in the west when Jem started. It was late in the afternoon when Mrs. Wallace left the house and though she was not gone half an hour that delay and the few minutes occupied in giving Jem his instructions allowed the kidnappers sufficient start to make it impossible to overtake them unless they stopped somewhere during the night, and of course their route could only be conjectured.

The stars were beginning to show themselves when Jem stopped his hard-ridden horse at the gate and dismounted. With a caution born of his experiences in the past he

* One incident of the past few years which should have been noted elsewhere was the establishment of a military post near Salt Lake. The small body of federal troops quartered there did their best to afford protection to non-Mormons but official red tape, made it difficult for them to afford assistance in most cases.

led his horse to the stable and went quietly to the back door as though returning from ordinary business. The two anxious watchers inside met him at the same moment and he answered their unspoken question in a whisper.

"Mr. Wallace is away. Went North five days ago. Will be back the day after to-morrow. General Connor will be here in an hour. But I have better news. I met Harris at the cross-roads and he gave me this." He handed his mistress a crumpled note, written in pencil. She unfolded it and read:

MRS. WALLACE:
I know where your daughter is, No harm will come to her for the present. To-morrow night at midnight let Jem meet me at the mouth of Big Cottonwood Caynon. He must come alone and ride a horse that will carry double. Be up and waiting at home, but don't show a light and if God helps me, before sunrise the next morning your daughter shall be with you.

HARRIS.

"You say Harris gave this to you yourself?" she asked

"Yes. He was coming here when I met him. He tore a leaf from his pocket-book and wrote this, sitting in his saddle."

"We can trust Harris and you, too, Jem."

"Mrs. Wallace, you saved my life, and I would give it back to-night to help you."

"I know it."

At this moment there was a loud and startling ring at the front door "General Connor I think" said Jem "but I'll make sure before unlocking."

A look through an aperture in the hall shutters dispelled all doubt, and a minute afterwards Jem ushered a gentleman into the parlor whose uniform was the most welcome sight which had greeted that household for many a day, for it promised protection in the name of the great government whose badge of service it was.

"I have the pleasure of addressing Mrs. Wallace?" he said rising and bowing.

"Yes General I have taken the liberty of sending for you because we are in great trouble and needed help."

"I am at your service Madam, and I have not come alone. I have half-a-dozen men at the gate, all well armed. Will you tell me just what has happened?"

Mrs. Wallace detailed the events of the afternoon just as rapidly as possible, and ended by giving him the note just received.

He scanned it attentively.

"You know the writer of this?" he said at length.

"Yes.'

"Can you trust him?"

"Implicitly."

"Well, then I think we see light ahead. Do your suspicions point to any one person as the author of this outrage?"

"Yes. I more than suspect, I am almost certain that a man named Harwood, a Mormon elder, who has been our evil genius for ten years past is the principal actor; at least he is the author of it."

"I know the fellow. A villian by nature and a brigand by profession. I would like to get just one good shot at him."

Mrs. Wallace smiled faintly at the thought of the cautious Harwood, whose valor consisted in always sending others to the front, exposing himself to Federal bullets, and the General continued:

"This Harris most probably knows the country better than we do, and has a far greater advantage in being acquainted with the place to which your daughter has been taken, so it may be best to leave the rescue altogether to him; still I think I will contrive some errand for a dozen of my men that will oblige them to pass the mouth of the canyon near the hour named. It will do no harm to have them within call and I will instruct your man how to summon them if he needs help."

"I hope that no such necessity will occur, but I shall be relieved of much anxiety if I know that help is near. Our lives here, as you must know, are passed in a state of continual apprehension."

"I do know, and I think, Mrs. Wallace, that after the occurences of today, you are no longer even partially safe here. My advice, which I hope you will accept, is that you remove at once with your family to Camp Douglass. Quite a large number of families in similar circumstances have already taken refuge there and a number of our officers have their wives with them. We will give you the best quarters at our disposal, with room for your servants and storage for your goods."

"Your offer is a kind one, and if my daughter is restored to me I shall accept it at once, for I shall not feel that we are safe for an hour here."

"I am very glad to hear your decision. Can I offer you any assistance in removing your effects?"

"I do not think we shall need any. We will only take such things as we are obliged to. The house and its contents will be safe enough in care of my tenant. I am not troubled about that nor about anything except my child. If I allow my mind to dwell upon her situation to-night I shall be incapable of doing anything to help her."

"Try to think hopefully of her. You have the assurance of one who seems to know, that no present harm will come to her, and in a little more than twenty-four hours she will be under your own roof."

"I believe so, for I trust in God."

The General bowed his head. "Madam, I honor and

at the same time envy your faith. Can I be of any farther service to-night."

"I think not. We will not be molested at present; at least I apprehend nothing and if Winnie is saved, we will remove to camp at an early hour the next morning."

With renewed offers of service the General took his leave, and the household retired, the mother to spend the night in prayer, Aunt Eunice to indulge freely in lamentations and self reproaches, and Jem in spite of his real grief and anxiety, to find the sleep that comes so easily to the young.

The longest night will wear toward morning, the saddest day must come to a close, and though the hours seemed endless they passed one by one until at length the clock struck nine on the evening of the next day. This was the time agreed upon for Jem to start. Brown Bess, the favorite of her young mistress was saddled and waiting. They all knew they could depend upon her fleetness and intelligence.

"If" said Jem, "I should be forced to get down and stop any one who followed us, the mare would find her way home at the top of her speed; and Miss Winnie knows how to ride."

"I hope no such thing will happen, Jem. What arms have you?" Jem threw open his coat and showed a heavy navy revolver and a knife.

"I pray that you may not need to use them, but if you do?"

"I won't waste powder. I'll fire to kill, if any man tries to stop us."

Jem did not wait to see how this was received, but hurried out, sprang into the saddle and was gone.

The mouth of the canyon was about twelve miles distant. He had ample time, and rode slowly, to save the speed of his horse for the return. There was no moon, and passing clouds lessened the faint starlight, but Jem knew every inch of the way and so did Brown Bess.

He had ridden about a mile out of town when he heard a pattering sound on the hard roadway, and looking down saw that Bruno, Winnie's faithful St. Bernard, had constituted himself one of the party. "Hi! Bruno, my boy, why did you not stay to take care of them at home?" he said.

The dog answered by a low whine and kept on close beside the horse.

"Well, old fellow, you know best. Maybe we shall need you with us to-night."

Jem always maintained stoutly that Bruno knew more than half the men in the Territory, and now he said to himself that if the dog had not the best of reasons for doing so, he would never have left the house unguarded to follow him.

It was near midnight before Jem, riding at the leisurely pace he had adopted, reached the mouth of the canyon. The entrance to the narrow defile was guarded on either side by large masses of rock that looked in the dim light, like castles and fortresses. Behind one of these Jem reined his horse and waited for the signal agreed upon. Before many minutes he heard it,—a long low whistle three times repeated. He answered it, and almost directly a horse bearing two riders emerged from the canyon. Jem, after one cautious glance from his hiding place, came out and met them.

"Just in time my good fellow," said Harris, "Well for all of us that we did'nt have to wait for you."

In less than five minutes Winnie was transferred to the pillion behind Jem's saddle. "Ride for your lives. You will be followed," Harris said as he swung himself upon his own horse.

Jem needed no urging, nor for that matter did Brown Bess. Her hoofs struck sparks of fire from the stony roadbed as she galloped homeward, making no account of the added weight she carried. They were already well out of the shadow of the mountain and near the point where the roads leading to the city and to Camp Douglass intersected each other, when Jem's quick ear detected a sound which made him lay his hands on his weapons.

They were followed, as Harris had warned them. Their pursuer gained on them. By the time they reached the cross-roads he was in plain sight. "Halt!" he called.

No answer.

There was a flash, a report, and a bullet whizzed past their heads.

Jem returned the fire without slackening speed.

Bess strained every nerve and still the horseman gained on them.

"We are lost," was Winnie's despairing thought, when help came from an unexpected quarter.

Bruno, left a little behind in their rapid flight, made a fierce spring at the horse's head and caught the bridle in his teeth, close to the bit.

The horse stumbled and fell, throwing his rider forward.

The man sprang up. The horse did not rise. Bruno, dragged down in his fall lay partly under him. The discomfitted rider, muttering a deep curse, discharged his pistol a second time, not at the fugitives, now out of his reach, but at the faithful animal that had saved them. As the report died away, another sound was borne on the breeze,—one most unwelcome to the midnight marauder.

It was a clattering of hoofs giving notice of approach of a body of horsemen, and in a minute more, around a bend of the road leading from the South, a dozen armed men came in sight. The starlight, faint as it was, showed plainly what they were,—a squad of cavalry returning to camp. Harwood, for the dismounted horseman was no other, believed with Hudibras that

> He who fights and runs away
> May live to fight another day.

It was the principle to which he owed most of his past success, and now, without waiting to be interviewed by the the new-comers, he slipped behind the nearest boulder, lowered himself thence into a gully, cut by the spring freshets, and following its bed made his safe and silent way back to the foot-hills.

The officer in command of the approaching squad quickened the speed of his men at the sound of pistol-shots. He had his private instructions from General Connor, and now feared he was too late at the scene of action.

A dark object lying across the road was the first thing that met his view. He turned the slide of a dark lantern at his saddle-bow so that a single ray fell upon it.

"A horse! Get down Saunders and see what is the matter. Here, take the light."

The man dismounted and after a hasty examination reported:

"The horse has both his knees broken, Captain. There is a dog, too—shot through the head"

"Well, put the horse out of his misery, while we look for the rider."

As the reader knows, the rider was by this time safe from their search but a close examination of the road, the tracks behind the fallen horse and those in front gave a clue to the facts. "Nobody hurt" was the Captain's final verdict. "There is no sign of any struggle and no blood in sight except that of the dog. That was a noble beast;" he added looking down upon the horse, "and the man that rode him deserved to be shot for leaving him to suffer, unless he had uncommon good reasons for getting out of the way in a hurry."

"Shan't we take the saddle Captain?" asked one of the men. "It might be useful in case that chap's friends should come round inquiring for him."

"Yes, take it. If the owner wants it he can advertise for it."

By the time Captain McKay and his men reached camp, Winnie was safe in her mothers arms.

Safe for the time, but neither mother nor daughter was willing to risk remaining another night in the city, and before noon the next day, General Connor received them at Camp Douglass.

\* \* \* \* \* \* \* \* \* \*

It is the month of June 1867, just eleven years from the ill-fated day when Esther Wallace and her daughter stepped on board the Western bound train that carried them from their home. Camp Douglass has become almost a city, so great is the number of refugees who have flocked to it to escape from Mormon tyranny and from the knife and bullet of the red-handed Danites—Brigham Young's Destroying Angels. Most of these refugees would gladly return to the States if they could, and orders have at length been issued for a military escort to protect such as are ready to undertake the journey across the plains. On the morning of which we write, a long train of more than fifty wagons, some loaded with supplies, others carrying passengers with their baggage, formed in line on the road leading out of the military reservation. Mrs. Wallace and Winnie are there, occupying the same carriage that brought them to the Territory, and with them is Theresa St. Clair. The two stalwart young men on horseback are her sons. Jem holds the reins that his mistress would not think of entrusting to other hands, and Aunt Eunice sits beside him and shakes her turbaned head solemnly as she points downward toward the city they are leaving.

"Sodom an Gormorrer! Dat's wat dey is. Sure's de sun shines dis bressed mornin', dere's a cloud o' fire an' brimstun gwine to bust ober dar. 'Pears like de Lord wor jest a waitin' for us to 'scape outen de valley."

\* \* \* \* \* \* \* \* \* \*

"AFTER MANY DAYS."

Time, September, 1870. Place, a little village nestled between the mountain and the river-bank, on the west side of the Hudson. Voyagers up and down that river know how many nooks, just large enough to hold a cluster of cottages, can be found on either shore along the base of the mountains that slope down to the water's edge. In one of these nooks, no matter which, and in the very prettiest cottage of the group, two ladies sat sewing in a cosy morning-room overlooking the river.

"Oh mamma" said the younger of the two, "there comes the morning boat from New York!"

"Winnie dear" said the elder lady smiling, "I shall have to put short frocks on you again. You are so enthusiastic over the boats, our neighbors will not believe you more than ten years old."

"Well mamma, you know I never saw one till I was twenty; I mean one like these."

At this moment the door-bell rang and the young lady, with the slightest perceptible hightening of color, began to sew again industriously.

A trim serving-maid appeared directly and ushered in a gentleman of about thirty, who was welcomed as Dr. Brownell.

"Always busy, Mrs. Wallace, and you too, Miss Winnie," he said after the first salutation, "but I know when I see you at work, that somebody is going to receive substantial benefit. I have just come from my patient at Hemlock Creek, and I think I could guess who made the new clothes the poor woman's children have on; — at least I have a recollection of seeing the pattern of the goods before."

"You must be very observing," said Winnie laughing, "and I wish you would exercise your gift in that respect for my benefit just now and tell me who lands from the steamboat. Mamma won't let me go down and find out for myself."

The doctor looked out of the window and reported:

"One fat woman with a bundle, three children and a young man in a blue blouse."

"Anybody else?"

"No—stop—I see a tall gentleman in a gray traveling cloak and felt hat. He stoops slightly. Has a cane and walks slowly. I should say he is either ill or quite aged."

Why was it that such a sudden pallor overspread the elder woman's face; —that her heart throbbed so for a moment? She could not tell herself. She sat silent, scarcely hearing the lively, bantering words of her daughter, who was now asking the doctor for a description of something on the other side of the river. The windows of the room did not afford a view of the road leading to the front of the house and when the shrubbery hid the few passengers just landing from view, the doctor and Winnie found something else to talk about.

They were interrupted by the ringing of the bell. This time when Jane made her appearance she announced:

"A gentleman inquiring for Mrs. Wallace."

"Where is he Jane?"

"In the parlor. He said he would wait at the door, but I brought him in. He seemed ill."

Mrs. Wallace had already risen to go to her visitor. She stopped, overcome again by an agitation for which she could not account. In a moment she recovered her composure and walked quietly out to the parlor.

"I wonder who mamma's mysterious visitor can be," said Winnie. The words were scarcely spoken when they heard a cry, a fall, and in the same instant her mother's voice calling them. They hurried into the parlor. Mrs. Wallace was kneeling on the floor beside the figure of a man, recognized by the doctor as the tall stranger just landed from the boat. His face was ghastly and a stream of blood which Mrs. Wallace vainly tried to staunch flowed from his mouth. Winnie gave a startled scream then a second glance. "Papa" she cried and dropped down beside her mother.

Dr. Brownell did a much more sensible thing; — drew his medicine case from his pocket and taking Winnie by the arm ordered her, almost sharply, to go for water. In a little while the remedies, so providentially at hand checked the flow of blood and restored the sick man to partial consciousness. His eyes wandered vacantly around until they rested on the face that bent over him; — then, as in that other sickness long ago he said, faintly: "At home? Thank God!" and closed his eyes again.

"He must be got to bed directly," said the doctor. "If your man Jem is at home let him come in and help me."

Winnie went herself to summon the needed help, and Jem, too much astonished to ask any questions, carried his old master into the next room and with the doctor's help undressed him and made him comfortable in bed.

"I have done all I can do at present," Dr. Brownell said as he returned to the parlor, "I will come in again this afternoon, and in the meantime he must have perfect quiet. Let only one person sit with him and do not allow him to talk. The least excitement may bring on the hemorrhage."

"I will sit with him."

Mrs. Wallace spoke as calmly as though the patient were a stranger.

"We are much indebted to you, doctor. You will be certain to come early?"

"I will not fail."

Mrs. Wallace entered the bed-room, closing the door behind her.

Winnie looked up. "Dr. Brownell," she said, "You know something of our unhappy history and will not wonder at anything you have seen or heard to-day. I am so thankful that it was you and not a stranger who happened to be present."

"It is I who should be thankful for the privilege of serving you. The tone in which he spoke these commonplace words, brought the color into Winnie's pale face, but she only answered:

"You can serve us in more ways than one. I am certain we can reply on you to protect us from gossip which would be very painful just now."

"There is nothing in my power to do for you which you cannot reply on me for."

And having had the satisfaction of watching the effect of his words a second time, the doctor took his leave, repeating his promise to call early in the afternoon.

Two or three days passed and the sick man improved so far as to be able to sit up.

The doctor removed his interdict regarding conversation, only sipulating that his patient should not be excited.

This stipulaton was not likely to be disregarded by his wife who sat beside him outwardly as calm as though nothing had disturbed the smooth current of their lives, or by the daughter who, controlled by her mother, looked and spoke as though they had never been separated,

Thus far, the only allusion made by either of them to the

shadow that darkened this pathway was when Wallace first grew strong enough to speak.

It was night and waking from a brief slumber he saw his wife watching beside his pillows. "Esther," he said, bringing out the words with a slow, painful utterance: "I have come home to die. You will not send me away?"

For answer, she took his wasted hands, in both of her's and repeated solemnly:

"God do so unto me and more also, if aught but death part thee and me."

Since the end was so near, why not let the dark past be as though it had never been! Esther saw in the dying man only the husband of her youth, the father of her children. The face of the fair-haired baby that slept under the violets, that face so like the father's own, rose up before her whenever her eyes fell upon that other face lying so white and wasted on the pillow.

The sad violet eyes had in them the look which had followed her so many years;—the piteous, appealing look with which her baby made his mute plea for help when struggling with the destroyer.

She asked no questions about the intervening years; —would listen to no self-acusations from those white lips. The one thing that gave her disquiet, the only thing about which she wished to hear him speak, was the false faith, whose blighting power she hoped was forever broken. Was it so? Had the wanderer come to himself and found his way back to his father's house? How should she learn and yet keep the promise that nothing should be allowed to disturb him?

She was pondering this one bright afternoon when he was so much better that he asked to be moved to the windows overlooking the river.

His eyes wandered up and down over the autumn landscape, so unlike anything he had seen for years. The river-bank was a bewildering maze of orange and scarlet, of deep crimson and pale yellow, broken here and there by the dark green of a clump of cedars. He sat a long time silent: At length, pointing to a group of trees beyond the lawn he said:

"What a vivid color those trees have! It seems as though I never knew before what crimson and scarlet meant."

Then turning his head slowly and facing her:

"Esther, there were years when I could not bear to look on those colors,—you know why, — but now there is one verse of holy scripture that is above all price to me. 'Though your sins be as scarlet, they shall be white as snow; though they be red like crimson, they shall be as wool,'— and there is another,—one that has saved me from despair, 'Father, forgive them. They know not what they do.' Esther,—wife—there were many years when I knew not what I did."

She took his hands in hers. For his sake she must be calm, but in spite of every effort her eyes filled and her voice trembled as she answered:

"I know that and surely God knows. If I am so glad to have you here at home, think how glad He is that you have come home to Him."

There was a moment of silence, then Wallace said:

"Since I have been lying here so helpless, how thankful I have been that in my childhood I learned so many chapters of the Holy Book by heart. I have not dared to open it for years, but now the story of the prodigal who came home and was received so joyfully, and of the good Shepherd who went out into the mountains seeking his lost sheep, come back to me as though I had read them yesterday."

They talked freely of the past and of the future and the

pale face of the invalid grew so much calmer and brighter that Winnie said to Dr. Brownell:

"Surely papa is better."

The doctor looked grave. "Do you want me to tell you the truth?"

"Yes."

"I have tried to be candid with all of you from the first. There is not the shadow of a hope that your father will recover. With such care as he has, he may last a month but even that is doubtful."

Winnie's tears fell fast.

"Does my mother know?" she asked.

"Yes. She has known all along."

"Does papa know it himself?"

"He does. And if you could realize how glad he is to be so near the end of all strife and unrest, you would rejoice with him."

The days grew into weeks. The weather had become much colder, and the sick man no longer left his bed. The end was not far off. It came one wild November night when the rain beat against the windows, and fierce gusts shook the leafless branches of the trees outside.

Wife and daughter, one on either side watched every change in the beloved face. The servants who had shared their changing fortune so many years, stood at the foot of the bed. The doctor sat beside the dying man's pillow.

He looked from one to the other. "God is so good,' he said, "so much better than my deserts, so much better than my fears, He lets me die at home." He closed his eyes and murmured indistinctly. His mind seemed wandering among the scenes of his boyhood. All at once a bright smile illumined his face. He held out his arms and said, "Arthur! Papa's boy! Come to papa, darling!"

Then sinking back he slept again.

Rousing after a few minutes, he fixed his eyes on his wife's face with a clear, conscious look.

"Esther," he said, "I thought I saw our baby—little Arthur. He held out his hands just as he used to, and was so glad to see me. I know he will be glad." Winnie's sobs made him turn towards her.

"Winnie, darling, come closer. Say good-bye to papa. Papa always loved his little daughter. Esther, beloved, it grows dark but I see your face yet."

There was a single deep drawn breath;—his head fell back upon his wife's bosom, and there was silence.

The storm-tossed soul had reached the desired haven.

THE END.

www.ingramcontent.com/pod-product-compliance
Lightning Source LLC
Chambersburg PA
CBHW031248250426
43672CB00029BA/1384